Medieva

and Mor.

MW00785094

Medieval Monks and Monasteries

HUNT JANIN *AND*
URSULA CARLSON

McFarland & Company, Inc., Publishers
Jefferson, North Carolina

ISBN (print) 978-1-4766-8732-2
ISBN (ebook) 978-1-4766-5005-0

LIBRARY OF CONGRESS AND BRITISH LIBRARY
CATALOGUING DATA ARE AVAILABLE

Library of Congress Control Number 2023002987

Panoramic view of famous Le Mont Saint-Michel tidal island with deep
blue water and clear reflections in golden evening light at sunset in summer,
Normandy, northern France (Shutterstock/canadastock)

Printed in the United States of America

*McFarland & Company, Inc., Publishers
Box 611, Jefferson, North Carolina 28640
www.mcfarlandpub.com*

"A white mantle of churches"

This is a lightly-edited translation of a famous account written in about the year 1000 by the French medieval monk and historian Raoul Glaber. He tells us:

Three years had not passed into the millennium that, throughout the whole world, and more particularly in Italy and in Gaul [modern-day France, Belgium, Luxembourg, and adjacent parts of the Netherlands, Switzerland, and Germany] the rebuilding of churches commenced, although for the most part, many of the existing ones were well-built and quite suitable.

It seemed that each Christian community sought to surpass the others by the splendor of its constructions. It was as if the whole world was breaking free, shedding the weight of the past and donning a white mantle of churches. Almost all of the churches and monasteries, and also the small oratories of the villages, were rebuilt better than before by the faithful.—After Haverkamp, *Images of Saône-et-Loire*, pp. 20–23

Table of Contents

Preface

The Middle Ages extended for about a thousand years—from roughly 500 to 1500. They witnessed huge social changes; political, military, economic, and religious upheavals; technological advances; intellectual and religious debates; artistic innovations; and, in 1470, the first printing press was installed in Paris. As part of this ongoing process, Western European medieval monasticism would be very much affected.

Thousands of monastic communities, large and small, were founded during this era. There were many different types of them, with very different emphases and goals, ranging from monasteries and nunneries that offered relative comfort and security to those that specialized only in the most ascetic lifestyles.

By the end of the 15th century in Western Europe, the prestige of the Church would be in sharp decline, due largely to financial scandals and corruption. Indeed, these failings would set the stage for the rapid growth of Protestantism after the end of the Middle Ages.

Long before then, however, if there was one common theme that emerged, time and time again, during what we may call the "monastic centuries" of the Middle Ages, it was that many of the men and women attracted to the monastic life were drawn to it because they wanted to live under strict rules that stressed the importance of pursuing only a simple and a God-oriented lifestyle.

Moreover, continuous monastic reform was also believed by many monks and nuns to be an essential part of their lives. They understood very well just how human weaknesses continually battled against—and so often lost—the fight against monastic rigor. One of the best examples of such rigor comes from the great French monastery of Cluny in the 10th century where, we are told, the monks had to sing at least 175 psalms every single day in their church.[1]

In the end, however, human corruption could be a much greater problem than a top-heavy liturgy, and one which needed high-level reform. The modern medievalist Lynette Olson reminds us that in the 11th century the papacy "had its ups and downs, but the downs were very low" indeed. For example, Benedict IX bought the papacy in 1032 and then sold it in 1045. The need for reform was so great that the Emperor Henry III had to initiate the reform of the papacy from outside the papacy itself.[2]

The present work offers a wide range of unusual people, places, and events, most of which are related, either directly or by extension, to medieval monasticism. Some matters, however, are highlighted chiefly for their remarkable local color.

This book traces, on both a local and an international level, the consequences of monastic efforts to follow the Gospel of Matthew (19:21). In it, Christ is quoted as saying: "If you would be perfect, go, sell what you possess, and give to the poor, and you will have treasure in heaven; and come, follow me."

The authors have had in this book two ambitious goals. The first is to introduce the reader to some of the most significant monastic and relevant secular events of the Middle Ages, focusing chiefly on France and England because information on them is more readily available than on other European countries. The second goal is to look beyond the usual facts and illustrations put forward in introductory-level studies of medieval life.

Therefore, many unusual and lesser-known but nevertheless still remarkable medieval individuals and incidents are highlighted. A good example here is Eustache, a French monk who became a pirate and who was eventually captured and then beheaded at sea by English sailors.

The book does not try to cover monastic life in any detail after about 1259 since economic problems and other constraints, discussed later, had by then combined to limit the number of monks who could easily be recruited by the monasteries.

Finally, Eastern Christian monasticism, i.e., the ways of life followed by the monks and nuns of the Eastern Orthodox Church, the Oriental Orthodoxy, the Church of the East, and Eastern Catholicism, is a complicated subject, far afield, and is not covered in this book.

Introduction

Western monasticism itself evolved from Constantine's legalization of Christianity in the year 313, which resulted in its becoming the official religion of his empire. This legalization did not satisfy many of the Christian zealots, however, who wanted to set the religious bar much higher by replacing the physical martyrdom of the persecution era with a new form of devotion. This was the rigorous, self-denying, "private martyrdom" practiced by the early monastic ascetics.

In addition, Western monasticism drew heavily on the unshakeable belief of all devout medieval Christians in the power and, indeed, in the *absolute necessity*, of frequent prayers and good works in order to stay in close touch with God and to stave off the clever, endless, blandishments of the Devil. Because monasticism addressed all these issues so directly, monastic life appealed to a great many of the faithful.

Moreover, in more worldly and more practical terms, for the unmarried sons and daughters of prosperous citizens for whom no rich spouse or generous inheritance was in sight, monastic life also offered many positions of stability and dignity in this world, with high hopes of salvation in the next.[1] One result was that, during its heyday in about 1130, the famous Benedictine monastery of Cluny in Saône-et-Loire, France, mentioned frequently in this book, stood at the apex of an enormous far-flung monastic empire that embraced 1,200 monasteries and hundreds of smaller associated houses scattered all across Western Europe.[2]

Within the limits of his order, the Abbot of Cluny was empowered to create a fluid administrative structure under which he could assign any monk to any monastic house. This flexible, supple, system, built around the central and personal authority of the abbot, would gradually become a key feature in the royal chanceries of England and France and also a keystone of the bureaucracies of the great independent dukedoms, such as that of Burgundy. Moreover, Cluny's highly centralized hierarchy would also become the training grounds for ambitious Catholic prelates: four monks of Cluny, for example, would rise to become popes.

3

Memorably described by the *National Geographic* in a 2010 book published in French as "une architecture de la vertu" ("an architecture of virtue"),[3] the abbey of Cluny could, in this context, also be fittingly described as "an architecture of religious power." Its beginnings were modest enough, however. This later-to-be great monastery was founded on the modest site of Duke William of Aquitaine's hunting lodge—an event that seemed at first to be of such little importance that the Duke himself hesitated to clear out his hunting dogs in order to make room for the monks. Nevertheless, on the site of this little hunting lodge there eventually arose a monastery so extensive that it would become an international meeting place for religious leaders that would be better known to them than Paris itself.[4]

At its peak, this empire had a total of perhaps as many as 10,000 monks. Very few—if any—monastic houses ever rivaled Cluny in the magnificence and size of its buildings. Indeed, Salimbene de Adam de Parma (1221–1288), a Franciscan monk and chronicler, could record to his own astonishment that Cluny itself was so big that the pope with all his cardinals and all his court as well as the emperor with all his could lodge there simultaneously without requiring any monk to leave his cell or suffer any discomfort.[5]

By the mid–12th century, there were about 460 monks in Cluny itself but this huge total was most unusual. Probably much more typical was the small Benedictine abbey at Corbie, France. (An abbey is a monastery headed by an abbot or an abbess, whose title comes from the Aramaic word *Abba*, meaning "father.") In 1234, Corbie was instructed to limit its own size to a maximum of only 40 monks.

That said, it must be understood that even a small abbey was never entirely cut off from the outside world, but instead could easily become the vibrant focal point of local life.[6] Indeed, as the major landowner of the area and the major employer of all kinds of labor, it was often a bee-hive of economic activity. But that was not all. In addition to being the religious center of the region, it was also the key cultural, artistic, and intellectual center. Today, many of the modern towns in Western Europe are located where they are precisely because a monastery once flourished there.

Occupying a complex and impressive range of stone buildings, an abbey would have included a fine church with all of its supporting buildings, namely, kitchens, refectory (i.e., dining room), dormitories, cloister (an arcade around an open unroofed square space), infirmary, abbot's lodgings, and guest houses for important visitors.

As a result, it would soon become the concentration point of local wealth and education, and of relatively prosperous monks, the latter numbering somewhere between 40 to 200 men. There were also some joint monasteries (also known as double monasteries), where monks and nuns shared the same buildings but lived entirely separately within them. The point of this unique arrangement was that priests provided the liturgical and sacramental ministrations which the nuns could not handle alone, since none of them, as women, could be ordained. A priest was thus the only person who could offer the Eucharistic sacrifice. At the same time, the priests or their male employees also shouldered the heavy manual and managerial tasks thought, at that time, to be beyond the capabilities of women.

In early medieval Europe, such joint monasteries were always ruled by an abbess. Although these monasteries reached their height of influence and ubiquity during the mid–7th century and declined thereafter, the later Middle Ages witnessed their gradual reappearance and a gradual spread across Western Europe. In any case, regardless of their ages, virtually all of the men and women in these monasteries would have been recruited only from the better-off elements of local society—a result of the requirement that all applicants had to make a significant financial contribution to a monastery if they wanted to become a member of it.

The authors believe that this book provides a close, more intimate record of history's Western monastic tradition—one which places people and events in their historical context, though not necessarily in chronological order. To keep this text as spritely and free-flowing as possible, the 32 chapters and the eight appendices in this book are all short, well-focused, very diverse in subject matter, and easy to read. Endnotes have been used generously, not only for formal attribution but also to add relevant details without choking up the text itself.

The bibliography offers a wide range of sources for interested readers who want more details on points made in the text. In addition to keeping the dates straight, the Chronology provides a good summary of the contents of this book as a whole. Finally, the appendices cover points that are relevant, instructive, and interesting but would take up too much space if used in the text itself.

When the celebrated medievalist Eileen Power (1889–1940) wrote her short but brilliant book on the medieval English wool trade, the editor explained to her readers that she had achieved "the lucidity of her style and the clarity of her thought, by the relentless reduction of her topics to essentials."[7] In our own book, we have tried hard to follow this same policy, while at the same time highlighting many of medieval monasticism's most striking human interest accounts.

1

The Importance of Monasticism in Western European Medieval Society

Monasticism became a key factor of religious life in the West during the 6th century, which is when the formal rules governing monastic life were first formulated.[1] These rules attached great importance to what the French later called *le travail intellectual des moines* ("the intellectual work of the monks").

Even though their fundamental impulse was to *withdraw* from this sinful world, the men and women who lived, worked, and died in the monasteries of medieval Europe in fact had important impacts on their own societies. For example, they helped to establish social norms, religious rituals, legal procedures, liturgies, and church buildings that were entirely new in their own time. Moreover, these innovations have in many cases survived, and even flourished, down to the present day.

There were many other successful centers of monasticism in Western Europe, e.g., in Italy, England, and Ireland, but it was the monks' intellectual work that was largely responsible for the lasting excellence of university education in Paris. This academic excellence has persisted since then, though chiefly now in secular terms.

The physical location of Paris was its greatest initial asset: this is what ultimately made possible its growth and its economic and strategic importance during the Middle Ages. The first royal palace there was built on the same site that, much earlier, the Romans had chosen for their own settlement. Thanks to its position at the confluence of the Seine, Oise, Marne, and Yerres rivers, Paris would always be well-endowed with grain, livestock, and wine from the surrounding countryside. Its rivers also encouraged trading with other cities in France and with neighboring countries.

Although river tolls to local feudal landowners (feudalism can be defined as "institutionalized patronage") had to be paid no less than 18 times in the 46-mile-long stretch of the Seine between Roche-Guyon near Mantes, which was an important transit-point of the Seine, and Paris itself, trade on the Seine flourished, thanks of the ever-growing population and prosperity of Paris itself.[2] Indeed, by about 1328 there were up to 270,000 people living in Paris and numerous bridges across the Seine there.[3]

The modern French medievalist Sophie Astic-Haisserer has given us a good snapshot of daily life in medieval Paris. Translated and lightly annotated here, it runs along the following lines: Paris during the Middle Ages was girded by two protective defensive walls, but it rapidly expanded far beyond them. It was the opening and the closing of the gates in these walls (the gates were known as *portes*), that governed the ceaseless rhythm of daily life in the city.

This began at about 6 a.m. with the market-cries of the farm women, flocking into Paris to sell fresh milk for little children. All through the day, Paris resounded with the shouts of merchants proclaiming the excellence of their wares, with announcements of public events, with the ringing of the bells of the many churches, and with the noise and smells of thousands of animals being driven to markets. The tumult of the city ceased only at night, when daylight ended (there were no street lights other than an occasional candle) and the city's gates were firmly shut until dawn. In the darkness, the narrow, tortuous, and filthy streets—unpaved, unlit, and unmarked—were peopled only by criminals, never by the honest men and women of daylight hours. The gates of the city and the several landing places along the River Seine all were guarded by men whose senior leader, the *prévot* of Paris, was ultimately responsible only to the King of France.[4]

Because religion so totally conditioned life in Paris during the Middle Ages, from birth to death, there was of course no shortage of religious institutions there. These included about 40 churches or chapels; some 15 monasteries located within the city walls; and about six big abbeys located outside the walls. The streets of the city of medieval Paris were full of priests and other members of religious organizations—so many, indeed, that "it was difficult to count their numbers."[5]

The most fruitful and most long-lasting field of French monastic labor, however, was that of *education*. This process began when every monastery was required to have its own school—chiefly designed to teach its novices how to read and write but, secondarily and rather more rarely, also to teach the sons of the local dignitaries. From these modest beginnings, however, starting in the 6th century the larger and well-established cathedral schools and monasteries of Paris began to attract many thousands of scholars and students, who in turn would form the colleges that would coalesce into the University of Paris in the beginning of the 13th century.

Paris soon became famous as a school of ascetical theologians and was made quite famous by its extraordinary constellation of scholars. By the end of the medieval period, about 50 small colleges had been established in Paris, almost all of them located on the left bank of the River Seine. Few traces of any of them remain today.[6] Some of their brightest teachers, however, are still remembered by historians today. Among them were the monks Hugh and Richard of St. Victor in the 12th century, and the monk Thomas Gallus in the 13th century, who were the foremost spokesmen of the mystical theology of their times.[7]

In this context, we must remember that the university was indigenous to Western Europe and is the greatest and most enduring achievement of the Middle Ages. Much more than stodgy institutions of higher learning, medieval universities were exciting arenas of people and ideas. They contributed enormously to the economic vitality of their host cities and served as birthplaces for some the era's most impressive minds, laws, and discoveries.[8]

Monasticism was certainly an important part of this growth process. There are many possible definitions of monasticism, but one of the clearest can be found in the Castilian law code of the 1260s that is known in Spanish as the *Siete Partidas* ("Seven Parties"). This was a body of legislation that was laid out to formalize the teaching of the Roman Catholic faith and to standardize religious law within the kingdom of Castile itself. Translated and shortened for convenience here, it runs as follows:

> Some persons choose to live a life which is austere and secluded from other men, because they believe that in this way they serve God better without hindrance. And since the riches of this world are an impediment to this, they think it better to renounce them all....
>
> Such persons are those called the regular clergy [the monks], because they all have certain rules by which they are compelled to live, according to the regulations which they have received from the Holy Church at the origin of its religion, and, for this reason, they are included in the Order of the Clergy.[9]

The vital role of the monasteries in preserving and transmitting the then-threatened culture of Western Europe during the early phases of the Middle Ages must never be forgotten by modern readers. During the long, slow, painful decline of the Roman Empire in Western Europe, the monasteries became, by default, the chief producers and storehouses of written knowledge. Indeed, modern historians have long considered the 6th through the 9th centuries to have been "the monastic centuries of education."[10]

The great Harvard medievalist Charles Homer Haskins put this even more dramatically:

Throughout the earlier Middle Ages the chief centres of culture had been the monasteries. Set like islands in a sea of ignorance and barbarism they had saved learning from extinction in Western Europe at a time when no other forces worked strongly toward that end.

True, they too were affected by the localism of the epoch, as well as by the human difficulties of maintaining the ascetic life, but they were kept in some sort of relation with one another by the influence of Rome, by the travels of the Irish monks, by the centralizing efforts of Charles the Great, and by the Cluniac reforms of the tenth and eleventh centuries, so that books and ideas often passed over long distances with a rapidity which surprises the modern student.[11]

It must be noted in passing here that, in the above context, "barbarism" is a now-dated historical expression that only means *those parts of Western Europe where Latin was still not widely spoken by educated people.*

In its broadest terms and as used in this book, Christian monasticism, both past and present, centers on the devotional practices of the believers—both male and female—who lead ascetic and often cloistered lives that are dedicated, directly or indirectly, to what they see as the service of God.

Throughout the many long and highly-devout years of the Middle Ages, monastic life was the most demanding and most dramatic form of religious life in Western Europe. Its rules called on the believer to humble and to tame his or her body. In the late Middle Ages the Church increasingly exalted the image of the suffering body, in imitation of Christ.[12] Due to the subtle but constant influence that monastic life exerted on the rest of medieval society, its importance then for all the ranks of society cannot be overstated.

There were three of these major social ranks during the Middle Ages. Traditionally known as "the three estates," each of these could be defined—but only in the most simplistic terms[13]—in only two words:

1. The first estate consisted of *"the Clerks,"* the ordained clergy, who were backstopped, as it were, by the non-ordained monks and by the nuns who, as women, could never be ordained. The God-given task of all these men and women was to pray for the people of the society.

2. The second estate embraced *"the Chivalry,"* the lords and their knights, who were charged by God with being trained to use military force to protect the people of the society.

3. The third estate can be summarized collectively as *"the Commons,"* chiefly the peasants. This was by far the biggest and poorest social group, whose task, again ordained by God, was to support by its incessant labor the life-styles of the first two estates. As Étienne de Fougères, the chaplain to King Henry II Plantagenet and later the

bishop of Rennes, France, put it so very simply and so accurately in around 1178, "To till the soil and to feed the livestock is the peasant's lot in life: the knight and the cleric [the religious leader] live entirely off what he produces."[14]

The monks, for their part, formed what today might be thought of as a "sub-estate," that is to say, a small but nevertheless very influential social group. It interacted on a daily basis with the ordained clergy (although a small number of monks were also ordained); with the knights and their families; and with many of the farmers, merchants, and working-class men and women of the towns and countryside.

The very challenging and unique lifestyles of the monks and the nuns gradually became role models for spiritual achievement in both the clerical and the lay communities. As a result, these men and women were usually warmly supported—financially, socially, and emotionally—by the other estates of the Middle Ages. The most important single reason for this warm support was that a constant flow of sincere prayers and good works was held to be an exceptionally important "winning ticket" for a blissful heavenly life after death. Kings, queens, and rich aristocrats "withdrew to monasteries," not only at times of political embarrassment for them but especially when their own deaths were nigh.

Even if one had never been a full-time ascetic, to die in the borrowed habit (i.e., the borrowed clothing) of a monk was thought to offer a much safer pathway to heaven than trying to do so directly from the strife and drama of the workaday world.[15] The terrible alternative to a heavenly afterlife was to suffer, for all eternity, the endless pains of hell.

Monasteries made an enormous contribution to the Catholic faith and to the rituals of medieval life and death. Indeed, from the 8th to the 11th centuries, it was the moral and sometimes the life-sustaining physical support they provided, during all the difficulties of daily life, which enabled Western Europe to survive the very worst years of invasion, destruction, famine, or risk of death through illness or by the sword.[16]

Monasteries were not only refuges for the dying but were also schools for the living. For example, a 1076 account of life in Maule, a small but prosperous city in north-central France, reported that during their own lifetimes the local knights and other wealthy residents gladly donated some of their land and other valuables to the monastery there. The reason for this, we are told, is because they valued the monastic order during their lifetimes and, when they were at death's door, they especially wanted its spiritual support.[17]

These knights and residents met frequently with the monks in the cloister and often discussed important spiritual as well as practical matters, such as wine-making, with them. Since many of France's best vineyards were first planned, developed, and overseen by monks, the monks had a great deal of valuable practical advice to offer to local landowners. A later chapter in this book takes a closer look at monks and vineyards.

2

Some Defining Characteristics of Christian Monasticism

Historically, the term "monastic" comes from *monas*, a Greek word meaning "alone" and implies an inward and solitary quest to know and to comply with the will of God. Monks have often been guided by the famous Latin motto *ora et labora* ("pray and work"), which neatly sums up the two most traditionally-important monastic duties.

Christian monasticism began in the deserts of Egypt and Palestine towards the end of the 3rd century. As Jerome, one of the first converts to the Christian monastic life, explained to Paulinus of Nola, a fellow convert, "If you wish to perform the office of a priest, [you should] live in cities and townships, and make the salvation of others the gain of your soul. But if you desire to be what is called a monk, that is a solitary, what are you doing in cities, which after all are the dwelling places not of solitaries, but of the many?"[1]

The early Christian monks were following a tradition already deeply rooted in the New Testament of the Bible. In the first of the Gospel narratives (that of St. Mark), for example, we hear of John the Baptist crying out in the desert: "Prepare ye the way of the Lord, make straight his path!"

Most monks were not priests and thus would have to rely on the local parish priests to administer the religious sacraments to them and to others. Even the most isolated monastic communities, however, usually could arrange to have one or more of their best monks ordained if need be. Because such newly-ordained monastic priests were the cream of the crop, as it were, they were often later chosen by the Church to become bishops.

Writing in Latin in the 11th century, the French bishop Hildebert of Le Mans described the typical monastic building in these words:

> The house presents a four-square shape; the cloister-court is adorned with four open walls, which, enclosed by three buildings required for bodily needs and a

13

fourth which is the church, provide the monks with exercise, food and repose, so that here the sheep are kept, as in a fold.

The first of these buildings stores their bread [the staple food of most French people] and meat [usually only vegetables, since meat was rarely eaten], and the second, counting next, feeds them therewith. The third provides rest for their limbs wearied by the day's labor, and the next forever rings with the praises of God.[2]

Christian monasticism can take credit for constructive activities in an impressive range of historical fields. These include:

- The survival of classical learning, literature, music, art, and many other aspects of Western European culture during the somber twilight years of the Roman Empire in Western Europe.
- Safeguarding important Greco-Roman and early Christian manuscripts and documents in monastery scriptoria (the Latin plural of scriptorium).
- Charitable works such as providing shelter for travelers, nursing the sick, helping the poor, and developing medicines in early pharmacies.
- Advances in agricultural production, road-building, land reclamation, manufacturing, business law, and in the specialization of labor.
- Progress in the liberal arts, music, cooking, and household management.

Monasteries contributed significantly to social stability in both Western and Eastern Europe by offering honorable careers to the unmarried second sons and the daughters of rich aristocratic families. Benedictine abbeys, in particular, offered their recruits security, social status, and a lifelong religious career without the distractions of any pastoral responsibilities.[3]

Monasteries were often caught up in the long and very human drama of (1) an initial burst of religious enthusiasm; (2) an era of temporary stability and growth; (3) a gradual slipping of its most ascetic standards; (4) a growing laxness and wealth; and, finally, (5) the need for a reformation of a monastery or, indeed, monastic order. After this last step, however, the above cycle was not infrequently repeated.

By the end of the High Middle Ages, however, new developments had combined to limit the number of monks who were willing and able to follow the classic pattern of quietly spending their entire lives in one monastery. These developments included rising economic costs; declining endowments; longer waiting times for new postulants, which made this way of life less attractive; and an end to child-oblation, i.e., the practice of parents donating a young boy to a monastic community to be brought up as a monk. Child-oblation had become the predominant gateway into monastic life during the 9th century.

By taking such a drastic step, the parents made what could best be called a "living investment" in a given monastery, and one that they expected would earn them very rich if intangible spiritual rewards over the child's lifetime. This certainly was a common practice: the surviving rent-rolls of the priory of Canterbury Cathedral in England, for example, reveal that in the 12th century many Canterbury families donated a young relative to this priory.[4] (A priory was a smaller monastery that did not have the status of an abbey. Its superior was known as the prior.) However, in a decretal, i.e., a papal directive, Pope Celestine III (1191–98) established that a boy who had been donated to a monastery by his father was free to leave as soon as he became an adult. Only a formal solemn vow taken by him as an adult could then turn him into him a monk.

Probably profiting from such sweeping changes were the mendicant friars. "Mendicant" means "a beggar"; "friars" means "brothers" in Latin. These men were addressed as "Brother," followed by their first name, as in "Brother John." However, other male members of a monastery, not just the mendicants, could properly be addressed as "Brother" as well, on the grounds that they were also "brothers in Christ."

Unlike monks, the mendicant friars did not live permanently in any specific monastery but were instead sent far afield and had to beg publicly for their daily food in order to be able to survive and preach in the towns and to help the poor there. Virtually all of them came from what we would now call middle-class families, were relatively well-educated, and almost all of them were quite devoted to their challenging way of life.

Being a mendicant was in fact a surprisingly popular way of religious life. In 1330, for example, in France alone there were 226 small cities that had mendicant monasteries, of which 28 cities had four monasteries and 24 cities had three monasteries.[5]

The medieval Franciscan monk and chronicler Salimbe de Adam de Parma assures us that the attractions of this calling were sufficiently great to bring forth a stream of high-quality recruits. He writes:

> There are many in both orders of friars [Franciscans and Dominicans] who, if they had been in the world, would have possessed the prebends [the ecclesiastical offices] they hold, and perhaps much better, for they are just as nobly born, as rich, powerful and learned as they, and would have been priests, canons [clerics living under an ecclesiastical rule], archdeacons, bishops and archbishops, perhaps even cardinals and popes like them. They should recognize that we have given up all these things to go begging.[6]

These mendicant friars may have been the most energetic part of the medieval Church in Western Europe during in the later Middle Ages.[7] This was an era in which most of the old monastic orders, which had been among the first transnational organizations in the world, were slowly decaying from a lack of postulants and a decline in endowments from wealthy believers.[8]

Nevertheless, during the Middle Ages the major monastic orders did leave an impressive trail of physical monuments sprinkled throughout Europe. The cultural impact of these buildings, both in cities and countryside alike, diffused architectural and artistic forms and techniques, thus linking this material heritage to the broader sweep of Europe's cultural and artistic history.[9]

The old orders were also hindered by their inherent and profound conservatism, which tied them tightly to their own monasteries. As the great medievalist Helen Waddell wrote of Brother Rupert, one of these traditional stay-at-home monks (i.e., he was not a friar), "the natural state of the clerical soul is static. Brother Rupert went about but little and hardly wore out two pairs of shoes in the year.... The stability of the Church goes far to stabilize Europe; it is seen in so concrete an instance as the growing of the towns round the episcopal palaces."[10]

The only great innovation in the ecclesiastical life of Paris itself toward the end of the High Middle Ages was the arrival there in 1217 of the two most remarkable mendicant orders, namely, the Dominicans (the Black Friars or Friars Preacher), and the Franciscans (Grey Friars; Friars Minor; or, in French, the *Cordeliers*—named after the cord they used to tie their long robe close to their bodies).

From the middle of the 13th century on, the Carmelites ("White Friars") and the Augustinian or "Austin" friars who wore black habits, were mendicant orders, too, but are perhaps not as well known today as the Dominicans and Franciscans, probably because much less has been written about them.[11] All these friars demonstrated strikingly new ways to preach Christianity, earning their daily bread by preaching in the streets, and by the genuine poverty of their personal lives. Their overriding goal was to preach the Gospel to the laity in the streets and squares of the big cities, that is, wherever they could draw a crowd of the faithful or just of the idle and the curious.[12]

However, this very simple and noble idea, which was the insight of St. Francis, all too easily lent itself to considerable abuse. The mendicants were supposed to beg for their own modest subsistence and then to give all the surplus donations only to the poor, the homeless, and the sick. By the time the great poet Geoffrey Chaucer was writing *The Canterbury Tales* in about 1386, however, the friars were being widely criticized for profiting personally from their supposedly-selfless calling.[13]

The French theologian William of Saint-Amour (1202–1272), for example, deplored the eagerness of mendicants to visit the homes of their parishioners who were ill and dying. The mendicants had hit upon this strategy because it brought them a more intimate contact with the patient's family, particularly the sorrowing womenfolk.

Indeed, these women themselves became passionate supporters of what we might, only half-jokingly, call these "death-bed mendicants." As part of this process, the practice of making legally-binding wills became more widespread and, not surprisingly, included "guarantees" of generous donations to convents.[14] Together with other orders, the mendicants are discussed again later.

It remains to be noted here that, in the Middle Ages, ordinary Christians usually regarded monks and nuns with mixed feelings. On the positive side, they granted them a certain degree of awe and respect as holy men and holy women whose lives and prayers were especially pleasing to God. On the negative side, however, as self-designated spiritual elites, these religious men and women may have looked down a bit, if only unconsciously, on all those rank-and-file "unholy" people who constituted the vast majority of the society and who could not live such austere lives.

Moreover, as the numbers of monasteries grew larger over time and attracted from the faithful more and more valuable donations of land and other worldly goods, the potential for monastic abuse of this largesse also grew. The problem here did not arise from any *shortage* of regulatory law but rather from a *superabundance* of often-contradictory legal rules and regulations.[15]

The medieval monk Gratian, discussed later, was one of the first to try to impose logical order onto the study of canon law, i.e., ecclesiastical law. Nevertheless, perhaps it can be joked here that canon law itself, which straddles the borders between law and theology and which is discussed later, was both part of the solution and part of the problem because of its complexities.

Canon law formed the governing principles and rules ("canon" in Greek) of the Western Church. It was based an amalgam of papal decretals, papal promulgations, and Roman civil law. What is most clear today is that, as the modern medievalist James Brundage put it,

> Canon law occupied a unique niche among the legal systems that flourished in the high and later Middle Ages. While most legal systems were confined to a particular region or locality, canon law emerged as a working and often quite effective international law. With relatively few exceptions, the same canonical rules applied everywhere in Latin Christendom....
> [Thus canon law] can tell us much about the sources of our own institutions and societies, as well as the vanished world of medieval Christendom, out of which the world we see around us ultimately grew.[16]

3

Early Western
European Monasticism

This chapter highlights, briefly, some of the most relevant historical background of the Western European way of monastic life. The beginnings lie in the ancient Jewish literature which mentions the existence of a group known as the "Nazirites" in what is now Israel. A Nazirite was a man who vowed, for a specific period of time, to abstain from grapes and any products thereof, whether intoxicating or not; not to cut his hair; and not to touch a corpse.[1]

"Nazirite" comes from the Hebrew word *nazir*, meaning "consecrated" or "separated." In daily Jewish life, such a man had a special status, resembling that of a priest, in that he was publicly known as being "holy to the Lord." The long uncut hair of the Nazirite was his special feature and his special distinction. It was, in fact, considered to be the real focal point of a man's own vitality and his life-force. During a Jewish religious ritual, a strand or two of it might have been able to substitute for him, symbolically, even if he could not be physically present himself.

The folk-heroes Samson and Samuel were lifelong Nazirites. It was believed by the faithful that their dedication to religion began not at their birth, but even earlier—at their very conception. They themselves were not monks, but perhaps we can think of them as having set the religious stage, as it were, for the later arrival of the early Christian monks.

During the Late Second Temple period (200 BCE to 70 CE),[2] the contemporary historian Flavius Josephus divided the Jews of Judea, conceptually, into three main groups: the Sadducees, the Pharisees, and the Essenes. Only the Essenes, however, are relevant to this present book.

The reason is that they formed a separatist group in the late 2nd century BCE, some of whom became an ascetic monastic community by the process of retreating into the wilderness of Judea. There they shared their meager material possessions and devoted themselves to disciplined study, worship, and hard physical work. They practiced communal ownership, ritual bathing, isolation, special oaths, and special food practices. They also carefully studied the Jewish mystical and apocalyptical writings of the period. They ate their meals together. One branch of this group did not marry.[3]

Philo of Alexandria describes the early Jewish hermits and communities who lived in Egypt in the 1st century CE. They practiced solitude, ritual cleansing, prayer, and fasting. Philo viewed them as good examples of a contemplative religious existence because they also studied Jewish allegorical and mystical readings from the Old Testament and from Apocryphal works.

Real-life Jewish and early Christian role models for medieval monastic life are said to have included:

- The Old Testament prophets Elijah and Elisha.
- John the Baptist, whose rigorous lifestyle and prophetic activities made him a forerunner of Christianity in Europe.
- Mary, hailed as the Mother of God, whose obedience, total submission to the divine will, and chastity were all seen as important aspects of the ascetic life.
- Paul, whose celibacy and practical tent-making skills were prized as monastic virtues.
- Jesus, whose life of celibacy, prayer, and self-sacrifice was revered as the highest possible role model.[4]

Historically, there have been two fundamental kinds of early Western monasticism: the eremetic and the cenobitic. These were not mutually exclusive, however, and some monks first followed one, and then the other, way of life.

The eremetics were hermits living alone, surviving either by the food and other supplies their supporters freely brought to them, or by earning a tiny income on their own from such rudimentary desert skills as tent-making and rope-making. Their diet was undoubtedly quite similar to that of the Egyptian peasants in the earliest centuries of Christianity: namely, bread, lentils, peas, beans, seasonal fruits and vegetables, dried figs, and honey.

The first Christian monk known to history by name was Paulus the Hermit (c. 230–342). As time went on, many such early hermits modified their lifestyles slightly—by continuing to live alone, but now by living close enough to each other so that mutual support and occasional religious meetings were possible.

The cenobitics, on the other hand, whose name in Latin means "community," were monks who lived very closely together as a unified group and who followed a common rule of life, i.e., a systematic ordering of that way of life. For example, at Dandara, on the Nile, Pachomius of Egypt

(292–346) is traditionally considered to have organized the first community of Christian monks, but his community may well have been only one of several other very loosely-organized Christian groups.

The famous "Desert Fathers," the desert-dwelling Christian monks of Egypt, were some of the earliest monks who variously followed both the eremitic (solitary) and the cenobitic (community) ways of life. These Desert Fathers are said to have arisen in reaction to the relative luxury, laxness, and excesses that developed after Christianity had been declared to be, first, a *tolerated* legal religion of the late Roman Empire, and then, later, the *official and most-favored* creed of that empire.

The Desert Fathers never lacked a dry sense of humor, as the following story shows:

> There were two old men who had lived together for many years and had never fought with one another. The first said to the other, "Let us have a fight like other men do." The other replied, "I do not know how to fight."
>
> The first said to him, "Look, I will put a brick between us, and I will say it is mine, and you will say, 'No, it is mine,' and so the fight will begin.
>
> So they put a brick between them and the first said, 'This brick is mine,' and the other said, 'No, it is mine,' and the first responded, 'If it is yours, take it and go'—so they gave up without being able to find an occasion for argument.[5]

One of the earliest and most famous desert hermits was Anthony of Egypt (251–356), a notable figure in Western monasticism who is said to have spent 80 years living as a hermit. He is remembered today chiefly because of the foundational writings of Athanasius, which were entitled, and which focused on, the *Life of Anthony.*

Anthony's decision to commit himself to the unforgiving harshness of desert life, his ascetic practices, and the many stories told about his spiritual struggles with diabolical forces all combined to encourage other devout men to follow in his footsteps. Athanasius tells us that young Anthony at first lived a very conventional and very normal Christian life until, one day on his way to church, he was suddenly emboldened to adopt a much more demanding lifestyle. This is what happened:

> [Anthony] communed with himself and reflected as he walked how all the Apostles left all and followed the Savior; and how in the Acts [the Biblical Acts of the Apostles] sold their possessions and brought and laid them at the Apostles' feet for distribution to the needy, and what and how great a hope was laid up for them in heaven.[6]

As the modern scholar John W. Baldwin has written,

> The great beauty of monastic manuscripts is testimony to the monks' patience and devotion. Unconcerned by the passage of time or the conflicts of the world, secure in his rural seclusion, the monk cultivated his learning in

isolation. His ideal habitat was best explained by Anthony of the Desert, who memorably advised a monk: 'Sit in thy cell and thy cell will teach you all things. The monk out of his cell is like a fish out of water.'[7]

Other early shapers of monasticism include Basil of Caesarea (c. 330–379), Benedict of Nursia (480–543), and an anonymous monk known only as Pseudo-Dionysius, who lived in Syria around the year 500 but whose religious influence extended into the Renaissance.

Basil of Caesarea, referred to as Basil the Great, was the founder of monasticism in Eastern Europe. Unlike most of the other Egyptian ascetics, he was a well-educated man from a professional family and had studied at Caesarea, Constantinople, and Athens. His writings, entitled *Aescetica*, laid down the foundational rules that still guide Eastern Orthodox monastic practice today. One of the chief theologians and preachers of his time, he also served as a bishop during the last seven years of his life.

Benedict of Nursia (480–543) is discussed again later in this book. Suffice it to say here that he is now widely considered to be the father of Western monasticism, having founded the monastery of Monte Cassino in Italy in 529. Indeed, until the end of the 12th century, which saw the rise of the Franciscan and Dominican orders, the Benedictine way of life was by far the dominant force in Western European monastic life.

Benedict began his monastic life as a hermit but after being surrounded near Sabiaco, Italy, in about 525 by enthusiastic crowds of his followers, he decided to found a communal monastic house at Monte Cassino in Italy.[8] He wrote a rule for monks that would become the bedrock on which the Benedictine Order is still based today. He understood the real need for a monastery and explained that "Therefore, we intend to establish a *schola* [this Latin word literally means 'school' but also carries the strong connotation of 'a military combat unit' for the Lord's service]."[9]

Benedict decided that his order must be governed by the rule of Saint Augustine. He laid a heavy responsibility on believers by telling them very firmly:

> Let a man consider that God is always looking at him from heaven, that his actions are everywhere visible to the divine eyes and are constantly being reported to God by the Angels.... In order that he may be careful about his wrongful thoughts, therefore, let the faithful brother say constantly in his heart: 'Then shall I be spotless before Him, if I have kept myself from my iniquity.'[10]

This rule embodies the three fundamental vows that monks were required to make, namely, *poverty* (i.e., communal, not personal, ownership of all property; very simple dress; and very simple meals); *chastity* (i.e., celibacy; self-control; and purity in life, thought, and body); and *obedience* (i.e., immediate and unquestioning submission to all superiors and to all monks who have entered the order earlier). In addition, Benedictine monks also took a fourth vow—namely, *stability*, which meant that they promised to live in one place only, usually their own monastery.

The influence of Pseudo-Dionysius on monastic thought was profound. His works were first used in public debates in the Eastern Christian Church during the rule of the Roman Emperor Justinian (who reigned from 527 to 565), but continued to be cited by major Western theologians well into the Renaissance. We do not have space to discuss all the elements of this monk's complex but very interesting theological speculations, but will note here that he believed *both positive and negative terms* must be used to describe God. This in turn, however, required a very careful use of language.

Pseudo-Dionysius offered to his monastic and other religious readers a "positive theology." This centered on attributing to God all those good attributes of human beings which may also be said to apply to God as well. However, since God is considered to be both unlimited and transcendent, a medieval theologian had to choose his words here with some care. For example, it would be incorrect for our mythical theologian to say that "God is good" in precisely the same sense that "a human being is good." God and human beings do not operate on the same plane and thus cannot ever be described in the same terms. It would therefore be more accurate for our theologian to explain, in this context, that God is in fact "super-good."

The "negative theology," or the "negations," of Pseudo-Dionysius, on the other hand, tell the reader that *God is not good* in the very limited sense that a mere human being can be considered as being good. Indeed, this negative theology argues that all names and all theological representations must be *negated*, i.e., they must simply be ignored.

The reason for this assertion is that the ultimate mystical religious experience is held to be far "beyond light and darkness: it is utter silence."[11] If such a religious experience should ever occur, according to Pseudo-Dionysius, there would be only *divine silence, total darkness, and a timeless "unknowing."*

Moving from the cosmic to a more mundane level, one can note that, under the procedures of Benedictine monasticism, monks carefully organized their day around a tightly-fixed schedule of religious services that were sung or recited at eight fixed times of the day. These were variously known as the canonical hours; as the Divine Office; or, in Latin, as *Opus Dei*, literally, the "Work of God." The detailed liturgy used in them was drawn primarily from the Psalter, a collection of poetic songs traditionally attributed to the Biblical King David. During the 24-hour day, each eight-hour segment had its own time-slot and its own prayers:

- During the night: Matins
- Morning prayer at dawn: Lauds
- Early morning prayer: Prime (6 a.m.)
- Mid-morning prayer: Terce (9 a.m.)
- Mid-day prayer: Sext (12 p.m.)
- Mid-afternoon prayer: None (3 p.m.)
- Evening prayer: Vespers (at the lighting of the lamps)
- Night prayer: Compline (just before going to bed), which marked the beginning of the Great Silence, i.e., the night hours during which talking was forbidden. During this period, only sign language was permitted. Known as "the language of the fingers and eyes," this was so highly-developed, however, that it was almost as quick and as accurate as spoken words.[12]

The Carthusian order, for its part, was founded by the religious leader Bruno in 1084 in Chartreuse, in the Alps. It adopted a radically reformed and much stricter new rule, known as *The Statues*, as distinct from the traditional Benedictine rule.

The Benedictine rule, however, was far more widespread, and it was this rule that was normally followed in Western monasticism by the early 11th century. Functioning both as a spoken text through readings at monastic meals, and as a written text for solitary monastic study, it was relatively gentle.[13] Indeed, a 15th-century illustration by the medieval artist Jean de Stavelot, now held by the Musée Condé in Chantilly, France, shows a kindly St. Benedict dictating his rule to a monk to copy and to promulgate.

Benedict's rule struck a very gentle and very kind paternal note in its opening words to the attentive postulate or monk:

> Hearken, O my son, to the precepts of the Master
> and incline the ear of your heart;
> freely accept and faithfully fulfill the instructions of a loving Father,
> that by the labor of obedience thou mayest return to Him
> from whom thou has strayed by the sloth of disobedience.[14]

Drawing considerable healing power from its time-tested liturgical rituals and from its extensive involvement in daily medieval life, this rule governed the monk's existence within a carefully-structured and like-minded 24-hour-a-day community run along the following lines[15]:

- Sleep (in two divided shifts, totaling 8½ hours)
- Religious offices (3½ hours)

- Reading and meditation (4½ hours)
- Manual labor (6½ hours)
- Eating (1 hour)

One of the best modern descriptions of the Benedictine rule came from the great French historian Marc Bloch (1886–1944). He described it as applying to

> a divided and pulsating world, ceaselessly tossed to and fro between pure asceticism and the more mundane cares inseparable from the administration of great wealth, or even from the humble business of gaining a livelihood. Moreover, we must not picture this body as separated from the laity by impossible barriers. Even those rules which embodied the most uncompromising principles of reclusion had at the last resort to yield to practical necessity. Monks had the cure of souls in parishes. Monasteries opened their doors to pupils who would never assume the cowl; especially after the Gregorian reform they became a nursery of bishops and popes.[16]

This very civilized and humane version of monastic life was highly valued by its conservative traditionalist supporters, but it was also strongly criticized by the most ascetic reformers, such as the Carthusians, an order founded in Germany in 1084. They saw it only as an inevitable slide toward an ever-softer and easier lifestyle.

Still considered today to be one of the strictest orders of the Roman Catholic Church, the Carthusians therefore rejected the more convivial dormitory-style common sleeping quarters used at the huge French monastery of Cluny. Instead, each monk lived and slept in the solitude of his own cell. Their austere lifestyle, which will be described later in more detail, was a very simple and Spartan existence, with plenty of hard manual labor, a scanty diet, and a minimum of warm clothing.

The Carthusians also stressed the need for simplicity and opposed the use of any special insignia to identify themselves. Indeed, they consciously returned to the earlier traditions of the Desert Fathers by serving under this motto: *nunquam reformata quia nunquam deformata* ("that which has never been deformed needs no reform now").[17]

As late as the 14th and 15th centuries, there was a small but steady growth in the number of Carthusian monasteries. This trend is thought to reflect the fact that, during the later Middle Ages, believers had decided to break away from the most structured and impersonal religious movements of the past. They now welcomed the chance to experience a *personal piety* of their own making. As the medievalist C.H. Lawrence put it, "It was an outward and visible sign of the spiritual kinship between the eremitical [monastic] ideal and the religious individualism of the townsmen that, at this period, patrons of the Carthusians began to erect

Charterhouses [monasteries] in the center of cities like London, Paris, and Cologne."[18]

The Cistercian order (its name comes from "Cisterium," the Latin name for the village of Cîteaux near Dijon in France) dates from 1098, when the monk Robert of Mosleme left the Benedictine order and set up a reform movement at Cîteaux. This new order, which has been aptly described by a modern scholar as "an offshoot of the Benedictine tree," came into being at the turn of the 12th century and as part of a radical monastic renewal that was then picking up speed.[19]

The Cistercians called for a return to the Benedictine rule in its original and exceptionally strict form. This order would soon become famous for its innovations in clearing land and developing new methods of agricultural production. Today Cistercian architecture is still hailed as one of the most beautiful styles of medieval architecture. Indeed, the Cistercians believed that a monastery, in its design, execution, and use, must be a "taste of paradise."[20]

This order stressed the importance of manual agricultural work in remote retreats (especially raising sheep for their wool) which could in time become largely self-sufficient. As the modern medievalist Gillian Hutchinson told us,

> Wool was the principal export of England and Scotland from before the [Norman] Conquest. During the 12th century, sheep farming grew rapidly, partly as a result of the new monastic houses, chiefly Cistercian, which specialized in it. For a great part of the Middle Ages, England was the largest and most important source of fine wool, supplying a good part of the Italian cloth industry and nearly the whole of the industry of the Low Countries.[21]

To avoid being caught up in the prosperity generated by their intensive sheep farming, the Cistercians always refused to accept any gifts to their wealthy, devout believers. In fact, the very high religious aspirations of this new order prompted its many critics to denounce it as being "insanely conceited."[22]

Under the leadership of Bernard of Clairvaux (1090–1153), an eloquent strong-willed mystic who became one of the most famous medieval monks, the number of Cistercian houses soared from 30 to 280 and later, after his death, to 344 houses in 1153. By the 15th century, there were over 750 Cistercian houses spread out across Europe.

A charming contemporary but unattributed first-person account of the Cistercian abbey of Clairvaux, located in Burgundy in what is now France, includes the following observations:

> Should you wish to picture Clairvaux, the following has been written to serve you as a mirror. Imagine two hills and between them a narrow valley, which

widens out as it approaches the monastery. The abbey covers one half of one hillside and the whole of the other. One is rich in vineyards, the other in crops, they do double duty, gladdening the heart and serving our necessities, one shelving flank providing food, the other drink....

Farther on, the rear of the abbey extends to the wide valley bottom, much of which lies inside the great sweep of the abbey walls....

The meadow [of the monastery] is refreshed by floodwaters of the Aube [a local river], which runs through it, so that the grass, thanks to the moisture at its roots, can stand the summer heat....

Two granges [associated monastic farms]] divide this meadow between them, the Aube serving as an equitable judge and surveyor in the settling of disputes. Assigning to each its share, like a marking-rope it sets the bounds that neither dares cross to invade the other's portion....

As regards the monastic buildings themselves, you will admit that they are well-fitted in size, location, and appearance for a large community of monks.

In the part of the meadow nearest the wall, a watery lake has been created from the solid field.... A brook some thirty feet distant keeps the water-level constant by means of feeder ditches, which carry and regulate both inflow and outflow.[23]

During the 13th century, to support their rapidly-expanding wool industry, the Cistercians even created a new order of lay brothers, who were not monks but who were instead highly-skilled herdsmen and field workers.

In this process, the Cistercians hit upon an effective policy that was midway between the total centralization of the Cluniac monks, on the one hand, and the complete independence of the Benedictine houses, on the other. At an annual meeting, for example, the abbot of Cîteaux would preside over an association of all the houses that were administered on his behalf by their resident Cistercian abbots.

To some extent, though, this midway policy was highly controversial. The Cistercians claimed to have unilaterally revived the pure and strict observance of the Benedictine rule which, they asserted, had been ignored over the years by the softer and more comfort-loving monks of Cluny, who were too fond of good food and of their gorgeous vestments for Mass, which were made of silk studded with semi-precious stones.

Any hard feelings between the Cistercian rigorists and the Cluniac traditionalists, however, tended to resolve themselves over time as both parties increasingly recognized their common inheritance and their common quest for a holy way of life. In practice, by the 1160s their dispute would settle down into a much less passionate intellectual debate.

However, in the early 12th century an English monk, known as William of Malmesbury and writing in Wiltshire, waxed eloquent over the remarkable abilities and motivation of the local Cistercians monks:

These men ... love bright minds more than gold vestments, knowing that the best recompense of good deeds is the enjoyment of a clear conscience. But if the laudable clemency of the abbot either wishes or pretends to wish to mitigate anything in the letter of the rule [i.e., by making it easier], these men strive against it, saying that there is not much time in life, nor will they live as long as they have done already; that they hope to maintain their purpose, and be an example for their successors in the future, who will sin if they should waver ... the Cistercian monks of today are an example for all monks, a mirror for the zealous, a goad for the slothful.[24]

During the 11th century, numerous independent monastic houses arose and organized themselves under the rule of St. Augustine, which was the early fifth-century work of the theologian, philosopher, and bishop Augustine of Hippo, North Africa. It was the monastic leader Augustine of Canterbury, however, who first brought Christian monasticism to England. In 597, he led a party of monks from Rome to Canterbury, where he was well-received by the pagan (the non–Christian), king of Kent.

Much later, between 1243 and 1256, the scattered Augustinian monasteries were officially consolidated by Pope Innocent IV during a lengthy process known as "The Great Union." In modern times, inspired by its ideals of "modesty and service," the order of Saint Augustine has administered schools, hospitals, retirement centers, and musical institutions.

The Franciscan and the Dominican orders, for their part, both date from the 13th century. It has been said that the policy of the Dominican order has been to preach the Gospel *both* by word and by example, while the Franciscans have long exhorted *more by example* than by word. Perhaps as a result, it has been joked that the Dominican trusts first to *reason*, while the Franciscan trusts first to *feeling*.[25]

Perhaps the best example of this latter point is a medieval religious song, the Canticle of the Sun, which is also known as *Laudes Creaturarum* ("Praise of the Creatures") and as the *Canticle of the Creatures*. Written by Francis of Assisi in about 1224 in the Umbrian dialect of Italian, it has since then been translated into many languages and is believed to be one of the first important works of literature—or, indeed, perhaps the very first work—ever written in Italian. An English translation of this song is given in Appendix 2.

Begun in Italy by Francis and by Clare of Assisi, the Franciscans were a preaching order most concerned with the poor. They became best-known for their work with the sick, the destitute, and the disenfranchised, and for their unquestioning obedience to the Pope. As Francis himself prescribed in his rule,

The brothers shall appropriate nothing to themselves, neither a place nor anything; but as pilgrims and strangers in this world, in poverty and humility serving God they shall go with confidence seeking alms. Nor need they be ashamed, for the Lord made himself poor for us in this world. This is that summit of the most lofty poverty which has made you, my most beloved brothers, heirs and kings of the kingdom of Heaven.[26]

Under Francis' charismatic leadership, the order expanded rapidly and became most active in the fields of evangelical poverty, in compassion for the downtrodden, and in its missionary projects. After his lifetime, however, the order split into stricter factions and laxer factions.

The scholar Bonaventure was the leader of the Franciscans from 1257 to 1274 and charted a new and more publicly-acceptable course by reining in the excesses of the much stricter "Spiritual" faction. In the end, however, the moderate "Conventuals" prevailed, and the "Spirituals" were declared heretical in 1322.

The Dominican order, also known as the Order of Preachers (in Latin, *Ordo Praedicatorum*), was founded by Dominic in the 13th century as a mendicant order—a name that comes from the Latin word meaning "to beg." This name refers to the orders of friars who did not settle down in the monasteries of the countryside but who lived instead in whatever modest temporary housing they could find in the cities, where they begged for their food.

Their goal was to serve God, and at the same time to work for their own salvation, not by cloistered asceticism in one given place (the monastery) but by working for others in much bigger geographical areas known as "provinces." Typically, they moved frequently, spending time in different houses of the communities located within a given province. They set themselves the tasks of preaching and ministering to city dwellers, and refused to own any collective or personal property at all. In order to survive, they relied on temporary jobs and, above all, they depended chiefly on their well-organized and socially-approved begging.

The Dominican order began with the vastly overly-ambitious evangelical goal of trying to convert all the local Muslims, Jews, and heretics to the Roman Catholic faith. Clearly, this goal could never be achieved. In more practical and more attainable terms, Dominic himself stressed that his monks needed to have a very strong *academic education*, especially in theology. This subject was at first the specialty of the monastic schools (the schools which since the 6th century had been closely allied with the monasteries). Then it flourished in the cathedral schools themselves. These latter were the schools associated with the seat of a bishop, i.e., a cathedral; some of these cathedral schools would later evolve into the medieval universities.[27] Dominic also wanted his monks to have the ability to speak fluently the languages most familiar to their audiences. Moreover, to avoid the charge of hypocrisy, they also had to lead personal lives of genuine simplicity and poverty.

The Dominican order itself grew quickly during its first centuries of existence, and its influence expanded rapidly because its brightest monks were selected for religious offices. Two of the most famous Dominicans were the friar Albertus Magnus and the monk Thomas Aquinas. Eventually, because of the intellectual skills of its best members, this order was put in charge of running the Inquisition in Rome.

The great Benedictine monastery at Cluny in Burgundy, France, was founded in 909 by Duke William III of Aquitaine to be an abbey that would be free of control by any secular states and that would endure forever. It was led by a series of seven powerful and intelligent abbots, who practiced a very centralized form of government which made all of Cluny's monastic houses answerable to Cluny's mother house.[28] As Duke William had explained his plan,

> Desiring to provide for my own salvation while I am still able, I have considered it advisable, indeed most necessary, that from the temporal goods conferred upon me I should give some little portion for the gain of my soul … which indeed seems attainable by no more suitable means than that, following the precept of Christ: 'I will make his poor my friends' … and making this act not a temporary but a lasting one, I should support at my own expense a congregation of monks.
>
> And this is my trust, this is my hope, that although I myself am unable to despise all things, nevertheless by receiving those who do despise the world [i.e., monks], whom I believe to be righteousness, I too may receive the reward of my righteousness.[29]

The net result was that Cluny flourished. It became a major center of liturgy and of art and was responsible for the training of popes and other key church officials. In the process, the Cluniacs, as an order, became quite rich, very influential, and well-traveled. Cluniac monasteries, for example, dotted the overnight stops of the great pilgrimage roads leading from northern Europe to Compostella in Spain.

The importance of these pilgrimage routes must not be overlooked. As the great medievalist Charles Homer Haskins reminds us,

> Stations of call and entertainment for very traveler, refuges of healing and consolation, shrines of devotion and even of miracles, [the religious establishments along these routes] collected distant fact and rumor for their local annals, spun their narratives of the wonders wrought by local saints and relics, and passed on the rich material for the popular epics which grew up along these roads and about these shrines. They were the natural meeting points of the world of the monk and the sacristan with the world of the pilgrim, the trader and the jongleur, of sacred and profane, Latin and vernacular....[30]

In marked contrast to the very peaceful dispositions of most monastic orders, some monks were in fact very warlike. These are discussed again in a later chapter, but here we can introduce some of the key players, beginning with the Knights Templar (c. 1119–c. 1312)—the best known of the monastic military orders.

This organization was set up after the First Crusade, thanks to the inspiration of Bernard of Clairvaux, and was designed to protect pilgrims in the Holy Land. It included both lifetime members, who were celibate, and temporary members, who could be married. Templar knights, wearing their distinctive white mantles marked with a red cross, were among the most skilled fighting units of the Crusades. There were up to 20,000 of them at their full strength, of whom only 10 percent were knights.

It was the remarkable achievement of Bernard and other religious activists to be able to fuse the military talents of the knightly class with their own more passive religious aspirations. The result was the birth of new orders that could best be called "monastic knights" or "fighting monks." These sanctioned the ideal of a new Christian knighthood dedicated to holy war, and made it possible for aggressive men who had no interest whatsoever in the quiet life of a secluded monastery to become active members of respected monastic orders.[31]

The 90 percent of the Templars who were not knights themselves were instead intelligent laymen that managed, very successfully, the Templars' large economic and financial infrastructure that was dotted throughout the Christian world. Indeed, the Templars' network of 1,000 *commanderies* (these were the smallest administrative units of their order) and all its forts across Europe and in the Holy Land may well have been the world's first truly multinational corporation. The order's visible successes as international bankers, however, soon led to its own downfall.

The Templars were so closely entwined with the Crusades that, after the Muslims recaptured Jerusalem in 1187, Western political and economic support for the Templars began to dry up. At the same time, King Philip IV of France, who was deeply in financial debt to the order, seized this unique opportunity to erase his debt by murdering the Templars. This process he began in 1307, when he had many of the Templars in France arrested, tortured into giving false confessions, and then burned at the stake. Under intense pressure from King Philip, Pope Clement V disbanded the order in 1312.

In 1318, however, a new "Order of Christ" picked up the fallen banner of the Knights Templar and absorbed many of its men. Headquartered in Portugal, the Order of Christ evolved over the centuries into both a religious order answerable to the Pope and a civil order answerable to the king.

Yet another armed-monk group, the Knights Hospitaller, a 12th-century order working with the sick, also pledged itself to protect pilgrims, militarily, when they were en route to and from the Holy Land. This order also fought in the Holy Land and later absorbed much of the property of the Knights Templar after they were suppressed. The branches of the Knights Hospitaller eventually became free-standing military enclaves, such as those of the Knights of Malta. Today, several other international non-military orders continue the Hospitaller tradition of service to others.

4

An Overview of Medieval
Monastic Callings

This chapter looks very briefly at a remarkable range of men and women, some of whom are discussed again in later chapters.

By using the term "monastic calling" very broadly, we can profitably interview, as it were, some of the hermits, monks, friars, clerics, nuns, and those following less structured religious lives. These latter included both the Beguines (groups of devout Christian lay-women who came together to practice a new form of nun-like religious life), and the reviled wandering monks known as *gyrovagi*. All these terms will be defined and discussed.

Hermits have already been mentioned in earlier pages, but more can usefully been said about them here. These were men who, for reasons best known to themselves, had chosen to follow *literally* the New Testament exhortations that spiritual salvation could best be achieved by living a totally isolated holy life, far removed from any worldly temptations, and by focusing single-mindedly on solitude and religious meditation.

Originally known as "anchorites," they divided their lives between prayer, asceticism, and hard physical work. They must have been very tough men: indeed, it was even joked by outsiders that they lived such lonely and intense lives that "their urine would etch glass."

Although Benedict's masterplan for the monastic life was in essence cenobitic, i.e., communal, he did leave room in it for some hermits. He warned his readers, though, that any aspiring hermit would first have to undergo some basic training by living for a time in a monastic community. This was so important, he wrote, because it was only in this way that those "who are not in the first fervor of the ascetical life [when they would be dangerously inexperienced], but in the daily testing of the monastery have been taught to fight the devil, [can] go out well armed from the battle-line of the brethren to the solitary combat of the desert."[1]

It was not unusual for a Benedictine abbey in the Middle Ages to have one or more hermits living near but outside of the monastery itself. Even the huge monastery of Cluny had some hermits associated with it, who had been given permission to move to remote mountainous regions elsewhere in France, e.g., to the Jura and the Pyrenees.

What was classically called "the pull of the desert" in the Middle East had its parallel in Celtic practices, too. There "the pull of the sea"—described as "the wave cry, the wind cry, the vast waters of the petrel and the porpoise"—enticed a few monks to settle precariously, as hermits, on some of the cold and most desolate islands and rocks flanking the shores of Ireland and northern Britain.[2]

Perhaps the best example of this watery "pull" is Skellig Michael, a tiny island located off the southwest coast of Ireland. Rising steeply 715 feet above the Atlantic Ocean, it once housed a small Christian monastery, eventually earning it a World Heritage listing in 1996. The island had been known since pre–Christian days, and the first monks settled on Skellig Michael during the 6th century. Their monastery managed to survive until the 13th century, when climate change brought lower temperatures and stronger storms to the southwest coast. As a result, the monks were finally forced to move to the mainland at Ballinskelligs. Skellig Michael itself probably continued to be a dependency of the Augustine Abbey there, and from it the monks could organize summer pilgrimages to the island. In the past, the papacy designated these monks as the "Augustinian priors of the rock of Saint Michael."

Hermits, monks, and friars were not mutually exclusive callings. Monks (and nuns) committed themselves to live and to work permanently in a given place, such as a monastery, and never left it without permission, during all the years of their duties.

The friars, on the other hand, were mendicants who were self-selected to live and work in the rough-and-tumble world of society at large, rather than choosing to live only in an ascetic cloistered monastery. They were therefore usually assigned to a broad-based community that was spread out across a large geographical area and was known as a Province. For this reason, friars typically moved around a great deal, spending time and discharging their duties in different monastic houses within a large Province.

In England, for example, the Dominican Province of England officially commenced at the second general chapter meeting of the Dominican order in Bologna during the spring of 1221. Dominic then sent 12 friars to England under the guidance of their English prior, Gilbert of Fresney. They landed in Dover on 5 August 1221; the Dominican Province of England officially came into being at its first provincial chapter meeting, held in 1230.

A monastery, together with all the bustling commercial and peasant communities that supported it, was usually self-sufficient in most items. Indeed, it often had considerable surpluses of grain and other farm products, cloth, and wine that could profitably be sold on the open market. The Benedictine and Cistercian monastic houses, for example, became vibrant centers of agricultural and industrial production in Western Europe. These and other prosperous monasteries were not slow to look for new ways to sell any surpluses they had on hand during and after the harvests.

Their sum of their commercial undertakings was quite important in broad economic terms because, without it, the towns themselves could not have grown bigger, and their specialized rural handicrafts could never have flourished. As a modern economic historian tells us,

> We must visualize a great many petty dealers going from village to village, buying up the peasants' surplus and doubtless making loans on the security of the next crop, while merchants operating on a large scale bought up the stores [surpluses] which accumulated in monastic tithe barns, and shipped them by cart and boat to distant markets.
>
> Thierry d'Hireçon [one such merchant] was able to sell his own considerable surplus to the towns of Flanders, and on one occasion he even shipped two boat loads [of agricultural produce] from the small river port of Aire to [the city of] Ghent, a distance of 100 kilometers.[3]

It was only in the monasteries that the classical Greek and Roman learning was preserved and therefore was able to survive for several centuries after the decline of the Roman Empire itself. During this long era, the monastery gradually became less and less a hiding place of refugees from an unstable, violent world, and more and more a wellspring of religious, economic, and political influence that was ushering in a more self-confident and more prosperous era.

Another important religious calling in the medieval world was that of the secular clerics, who were also known as "clerks." (This and some of the other religious positions discussed below may be confusing because their medieval meanings and their modern meanings are often different.) In this context, secular means "non-monastic" rather than "non-religious." In Christianity, the term "secular clergy" refers to ordained deacons and priests who are not members of a religious institute, such as a monastery. Secular clerics do not take vows of poverty, chastity, and obedience. Since they live in the world at large rather than in a monastery, they do not have to follow any specified monastic rule of life.

Another possible source of confusion is that the undergraduates in medieval English universities were traditionally identified with the secular clergy and were known as "clerks." The reason for this was that, in parallel with the secular clergy, the English university student was always officially recognized as being, in Latin, a *clericus* (or "clerk" in Chaucerian

English). This meant that he was a cleric, even if only by virtue of the simple step of having been *tonsured* (see below). This single religious act officially made him a member of the lowest of the minor orders of the Church, namely, clerks, even if he was never ordained.[4]

Tonsure was a ritual circular clipping of the hair of the head, with a bald spot shaved on the top of the head, leaving just a fringe of hair around the bald spot. It was normally first performed by a bishop, by which process a young man officially received clerical status. Clerical status meant that no matter what laws they broke, clerics could only be tried by ecclesiastical courts, and never by any secular civil courts. Since for all practical purposes, scholarship in the Middle Ages was limited to the clergy, the word "clerk" came to be synonymous with "scholar."

In addition, the clerks were, in their capacity as clerics, entitled to "benefices." These were paid positions that received their own income through endowments from the faithful. There were some 9,000 parish benefices in England alone in the later Middle Ages, plus a large number of other benefices "without the cure of souls," i.e., without the cleric being responsible for any of the people living or working there. These latter benefices included stalls in cathedral chapters and in collegiate churches, as well as wardenships of hospitals and other charitable institutions.[5]

The bottom line of all this was that while a bright and well-connected university student might have only one small benefice to help him finance his studies, senior clergymen often held a sizeable number of more lucrative benefices, reflecting their own higher ranks in the Church. The downside of this highly competitive process, however, was that not all young clerical applicants were able enough, or lucky enough, to be able to secure a lucrative benefice. Many of them were therefore reduced to accepting a sizable number of poorly-paid benefices, or looking for a low-paying job as the secretary-servant of an older and well-established clergyman.[6]

Medieval clergy can technically be defined as those members of the church who administered the sacraments or who assisted in this process. Most medieval monks, however, were not clergy and therefore could not administer the sacraments themselves. They did, however, make life-long vows regarding obedience; stability, i.e., residing permanently in one place, such as a monastery, if they were not members of a mendicant order; living under a monastic rule; renouncing all their personal property; and withdrawing from the busy world, if they were not mendicants.

Clergy, on the other hand, could own property, did not necessarily have to live under a rule, and were encouraged to engage actively with the world, e.g., by teaching in the cathedral schools long associated with monasteries. Historically, however, clergy faced criticism, often harsh criticism, from the monks themselves who—judging entirely by their own very strict monastic standards—strongly deplored what they saw as the unacceptable clerical laxity and clerical disobedience.[7]

It is worth noting that a large number of monastic leaders had been trained as clerics in their youth, opting to become monks only in adulthood. The reason was that a clerical background was found to be much better at encouraging personal initiative and leadership skills than the very passive monastic background.[8]

Concerning medieval *nuns*, it should be noted that, historically, nuns took solemn vows and led secluded lives of prayer and contemplation in a nunnery. *Sisters*, however, took much simpler vows and lived a very active life of charitable work in the wider world outside of any nunnery. In these latter cases, they usually specialized in education or in health care.

Medieval nunneries played a number of different social roles. For women who had a very strong religious motivation, they may have been an ideal choice on those grounds alone. In many other cases, however, their families may have despaired of ever being able to find them suitable husbands and therefore decided to offer these women as "gifts to the church." Widows could also be sent into the welcoming arms of the church.

All such women would be happily accepted, however, only if they could bring with them a very ample financial endowment for the nunnery. For this reason, virtually all of them came from relatively prosperous and socially well-connected families. If accepted at all, any poor women who applied had to be willing to work with and to live with the convent's servants. While the convent may have been a welcome port in a storm for some women, their lives there were not always very happy ones. The historian Barbara Tuchman tells us, for example, that "cloistered nuns were said to be melancholy and irritable, 'like dogs chained up too much.'"[9]

Less-structured medieval religious callings for women include the very interesting and usually relatively prosperous women known as the Beguines, who are discussed in later pages. They had no identifiable founder, point of origin, or papal endorsement and thus never constituted a formal religious order themselves. Technically speaking, they were not really nuns but were frequently confused with nuns because of their similar modes of dress and their charitable activities. To avoid this problem, the clerical supporters of these women sometimes referred to them, in Latin, as *mulieres religiosae* (i.e., "religious women").

By the middle of the 13th century, gatherings of these devout laywomen, supported by local secular and church authorities, began to present themselves as formal religious institutions. The net result was the founding of hundreds of Beguine houses known as *beguinages*, many of which still survive today as cultural heritage sites in the Netherlands and elsewhere.[10]

Their male counterparts were known as the Beghards. They were similar in organization to the Beguines but they were all working-class men of very humble origins, e.g., weavers and dyers, who had been part of the urban textile trade. These men were now down on their luck, due to old age, ill health, or an accident of some kind, and they needed a charitable helping hand in order to survive. Their numbers declined sharply before the close of the Middle Ages, however, due to the waning of the textile trade itself in their home countries.

Last on our list of medieval monastic callings were the endlessly-wandering, always-hungry, and always-thirsty "failed monks" known as *gyrovagi*, a name that comes from the Greek word for "rotation." St. Benedict held them in great contempt because they were supremely lazy and did no work at all during their travels; never stayed in the same place for very long; always gave themselves up to "the snares of gluttony"; and, finally, invariably showed up at monasteries—as self-invited guests—just as food and drink were being served. Benedict concludes, charitably, that these are men "of whose unhappy conversation it is better to be silent than to speak."[11]

An anonymous commentator in the 8th century also made some highly critical points. This account runs along the following nearly-verbatim lines and echoes his own cadences. He wrote:

- These vagabonds count on the hospitality of the monastery they are about to visit, though they have never been invited there. They look forward to receiving the hospitality which the New Testament commands that a monastery offer to all its guests. They know very well, that forced by the requirements of monastic courtesy to respond to their unwelcome and unexpected arrival, their host will have no choice but to offer them kinds of exquisite delicacies, and that many chickens will have to give up the ghost under the knife.
- They complain that their feet are so sore from the rocky road they had to follow to get to the monastery that they want now to have them washed. First, however, they would rather have their stomachs drenched with infinite refillings of cups of the host's wine.
- Once their host, who because his own supply of food is so limited has to go hungry while they stuff themselves, has cleared the crumbs off the table, they shamelessly insist on their almighty thirst. They tell him that, if no wine goblets are handy, they will just slurp up their wine directly from their eating bowls, which still have bits of uneaten food clinging to them.
- Once they are stuffed and sodden to the pitch of vomiting, they say that their discomfort is due to the very hard life they must follow

as monks. Before they go to bed, more exhausted after their labors at the table than by their journey, they tell their host about all the problems they had to face to get to his monastery, and then ask for even more to eat and to drink.

- Soon they will also be asking him for directions on how, the next morning, they can easily find their way to any other monastery that is very close to where they are now. To that place they will go, and there the great thirst they have just experienced as "long-distance travelers" will demand goblet upon hurried goblet of wine: they are pilgrims for their bellies' sake rather than for their souls' sake!
- Once arrived at the next monastery, they hear a hearty voice from the abbot, crying: "Benedicte!" ["Blessings be upon you!"], and hardly inside the monastery, what a thirst they have! … They go to bed … in the morning, their bones are so tired by the fatigues of the road; they cannot rise, though they were strong and hearty at table the night before.
- But matins [the first office of the day, sung during the night, commonly called Nocturnes in medieval text] once safely over, they get up, groaning and exhausted. A little wine warms them, however, and just a morsel of bread: they creep around the monastery, bowed with their infirmity, though their step livens wonderfully out of sight…. Forever wandering, they know not when the last weariness will come upon them: nor do they know the place that will give them burial.[12]

On a more upbeat note, it must be remembered that medieval men and women were drawn to the monastic life for a wide variety of good reasons. These can be listed as follows:

- Genuine piety.
- Family connections with and strong financial support for a local monastery.
- Becoming a monk was a respected and very honorable career choice. Moreover, the most intelligent recruits also met an increasingly important monastic need. By 1150, all the monasteries felt the need to have men on their staff who already had, or who could master in the future, the very difficult advanced academic training known as *scholasticism*, which was also known as scholastic theology.

This was a new method of learning based on Aristotelian logic that dominated teaching in medieval universities from about 1100 to 1700.

Originating in the monastic schools that were the foundations of the earliest European universities, it focused on theology and on canon law, placing strong emphasis on extending scholarly knowledge through inference and on ways to resolve Biblical or other contradictions. Since it would become one of the most important fields of study at the medieval universities themselves, it is discussed at some length in later pages.

At the same time, however, the monasteries also wanted to recruit men who would have a single-minded loyalty to the interests of their own monastery.[13] Once chosen, such a monk could hope to rise sometime later to become an abbot and thus to enjoy a life of social and economic influence roughly equivalent to that of a medieval baron. Other pulls toward the monastic life included:

- Modest living accommodations, but highlighted by above-average meals with good wine, ale, and beer, together with educated, friendly companions. The monastery's servants and its employees did all of the domestic work and much of the heavy outdoor work as well. All these benefits were guaranteed to the monks for life.
- The second and later sons of the aristocracy were never going to inherit their father's title or lands, so they were often encouraged by their parents to join the Church instead. This was sound advice because monastery life was one of the surest paths to a successful career. At a time when most people were not educated at all, the monastery offered a solid educational foundation, namely, reading, writing, arithmetic, and Latin. These skills were increasingly in demand in the religious, financial, political, literary, and even military activities of the Middle Ages.

Recruits for the monastery tended to be the local inhabitants of a given region, but the bigger monasteries were also able to attract applicants from foreign countries. Because it was usually necessary for an applicant to make a substantial donation to the monastery upon entry, most monks came from a relatively prosperous and educated background and therefore got along with each other easily on a social basis. The bottom line was that although monks made up only a tiny fraction (about 1 percent) of the medieval population, there was never any shortage of applicants for this way of life.[14]

Moreover and not surprisingly, the rigorous social stratification of the wider world outside the cloister continued to persist in the cloister itself.[15] A vast social difference always separated the clergy and monks in a monastery from their dependent servants and peasants, who through their unremittent labor made it possible for their "spiritual betters" to devote themselves exclusively to quiet lives of prayer.

The same held true as well for the nunneries and for the different communities of canons. "Canons secular" lived a communal but not a monastic life; "canons regular," on the other hand, lived under a monastic rule. As Jacques de Vitry (d. 1240), who was a regular canon and later bishop of Acre in Palestine, explained in his *History of the Western World*,

> the renewal of the Western Church could only happen through the orders of [canons] regular or monasticism.... From the earliest times onwards there existed in the Western World two different kinds of [monastic] regulars, namely, the "Black Monks" [so named for the color of their clothing] following the Rule of St. Benedict, and the "White Canons" [a white-robed order known as the Premonstratensians, who were founded in France in 1120] living according to the Rule of St. Augustine.... They all had one and the same foundation, like a kind of cornerstone: they had to renounce the world, to have nothing of their own, to be obedient to their superior, and to remain chaste.[16]

5

Notable Medieval Abbeys and Monasteries

It is impossible to discuss *all* of the most important monasteries of the Western European Middle Ages: there were simply too many of them and, indeed, there is now no definitive count of their likely numbers. Instead, the present work looks at a representative sample of the very best.

The total number of medieval monasteries is not accurately known now, but its likely size is suggested by the fact that when the English king Henry VIII disbanded all the abbeys, monasteries, priories, convents, and friaries in England, Wales, and Ireland in the late 1530s, there were at that time approximately 500 religious houses in England alone.

These were variously staffed by about 12,000 monks; by canons regular, which were communities of clergy following a "canon" (a monastic rule),[1] especially the rule of St. Augustine; by friars; and by nuns. Earlier, in about 1300, there had been a national total of some 17,000 to 18,000 monks, canons, friars, and nuns in England.[2] A French source says that, out of an estimated population of 3 million people in England in 1300, at least 40,000 were clerks or priests, and that, counting both men and women, a total of about 65,000 people were part of the religious establishment there.[3]

When Henry VIII engineered his break with Rome in the 1530s, some his chief targets were the very rich monastic houses. A handful of abbey churches that were located near big centers of population managed to survive his onslaught, but only because they had already become cathedrals, i.e., they were the official seats of bishops, or were large well-established parish churches with sizeable congregations. Canterbury Cathedral, Durham Cathedral, and Westminster Abbey are good examples.

Most of the isolated abbeys, however, e.g., including almost all of the Cistercian monasteries, were be demolished and their assets were dispersed to new secular owners. Throughout the Tudor and later periods, the still-standing shells of these massive stone buildings were used by local people as a free source of best-quality stone blocks and of other useful building materials.

This chapter focuses, albeit briefly, on seven important abbeys and monasteries: the first two in Paris, and then five others located elsewhere. In order of their founding, these include: Sainte-Geneviève (502) and Saint-Germain-des-Prés (540s), both in Paris; Moissac in France (before 680); St. Gall in Switzerland (719); Fulda in Germany (744); Cluny in France (910); and Mont-Saint-Michel, also in France (966). The imposing ruins of the remarkable Fountains Abbey in Yorkshire is discussed at more length later in this book.

First, a brief word about the importance of Paris itself because of its central role in French monastic history. The first Parisian monasteries were established during the Merovingian Dynasty of 481–731 and were clustered around the hill of Sainte-Geneviève, located on the Left Bank of the River Seine. This was the same site on which the Romans had built their own city, named "Lutetia."

In addition, the Abbey of Saint Laurent was founded in the first half of the 6th century. Later, in the early 7th century, the Basilica of the Saints-Apôtres (the Holy Apostles), which would become the Abbey of Sainte-Geneviève, was established near the site of the old Roman forum on the left bank of the Seine.

Further west but also on the Left Bank of the river, Saint Germain of Paris founded the Abbey of Sainte-Croix and Saint Vincent; after his death, it became the Abbey of Saint-Germain-des-Prés. Later, some of these abbeys became independent of the Bishop of Paris. They were then ruled by the pope and usually had direct contacts with the king as well.

These ties were very strong—possibly even stronger and certainly more immediate—than the ties between the pope and the king. The reasons were that these monasteries owned a large part of the Left Bank and thus played a decisive role in the economic life of the city as a whole.

Not only did they produce large amounts of food and wine, but they also organized the biggest commercial fairs, which attracted merchants from as far away as Saxony and Italy. For example, the important Abbey of Saint Denis, located near Paris, had been holding a large annual fair since the 7th century; the fair of Saint-Mathias began in the 8th century; the famous Lendit Fair dates from 1109; and the Fair of the Abbey of Saint-Germain-des-Prés started in the 12th century. The monasteries also led the city's cultural life by running all the local schools and colleges, by producing richly illuminated manuscripts, and by generating soaring Gothic architecture and other fine works of art of the Middle Ages.

Despite the civil wars, plague, and foreign occupation it suffered,

Paris nevertheless rose to become the most populous city in the Western world during the Middle Ages. The seat of political power was central Paris, on the west end of the Île de la Cité ("Island of the City"), but the center of religious authority, which was equally important, lay on the east end of that island.

There, by the 1300s, a visitor found the surpassing glory of the magnificent Cathedral of Notre-Dame de Paris; the cloisters of Notre-Dame; the Cathedral's school and its teaching community, which was in effect a small city enclosed by a wall; and, last but not least, the residence of the Bishop of Paris. The Bishop himself was assisted by 51 canons; each of the 33 parish churches of Paris also had its own religious staff, consisting of the *curé* (the priest in charge), the vicar, assorted chaplains, and numerous lay workers.

At the same time, there were also thousands of monks and nuns in the city's 88 monasteries and convents; many nuns, Beguines, and members of other religious organizations; and about 3,000 students who were technically ranked as clerics. All told, there were perhaps 20,000 members of religious institutions living and working in Paris, about 10 percent of the total population.

The modern French medievalists Boris Bove and Claude Gauvard touch on some instructive points when discussing the role of the monasteries in the rise of Paris during the 6th—12th centuries.[4] For example:

- The abbeys of Sainte-Geneviève and Saint-Germain-des-Prés were the principal leaders in the economic flourishing of the city. By the early Middle Ages, the main market of Paris was the Parvis, i.e., the square, located in front of the Cathedral of Notre-Dame. Other markets sprang up, too—most famously, after 1137, the huge market known as Les Halles. This would continue to be the main produce market in Paris until it was transferred to the Paris suburbs in the late 20th century.
- By concentrating the riches of the supporting countryside through their hard work and high degree of organization, and by amassing so many generous donations from the faithful, these and other abbeys in Paris were instrumental in supporting the growing numbers of artisans and the markets of the city. To respond to the needs of church leaders and the growing population of Paris, some entrepreneurs began to specialize in the foodstuffs and in the manufacture of the items needed by city-dwellers.
- On the intellectual front, these monasteries were governed by strict rules that put a very high value on the monks' mental work. Medieval learning profited from the training given to young men in the monastic schools, and by their production of illustrated

manuscripts. Some of the Parisian clerks became such experts in theology that their fame spread far beyond the walls of the monasteries and contributed markedly to the flourishing of other schools in Paris.

Sainte-Geneviève

Said to have been built in 502 by Clovis, King of the Franks, and his queen, Clotilde, this abbey was a center of religious scholarship in the Middle Ages. The first record of the Sainte-Geneviève library dates from 831 and mentions the donation to the abbey of three historic texts. Clovis and his wife were both buried there, and the patron saint of Paris, Sainte Geneviève, often went there to pray. When she died in 512, the saint's remains were buried in the abbey church near the tomb of Clovis; they were brought out of the tomb whenever the ferocious Vikings or other mortal dangers threatened Paris.[5]

Nevertheless, despite such spiritual precautions the Vikings raided Paris three times during the 9th century. Luckily, the very heart of Paris, i.e., the island in the Seine known as the Île-de-la-Cité, was protected by the river itself. The undefended abbey was sacked and the books of its library were carried away or were otherwise lost forever.

In around 1108, the theology school of the abbey joined forces with the school of Notre Dame Cathedral and with the school of the Royal Palace to form the future University of Paris. From 1108 to 1113, the famous intellectual Peter Abelard (d. 1142), who will be discussed in later pages, taught at the abbey's school.

All was not perfect at the abbey, however. By 1147, the secular canons, who did not live under a monastic rule and who could possess private property, were in charge of the church. King Louis VII of France and Pope Eugene III are said to have witnessed some "disorders" there and very much wanted to restore religious discipline. Odo, the prior of another abbey, was sent there to do just that. There were some difficulties in the process, but in the end Odo and his reformers prevailed: some of the secular canons joined them, and the abbey then became a house of canons regular living under the Augustinian rule.

Saint-Germain-des-Prés

Founded by Childebert I in the 540s, this former monastery is now a parish church located in the Saint-Germain-des-Prés quarter of Paris. It has a very long and very distinguished history as a link in what a modern French source describes as "the prodigious Benedictine monastic chain that since the 8th century has included 17,000 abbeys and priories."[6]

Moreover, the Benedictine order itself has produced 24 popes, 200 cardinals, 1,600 archbishops, 1,500 saints, 5,000 "blessed" (unusually holy) people, 43 emperors, and 44 kings. Originally situated beyond the outskirts of early medieval Paris, Saint-Germain-des-Prés evolved into a rich and important abbey complex that became the Parisian burial ground of kings.

In French, "prés" means "meadows." When the abbey was being built, its location on the meadows of the low-lying Left Bank of the Seine made it quite vulnerable to flooding and thus unsuitable as an extensive building site. As a result, the abbey stood alone in the middle of the meadows. The oldest part of the present-day church is the prominent and now partially-restored and modified western tower, which was built in the year 1000.

The church was frequently attacked, plundered, and set on fire by the Vikings in the 9th century. The great wall of Paris, which was added later and was built during the reign of Philip II of France, did not include the church, so the local inhabitants had to flee or to defend themselves as best they could.[7]

The good news was that the abbey gave its name to the famous quarter of Paris still known today as Saint-Germain-des-Prés. It was part of the Latin Quarter—so named because Latin was the language that all the students of the University of Paris had to be able to speak and to understand in their classes. Built on lands along the Seine donated by the abbey, these lands bore the lovely name of the *Prés aux Clercs* (the "Meadows of the Scholars").

Moissac

The French abbey of Saint-Pierre de Moissac has been listed since 1998 as a UNESCO World Heritage Site along the routes leading to the pilgrimage site in Spain of St. James of Compostella. Moissac itself is a small city located at the confluence of the rivers Garonne and Tarn at the Canal de Garonne in southwestern France.

The most famous part of this abbey is the tympanum, i.e., the semi-circular decorative wall surface over the entrance, which is bounded by a lintel and arch and which contains sculpture and other imagery. At Moissac, the tympanum, placed over the south portal of the church, was made between 1110 and 1130 and measures about 21 feet by 14 feet. It was inspired by the Biblical Apocalypse of John, and depicts the return of Christ to Earth in majesty and in glory at the end of time.

His figure is surrounded by symbols of the four evangelists (Matthew, Mark, Luke, and John), which are ranged around the bottom and on the sides of the piece. Fine carvings also show Saint Peter and the prophet Jeremiah, which echo the strong religious ties that existed between Moissac and abbey of Cluny. The magnificently sculpted and very gentle face of the prophet Jeremiah is widely known for the "sweet melancholy" it evokes in the mind of the viewer.

St. Gall

Known in German as *Kloster St. Gallen*, this was a sizeable Benedictine 7th century abbey located in St. Gallen in German-speaking Switzerland. Thanks to its excellent library, for several centuries it was one of the most important Benedictine monasteries in the whole of Western Europe. A nineth-century ground plan still preserved in the abbey depicts it as an idealistic structure designed to inspire and to encourage devotion.

St. Gall is named in honor of Gallus, an Irish companion of St. Columbanus, a renowned wanderer of the early Middle Ages who was a monk and a schoolmaster and who spread Christianity in parts of Western Europe. Monastic studies in letters, in the liberal arts, and in the sciences all flourished at the school established at St. Gall.

Under the leadership of Abbot Waldo de Reichenau (740–814), manuscripts were copied and became the basis for a famous library. Anglo-Saxon and Irish monks came to copy manuscripts, while other monks spread the use and the fame of the Gregorian chant. A ninth-century drawing of St. Gall shows a spacious scriptorium (writing area), with seven writing-desks for monks, located above the library.

The monks there were totally devoted to their duties. Indeed, when Emperor Otto I visited St. Gallen in 972, he dropped his heavy scepter— *on purpose*—among the monks who were then singing the *lauds* to welcome him. It made a very loud clattering noise, and he quickly looked around to see if any of the monks had been distracted. None of them had been, however, and just continued to sing. The emperor was extremely pleased![8]

Today, very little of the medieval abbey remains but its library is still recognized as one of the best survivors of the medieval era. In 1983, UNESCO enrolled the abbey as "a perfect example of a Carolingian monastery." The Carolingian dynasty reached its peak in the year 800 with the crowning of Charlemagne as the first Emperor of Romans in the West.

Very large abbeys were characteristic of this era, and have been described by a modern scholar:

> Their very size symbolized their wealth and power. Monasteries were prominent in the overwhelming rural landscape, harbouring hundreds of people; their economic, social, and cultural impact has been compared to that of towns in a later age. Moreover, the prayer of thousands of monks and nuns played a vital part in safeguarding the ruler and his realm. In other words, monasteries were indispensable to those wielding power.[9]

Fulda

Now a small city located in central Germany, Fulda has remained strongly influenced by its religious past because it is the site of the tomb of St. Boniface, who has been hailed as the "apostle of Germany."

The Benedictine abbey of Fulda was founded in 744 and its famous library of manuscripts made it into an important center of learning during the Carolingian Renaissance from the late 8th to the 9th century. During this era, there was a marked increase of literature, writing, the liberal arts, architecture, legal studies, and liturgical reforms. With a membership of about 600 monks by 842, Fulda also became a center of scientific studies in the Christian West.

In ninth-century Fulda, however, all was not well. The very ambitious Abbot Ratger courted the financial ruin of the monastery by constructing a huge church there, which his own monks denounced as "an immense and superfluous building." The monks complained to the Emperor Charlemagne about this extravagance, but they became even more unhappy when Ratger's expansionist policies forced them to spend much less time in prayer, which they felt was by far their most important daily duty.[10]

Louis IV of France gave to the lord of Fulda the sonorous title of "Archchancellor of the Empress" in 1356 but by then the monastery was already falling under the control of its more powerful neighbors. The net result was that by 1476 Fulda Abbey had ceased to exist as a major political and territorial entity.

Cluny

Not much more needs to be added here about Cluny Abbey. The gist of the matter is that, located in the Bourgogne-Franche-Comité region of central-east France and founded by Duke William of Aquitaine in 910, Cluny was famous for its size, richness, and very strict adherence to the rule of St. Benedict. Chiefly for this reason, it became the acknowledged leader of Western European medieval monasticism. Its abbots were internationally famous; in its heyday, Cluny was widely considered to be the grandest, the most prestigious, and most generously-endowed monastic institution in all of Europe.

Nevertheless, there was also within this monastery an inherent and increasing tension between two different facts of medieval life. The first fact was that Cluny had been a monastery founded on the principles of simplicity and helping the poor. The second fact was that, over time, it had become too rich and too powerful—even to the extent of encouraging a trend toward monastic *opulence* in Western Europe as a whole.

A sign of these latter times was that, beginning in about 1334, the abbots of Cluny maintained a huge, semi-regal, private townhouse in Paris that was known as the Hôtel de Cluny. Even though the monastery itself was disestablished in 1790, ever since 1844 the Hôtel de Cluny itself has been a museum in Paris, open to the public, and focusing on the Middle Ages.

Although it no longer possesses anything originally and directly connected with Cluny Abbey itself, it has recently been fully restored and is well worth visiting today. This museum now consists of the Roman-French cold-to-hot baths (*Thermes*) of the first through third centuries (purchased in 1330 by the abbot Pierre de Chaulus on behalf of King Philip VI), on the one hand, and the medieval exhibits now held in the Hôtel de Cluny itself, on the other.

By the time of the 1789–1790 French Revolution, the monks of Cluny had become so deeply intertwined with the totally-discredited *Ancien Régime* (the corrupt "Old Regime" of France before the Revolution) that their monastery was virtually demolished in 1810 and was then used as a stone quarry until 1823. In their heyday (about 950 to 1130), however, Cluny's abbots were the stars of the international religious stage. This monastery is most remembered today for the Cluniac Reforms (also known as the Benedictine Reform), which restored the traditionally super-strict patterns of Benedictine monastic life; encouraged art; and stressed the importance of caring for the poor.

These reforms were considered to be necessary because of the ever-increasing secular/feudal interference in monastic life. Because Benedictine monasteries needed to have land to lease to local farmers in order to generate some income for themselves, and also needed land on which to grow their own crops, these monasteries depended very heavily on the patronage and support of the local lords, who owned much of the land.

The lords, however, would often demand rights that interfered with the efficient operations of the monasteries themselves. Such abuses included demanding that their own relatives become the abbots, and by seizing for their own personal use the considerable revenues generated by the monastic properties which had been established by their ancestors on Church land in the distant past.

The Cluniac Reforms extended from about 950 to 1130, spreading throughout France, into England, and through much of Italy and Spain. As a modern medievalist has put it, "The Cluny reform was the clergy's declaration of independence from ignorance, concubines, and kings."[11] Cluny's new rules were so strict, however, that at least one monastic commentator (the French monk and poet Guiot) simply refused to join this reformed order. He complained: "They keep too closely to the vows which they make in there [their monastery]. They would insist, in truth, that when I wished to sleep I should have to keep awake, and when I wished to eat they would make me fast."[12]

In addition, the Cluniacs supported a pacifist movement known as the "Peace of God," which was probably the first mass peace movement in European history; promoted pilgrimages to the Holy Land; and resisted efforts by the secular community to bring Cluny under lay control. At the same time, however, the always-expanding liturgy of Cluny's monks stimulated a growing demand in Europe for ever-more ornate altar vessels, now made of gold; for finer tapestries and fabrics; for wonderful stained glass; and for rich, polyphonic choral music. Not surprisingly, Cluny's very opulence and success worked against its own long-term future by encouraging the rise of a rival and far more austere institution, namely, the Cistercian order.

By 1098, Robert de Molesme, a Benedictine monk from Cluny Abbey had tried—but had failed—to install the simple but severe qualities of the original rule of St. Benedict at a monastery he had just founded at Molesme, France. He therefore led a band of 21 other dissident monks to a new location—a very unpromising plot of marshland located at Cîteaux south of Dijon, France. Its name in Old French (*cistel*) was derived, in turn, from the Latin word for "reeds," namely, *cistellium*. Remarkably, however, before long this water-logged reedy site would become the abbey of the new and exceptionally austere Cistercian order.

Mont-Saint-Michel

The long history of Mont-Saint-Michel, which was built atop a rocky outcrop on the northwestern coast of France, begins in 708. It was then that Bishop Aubert constructed the first religious sanctuary on this 80-foot-high pinnacle, which is named in honor of the Archangel Michael.

It was not until 966, however, that Benedictine monks actually began to settle there, in response to a request from the ruling Duke of Normandy, Richard I.

Under their stewardship, the abbey quickly not only became a major place of pilgrimage in the Christian West but also developed into one of the key centers of medieval culture. Such a large number of manuscripts were written and stored there, in fact, that Mont-Saint-Michel was nicknamed the "City of Books."[13]

Because it became a political and intellectual crossroads, the abbey was visited by large numbers of pilgrims over the centuries, including several kings of France and of England. This masterpiece of Norman Gothic art bears permanent witness to the architectural expertise of its 13th-century builders.

After the French Revolution, the monks of Mont-Saint-Michel were driven out and the monastery, then renamed Mont Libre ("Freedom Mountain"), became in 1793 a prison for refractory priests. By 1811 it had become a reformatory housing both common-law prisoners and political prisoners. Its tours of duty as a prison, however, were all that saved the abbey from certain destruction: if it had not been so useful as a prison, it would surely have been destroyed because it was not then seen as being of any historical value.

In 1874 it was finally classified as a national monument and the long process of restoration could begin. In 1979 the abbey was listed as a UNESCO World Heritage Site, and in 1998 it was also listed as an historic highpoint in the pilgrimage route to Santiago de Compostela in Spain.

6

The Economic Roles
of Monks

Monks played extremely important economic roles in Western Europe during the Middle Ages. For example, from at least the 6th century on, the most powerful driving force behind the Church in England itself was not the secular clergy but the monks, i.e., the men and women living communally under some kind on monastic rule.[1] This was true in many other Western European countries as well.

Monasticism became a surprisingly attractive and popular way of life. In fact, it has been estimated that in 13th-century England the total number of monks, canons, nuns, and members of the military orders was approximately 18,000 to 20,000 men and women, i.e., about one in every 150 inhabitants.[2]

Western European monasteries were generally well-organized and well-run in administrative terms. They were staffed by many hard-working, low-cost, literate, very dedicated men and women who were able, as good and selfless managers, to produce surpluses of almost all of the food and drink their monasteries required. Anything that was not used in or near the monastery could readily be sold to the public.

Every monastery had its own school, chiefly for the education of its own novices (it was essential that they master reading, writing, and simple arithmetic) but sometimes for the sons of local dignitaries as well. Such schools were in fact the proto-universities of their era.

Moreover, on the commercial front, the monasteries could also gainfully employ large numbers of full-time and part-time rural workers themselves who had only the most rudimentary agricultural skills to offer prospective employers, and who therefore otherwise might not have been gainfully employed. For example, the extensive, labor-intensive, public works programs listed in the "Carolingian capitularies" (these were official Western European documents dating from the late 8th and early 9th centuries) focus on land reclamation, road building and maintenance, ironworks, and various ways to help the poor.

All these entries bear witness to the early and continuing importance of monks in the economic system. For example, in the endless and arduous task of draining waterlogged marshes and meadows—and then keeping them dry, especially those located in the always-soggy regions (for example, in and near what is now the Netherlands), it was the monasteries that played the major roles.

In fact, until the towns themselves grew much larger during the 11th century, it was the monasteries that took charge of pioneering commerce and industry in Western Europe. Their abbeys became very convenient social, trade, and information-exchange posts. Many of today's best French vineyards were begun, organized, and improved by the monks and their workers.[3]

The monasteries in France itself were much like those elsewhere in Western Europe. They tended to be large Benedictine houses with origins before the year 1000 and consisted of big, well-organized monastic estates. There was in fact a great flourishing of new monastic orders in France during the 12th century. The Cistercians had the strongest reputation for innovations in clearing land, in hydraulic engineering, and in developing new methods of wine production.

The monastic economic influence in England, already significant, expanded further with the arrival of new monastic orders there in the 12th century. These new arrivals included the Cistercians, the Augustinian canons, the Gilbertines, and the military orders of the Templars and the Hospitallers.

An era of the especially successful management of some monastic estates, a process known as "high farming," under the leadership of such able monks as Henry of Eastry at Canterbury Cathedral Priory and of John of Laund at Bolton Priory, led to rising manorial incomes and to higher profits for some monasteries. Moreover, new tenants settled on the lands colonized from woods and marshes, or located in the growing new towns of England. Labor services and payments in kind were being converted into more efficient cash payments.[4] Although, as individuals, the monks had almost no possessions themselves, their richest monasteries could generate vast revenues, chiefly by donations from the faithful but also by sound management of their very extensive lands.

In the early 14th century there were perhaps as many as 500 different religious houses in England alone. Monks sometimes lived in grand buildings there and elsewhere. In the richest of them, when celebrating Mass their priests could wear beautiful vestments and could use precious chalices and other ornate items. Understandably, such monks were usually closely tied to the political and economic elites of England and other prosperous European countries. Almost all of the inhabitants of the English counties supported the Church and thus, by extension, they were also will-ing to support its monks and nuns, sometimes in some luxury.

These elites believed that their contributing land, funds, and/or chil-dren to their local monastery would produce both important spiritual benefits in the future and, equally if not more important, some very useful social contacts here on earth. A good example of this practical approach was Leicester Abbey, an Augustinian monastery which the new earl of Leicester, Robert de Beaumont, set up in a very expansive and expensive manner in about 1138.

Many new monasteries were founded during this period. They included more than 60 Cistercian houses by 1200 in England and Wales; more than 150 Augustinian houses there; and, then by 1300, about 50 other assorted monastic houses located in Scotland. All told, the church's share of the landed wealth of England itself rose from about 25 percent of the total in 1086 to almost 30 percent in 1300.

By about 1300, there was thus in England a national total of about 17,000 to 18,000 monks, canons, friars, and nuns. Much later, in the middle years of the 15th century, there were 126 English monasteries that had very high annual incomes, £300 or more. This was easily enough to encour-age their abbots to function as landed aristocrats, and to live in an opulent style similar to that of any baronial household.

Monastic inputs at a more modest economic level can be seen very clearly in a c. 1290 report on the monks of Crawford on their 300-acre Northamptonshire manor in Wellingborough, England. There they employed eight plowmen, who had to handle four animal-drawn plows throughout the course of a year; two carters; three shepherds; a dairymaid; and a cowherd. In addition, some part-time servants, such as a swineherd and tithe-collector, were hired during the harvest season. Other employ-ees, e.g., ironsmiths and carpenters to maintain the ploughs and the carts; men to castrate the piglets; and common laborers to weed, thresh, mow hay, and harvest wheat were always needed as well.

A peasant on this monastic manor "owed labor to the monastery," that is, he was required by custom (which as a practical matter had the full force of law) to work hard for the monks, without any pay, for two full days a week throughout the winter, summer, and spring, and then for three full days a week during the very busy August–September harvest season.

Needless to say, since these manorial labor duties cut seriously into the already-limited amount of time available to the peasant to work on his own tiny patch of land, he undertook them only very grudgingly and with-out any enthusiasm. He certainly would not have done them at all if he could have found a way to avoid them without facing punishment.

However, while the peasants were beavering away, year after year, to maintain and improve the monks' and nobles' estates, the nobles themselves spent most of their lives simply *playing war games* (to use an uncharitable modern description). Although the theoretical justification for this activity was that the knightly class could not discharge its duties as one of the three medieval "estates" unless it was constantly organized to fight when mounted on well-trained horses, to modern eyes this was a great wasting of limited economic resources that could have been much better used elsewhere in the society. For example, the expense of maintaining the highest grade of war-horse in the stables of the Earl of Cornwall's manor in Wiltshire, England, for 82 days in the summer of 1297 amounted to more than an unskilled worker's annual wage.[5]

On the other hand, there was also a bit of better economic news. In this era, a peasant owning an annual rent to a monastery did not have to pay the monks in hard cash, but could instead agree do some harvest work for them or could "contribute" to them some on-the-hoof food for their kitchen, such as an old ox.[6] In general, however, the monasteries demanded from their tenants specific and sizeable quantities of good-quality "food-rent" that had to be produced on the small plots of monastic land that the tenants farmed.

For example, in England the food-rent that had to be paid on the Hickling and Kinoulton estate in Nottinghamshire when it was transferred to Ramsey Abbey in about the year 1000 consisted of 80 bushels of malt for brewing, 40 bushels of oatmeal, 80 bushels of flour for bread, 8 sides of bacon, 16 cheeses, two fat cows, and 8 salmon in Lent. This was enough food to feed the monks and servants of a large monastery for only about a week or two. In Wales, food-rents consisted of loaves of bread, oats, cattle, sheep, pigs, butter, ale, and honey.

It is important to note, however, that the Hickling and Kinoulton estate was not administered in order to squeeze the land or its people with any severity. The food-rents demanded constituted only a very small fraction of the total produce of the abbey's land, i.e., only about 30 acres worth. Larger estates could easily have produced many thousands of bushels of grain and dozens of healthy animals ready for the knife.[7]

More broadly speaking, it must be noted, too, that in medieval rural England the rich and the poor, and the religious and the secular, were all tied closely together into one complementary economic and social relationship. By making generous food or other seasonal gifts to the poor on major religious celebrations, the rich could show their mercy to the poor and their piety. At the same time, the poor could repay them, at no financial cost, with their public expressions of warm gratitude and with their private prayers for the well-being and salvation of the rich.[8] It was in this manner that the monks of the manor could believe that the rich were being morally improved, thanks to their generous gifts to the poor, while the poor themselves, by accepting with infinite patience and resignation their very modest lot here on earth, would surely win a starry heavenly life after death.

One of the most readable accounts of the relationships between the cloister and the rest of medieval society in Western Europe can be found in the fourth edition (2015) of C.H. Lawrence's definitive summary of medieval monasticism. It makes a number of relevant points, which are used here in the following pages.[9]

Perhaps the most important fact is that very close economic and political ties normally existed between every large monastery and its neighboring township or city. In Canterbury, for example, the priory owned, either by bequests from the faithful or by its own direct purchases, nearly half of the houses in the city and suburbs. Rents from these holdings were a steady source of local monastic income. The other side of the coin was that the monastery itself was a major employer of the region. In Canterbury alone, about 100 domestic servants lived there, as well as the owners and their staffs of the many small enterprises that provided legal advice; medical treatment; gold jewelry; home construction and repair; and room and board for retired clerics, domestic servants, and pensioned soldiers.

The oldest and therefore often the biggest abbeys could indeed have vast land-holdings, but because these had been acquired bit by bit, they were often scattered around the countryside in different local regions. Nevertheless, they were managed much as the secular lords managed their own large and more unified estates. The clearing, plowing, sowing, and harvesting of the land was done by the forced labor of large numbers of peasants or serfs, who basically were never free, during normal times, to leave their employers. The only major exception to this rule was the severe labor shortage that arose in the wake of the Black Death, i.e., the bubonic plague.

Some of the farmlands of a monastery were not leased to tenants but were instead retained "in demesne," that is to say, they were reserved for the use of the monastery itself. Historically, a demesne could include various kinds of uncultivated land as well as arable land: the total could extend to several hundred hectares.

The monks consumed most of what the demesne manors produced, and any surplus was easily sold. The primary role of these monastery manors was to feed not only the monks themselves but also the large numbers of hungry and thirsty servants and guests who were invariably waiting. In the Norwich or Durham priories, for example, most of the wheat that these manors produced was never sold to finance the running of these monasteries, but was instead consumed on the spot, as bread, by the monks, their servants, and their many guests.

At Cluny, Peter the Venerable set up a quasi-modern "just-in-time" production system, under which each group of workers was required to specialize by producing a given crop. Some farmers grew wheat for the fine white bread to be served to high-ranking abbots and guests; others produced rye for coarser bread for lower-ranking diners; and still others specialized in putting cheese, beans, ale, or wine on the tables. Each Cluny manor was earmarked as the sole supplier of a particular item for a specific period of time. The manor of Mazille, for example, had to supply, for one given night, all of the oats required for the many horses then stabled at Cluny.

Economic forces affected the monasteries as well as all the secular medieval institutions. Because of increases in the population of Western Europe and the corresponding increase in demand, both the prices of agricultural produce and the costs of farmland rose significantly. To deal with this issue of inflation, monastic and secular landowners alike had to focus on raising crops that could readily be sold and thus easily turned into cash. In the 13th century, Christ Church in Canterbury reorganized its demesne manors so that its wheat crop could be sold in bulk for long-distant shipment, either around the English coast or abroad.

The bottom line, however, is that many of the most celebrated monasteries were chronically in debt–Cluny after 1140 and, by the end of the century, La Charité-sur-Loire in France, and Monte Cassino in Italy, as well. However, there does not seem to be a simple or, indeed, even a *single* reason for this state of financial affairs.

The underlying reality, though, was that the monasteries almost always spent appreciably more than they earned. Excessive outlays on new buildings; the never-ending and ever-increasing costs of the year-round hospitality that was traditionally expected from the monks; and the hemorrhages imposed by the generous pensions (corrodies) which the monasteries had agreed to pay to their staff and supporters—all these were part-and-parcel of the financial problem.

In the end, as Chapter 31, "Limiting the number of monks," explains, it was not any shortage of postulants that held down the size of the major Benedictine monasteries in the Middle Ages, but rather the self-perceived need for them to economize in order to stave off the dangers of financial collapse.

7

Monks and Vineyards

We have the Greeks to thank for the introduction of wine grapes into what is now France, and the Romans to thank for turning wine into an internationally-traded commodity that has become such an important part of Western European and other cultures.

The real roots of French wine-making itself, however, date from the life of Martin of Tours (316–397), an ex–Roman soldier who had become a Christian and who founded the first monastery in France.[1] The highlights of his contributions were (1) developing the Chien Noir and the Chien Blanc grapes from the wild grapes growing in the Touraine forest, and (2) planting the first Vouvray vineyards.

Perhaps most remarkably, however, Martin also discovered—quite by accident—the beneficial effects of pruning the vines. He had quite forgotten, one day, to tether his donkey when he left it alone in a vineyard. When he finally got back to it, he was horrified to find that the hungry beast had eaten every single vine that extended above knee level. Instead of ruining the next year's harvest, however, it turned out that the wine made from these heavily-pruned grapevines was the best that the monks had ever tasted!

By the 8th and 9th centuries, the Church, especially in the form of its bishops and abbots, was the institution most likely to be the proprietor of extensive vineyards. The basic reason for this was not the need for small amounts of wine to be used in the ceremony of Mass. Instead, it was the need of all the important monasteries to serve good wine in lavish amounts to honor the many important officials and other travelers who visited them at all seasons.[2]

It was chiefly the Benedictine order that supported monasticism in France and thus, by extension, oversaw the development of the monks' wine-making skills. Their wine-making program was in fact a great success. The monks achieved it, over time, by carefully following three inter-related policies:

1. Educated by the experiences passed on from one monastic generation to the next, they learned how best to prune the vines, how to compare and choose varietals, and how to preserve their wines.

2. They marked out precise plots, each one known as a *territoire* (a micro-territory of land), as dictated by the local soil and the prevailing local climate. These small plots could produce wines of very different characters.

3. The monks also surrounded their plots with low stone walls, which protected the vines from animals; permanently reshaped the natural landscape of the region; and thus, in the end, made possible the long-term continuity and productively of local wine-growing traditions.[3]

By the 11th century, wine had become the single most widely traded commodity in Western Europe. It enriched monasteries and lay merchants alike; gladdened the hearts of the consumers; deeply affected European culture and social life; and created an extensive, ever-changing, and always-demanding international mega business.

The top quality wines preferred by prosperous English customers carried high profit margins, which ultimately benefited the monks and other wine-producers in France and elsewhere. During the 13th century, much of this fine wine came from the English king's possessions in Gascony in France, especially from the Duchy of Aquitaine in southwestern France. At the high point of this trade in about 1308, no less than 5 million gallons of wine were shipped by sea from Aquitaine to England and to other European markets.[4]

The monks not only produced a great deal of wine but they were required to give away a great deal of it, too. For example, between 1244 and 1257, Cluny Abbey entertained Pope Innocent IV; the French bishops of Senlis and Évruex; Louis IX (the King of France), his mother, his wife Blanche, his brother, and his sister; the Emperor of Constantinople; the King of Aragon and the son of the King of Castile. In addition, of course, the abbey also had to host the very large entourages of always-thirsty nobles, soldiers, servants, and clergy who were escorting and catering to the needs of all these distinguished and demanding guests.[5]

The Church had been quick to understand that wine could be sold very easily, especially if the vineyards were located close to a reliable and easy way, such as a river or the English Channel, of getting it to market quickly and in good condition.

The Cistercians, for example, who had first made their economic mark by producing and selling raw wool, now turned their attention to viticulture—not for their own use (they were a famously austere order) but solely in order to earn money to pay for the costly support and maintenance of their many beautiful monasteries.

In Burgundy, the monks' experience and hands-on wine-making skills that evolved in the vineyards of Meursault, Musigny, and Clos de Vougeot were justly famous. The monastery at Vougeot, for its part, even built a cellar over 100 feet long that was able to store at least 2,000 barrels of wine. Its volume cannot be estimated accurately now because, during the Western European Middle Ages, wine-volume terms such as "barrel" and "cask" did not have any exact, unchanging meanings.

In 1143, the vineyards of the Cistercian abbey at Longport, near Soissons, had been a generous gift to the abbey from the canon of Soissons. The abbey soon amassed a total of at least 13 vineyards, stretching along the right bank of the Aisne River and extending beyond Soissons itself. The wine that the monks produced was used in churches, in the refectory (the section of a monastery where the monks ate their meals), and to refresh travelers and the poor. By 1228, Longport had cellars in Noyon and was also actively selling wine there and at other nearby locations as well.

In the Auxerre region, the Cistercians produced such excellent wine that the Franciscan friar and writer Salimbene de Adam de Parma hailed it in 1245, in a chronicle of his travels, in the warmest possible words. It was, he marveled, "white or sometimes golden, aromatic and full bodied with an exquisite taste which fills the heart with joy and confidence."[6]

Wine was so important in medieval France that it influenced the growth of French towns and even the government of the country itself. For example, wine grapes had first been grown near the town of Bergerac in the Dordogne River valley in the 9th century. By the 14th century, taken as a whole, the overall *vignoble* ("vineyard") of Bergerac had become a very well-defined and prosperous area belonging to the townsmen and to the burgesses (i.e., the richest citizens).

The legal authorities of Bergerac, known as the Consuls, were the only ones who had the power to decide the date on which the grape harvest would officially begin. Their decision was backed by the full force of the law, even including the death penalty, for those disregarding it. Guards were posted to keep watch on the vineyards, and sentries were stationed at the gates of the town to make sure that no grapes from outside the Bergerac *vignoble* ever came into the town before a given day.

In the town itself, the retail sale of wine in taverns was also strictly controlled. However, foreigners and nobles could overcome most of these restrictions simply by paying a modest toll, which became an important and very welcome part of the town's annual income. Similar procedures were in force in many other towns in the wine-producing regions of France.[7]

Bergerac suffered as a wine-producer, however, because it was located in a region of western France that was often fought over by the English and the French during the Hundred Years War. Whenever they invaded France, the English armies were eager to find and loot the wine-holding cellars of the region, or to destroy the local vineyards. The Consuls of Bergerac dealt with this problem chiefly by paying off the English commanders—by offering them, for themselves and for their troops, large quantities of the new wine.

In the city of Liège and its nearby areas, the first vineyards were created and were operated by the cathedral chapter and its monasteries. This policy was so lucrative, that wine production gradually moved out of monastic hands as many of the wine-producing tenants became lease-holders themselves, and as rich merchants in the city began to invest in the local vineyards. One leading merchant, for example, leased at least three vineyards in the 1370s and hired skilled wine-makers to run them.

The national politics of France may have been turbulent during the 13th and 14th centuries but they did not stop the steady expansion of the wine-growing regions close to the Gironde River. The vineyards there that were owned by the Church, e.g., by the Archbishop of Bordeaux and the big abbeys, continued to grow fine grapes.

Some of the best wine producers were located in the Bordelais wine-producing district between the Dordogne and the Garonne rivers, which would later become world-famous and still is acclaimed under the trade name of *Entre Deux Mers* ("Between Two Seas"). In the 13th century, the monks of the Abbey of La Sauve Majeure had made this wine-production possible by clearing away the forests there and planting vines instead.

Rejecting what they considered to be the undue laxity of the Benedictine order, the early Cistercians opted instead for such a strictly ascetic way of life that the life expectancy of the average Cistercian was said to be only 28 years, rather than the 33 years the average medieval man could expect to live. The good news, however, was that the surviving Cistercians were credited with making some of the very best white wines in the world.

Many of France's most notable Bourgogne and Bordeaux wines still bear the names of the monasteries that survived for centuries—until the French Revolution ended many of them. Perhaps the most famous of the surviving "old timers" is Dom Pérignon champagne, named after the Benedictine monk who played such a major role in developing the art of blending it.

The Cistercian order, which had been co-founded with the Abbey of Cîteaux in 1098, owned excellent wine-making lands on both the Côte de Beaune and the Côte de Nuits, as well as vineyards near Chablis and

Chalon-sur-Saône. The Cluniac order was another major landowner on the Côte Chalonnaise and the Mâcon region. It also held some vineyards farther north, including the still-used plot of Romanée-Saint-Vivant. The monks of both orders first used their lands to produce only the amounts of wine necessary to celebrate Mass. Gradually, however, their hard work paid off and they managed to develop the art of wine-growing by improving both the quality and the yields. The result was that by the 15th century, the high quality of their wines was recognized all across Europe.

The records of religious communities can be an excellent source of information about their use of wine. The c. 530 Benedictine rule specified that wine could legitimately be served to a monastic community, although Benedict himself simply *tolerated* rather encouraged its consumption.[8]

He set the daily limit for each monk at a very modest amount (about a quarter of a liter), but nevertheless still had to urge his followers to remember that "those to whom God gives the strength to abstain should know that they will receive a special reward," presumably in heaven. Benedict personally believed that "wine is by no means a drink for monks" but, tolerantly understanding human weaknesses, he also concluded that "since the monks of our day cannot be persuaded of this, let us at least agree to drink sparingly and not to satiety because wine makes even the wise fall away."

In practice, the abbot or abbess of a monastic community ultimately had the last say on how much wine should be allowed but, except on days set aside for fasting, wine could usually be found on virtually all of the monastic tables. For example, a London merchant, Gilbert Maghfeld, has left for posterity his ledger covering the 1390s. It shows that some of his best customers were the religious houses of London and its environments, including St. Giles Holborn, St. Anthony's, the Abbey of St. Mary Graces, and Waltham Abbey. This reflects the fact that many monasteries in France and elsewhere in Western Europe now saw wine-making as a profitable commercial undertaking that could generate an income that could be used for their own religious purposes.

Monastic bursars' (treasurers') accounts from England can give us more details on what monks and their important guests actually drank. At Durham Cathedral Priory, most of the wine purchased was red wine, plus a small amount of both white wine and claret (the latter was a light red wine from Gascony in southwestern France). These three wines were all about the same price, so in 1504–1505 the priory's bursar ordered "two tuns of red, claret wine and white wine at £5 6s.8d" per tun. At that time and place, a tun was 256 gallons of wine.

Sweet wines such as malmsey were much more expensive. They were not drunk in such quantities as red wines and were bought in smaller amounts. In the 15th century, this bursar bought most of his stock from Newcastle, but sometimes ordered it from Hull if prices were lower there. Even if wine prices rose at times of higher tensions between England and France, he usually did not change the amounts he ordered.

If we exclude the small amount of wine used each day in celebrating Mass, it is thought that in a community of, say, 40 monks each one would have been given just over one pint of wine per day. This is twice as much as St. Benedict thought proper, but it does not reflect the fact that, due to the great many fast and wine-free days on the monastic calendar, it is probable that wine was not served to them every single day, but perhaps only about 100 days per year. There does not seem to be much scholarly agreement on how much wine the monks actually drank. At Westminster Abbey, they received only a quarter of a pint per day. The monks of Battle Abbey, near where William the Conqueror came ashore from Normandy in 1066, however, may have received nearly one and a half pints per day.

On one special Sunday in 1535, the 40 monks at Westminster were allowed one gallon of malmsey wine, plus three and a half gallons of Gascon wine—all to be shared between them and their servants. However, since virtually all of the drinking water of that era was very likely to be polluted, the monks also usually drank up to one gallon of ale per person per day.

The drinking policies of the monks readily lent themselves to satire. In the Digby Collection in the Bodleian Library in Oxford, for example, there is an amusing if unkind description of an abbot in his cups after dinner. It can be summarized as follows:

- First, the abbot had two pitchers of wine placed by his seat at the dinner table, with white wine on his right and red wine on his left.
- He then sampled each wine, and drank deeply from goblets of each, toasting "the peace and stability of the Church."
- He continued to drink a series of other toasts for many different purposes, such for the well-being of priests, and for good weather to keep travelers and pilgrims safe from any harm.
- The last big goblet of wine that he consumed (it was his fifteenth) was in the hope that dew would fall on a nearby vineyard so that the grapevines there would flourish.
- By the end of the dinner, this revered abbot was so drunk that he was quite unable to stand up unaided. Indeed, it was written of him then that "he cannot rise from his seat unless he be raised by both arms like a cow stuck in a muddy slough."[9]

Less dramatic information can been found in a document of 1364–1365 which gives details on all the food and drink supplied for the masters, pupils, and servants of a religious study center set up by Pope Urban VI near Aix-en-Provence in France.

There were 180 young men, aged from 12 to 18, at that study center. Virtually all of them, plus an unstated number of masters and servants, were present at each meal. There was enough wine so that, for planning purposes, each diner was allocated 210 liters of wine for the whole year—a total which is thought to have equated to more than half a liter of wine per person per day.

This figure seems quite reasonable in light of the enormous wine consumption at the huge papal court itself. There, even during the weeks without any important religious feast-days to celebrate, the butler, i.e., the official in charge of buying wine for the papal court, was expected to serve from 10,000 to 10,500 liters of wine per week, of which 10 liters were reserved for the table of the Pope himself.

Most of the staff and guests of the papal court were almost certainly men, but what, then, can we say of the women? As Susan Rose tells us in *The Wine Trade in Medieval Europe*, religious houses for women were also governed by the Benedictine rule or by a version of it. What is clear is that wine could be, and certainly was, served and drunk in the convents. The author of the Rule of Caesarius of Arles, which dates from 512 to 534 (the same period of the Benedictine rule), tried to prevent nuns from buying wine secretly or, at minimum, to share equally whatever wine they received in some other way. This was a task important enough so that a "wine-mistress" was sometimes appointed.

One of the responsibilities of an abbess was to always have at hand some best quality wine for any of her nuns "who are ill or were raised more delicately." Moreover, noble or royal ladies living in a convent got also preferential wine-treatment. We learn, for example, that at the convent of Fontevraud at Nuneaton in England, when King Edward I's daughter Mary lived there, three gallons of wine were provided specifically for her use in celebrating Easter. Large quantities of ale were of course the normal drink for all the lower-ranking clerks, guests, and servants of this convent.

Among other sources of information on wine consumption by religious women is a brief account from Wilton Abbey covering 16 weeks from June to September 1299. This convent, which had been founded by King Alfred, often housed women of very high social standing. However, wine was reserved for very special occasions, e.g., when important male guests were being entertained, or when a new abbess was being installed.

On 13 September 1299, for instance, the new abbess was welcomed by a great feast. The nuns had to buy 800 new plates and dishes to hold the food of their many guests, who dined on swans, peacocks, and 166 capons. Wine was certainly served, but we do not know how much.

Visitations, i.e., official inspections, of convents for women in France were conducted by Bishop Eudes of Rouen in the mid–13th century. He could not have been overjoyed by what he discovered in his travels. At the convent of St. Armand de Rouen, for example, he learned that some of the nuns were receiving much more than their fair share of wine. They were then secretly selling, to buyers outside the convent's high walls, all of the "surplus" wine they could not easily drink themselves. The bishop also discovered, probably to his horror, that some even more deplorable things were going on at the nearby priory of Villarceaux. There, it was said, most of the nuns had lovers, and the prioress herself was drunk nearly every night.

The monastic wine trade is, for better or for worse, much better documented—if much less interesting—than these escapades. Writing in 1976, for example, the French medievalist Alain Sadourny summarized the late medieval monastic wine trade along the River Seine as follows. His account has been translated, annotated, and considerably shortened for use here.

The Seine wine trade was the most important of all the local river traffic of the time. It was often small-scale and usually carried relatively modest quantities of wine. The abbeys of Normandy, such as the monastery located on the Seine upstream of Rouen, owned vineyards in the Seine valley and usually transported their new wines in autumn, using sailing vessels of only modest size.

In 1372, however, this monastery hired a much bigger cargo ship known as a "nef" (typically, this would have been a lateen-rigged round-ship with two masts) which could transport both empty wine barrels and full barrels brimming with new wine. Although the monks alone were responsible for arranging and supervising the production of wine, their duties ended at the water's edge, where professional longshoremen and navigators took over.[10]

8

Armed Monks

The kings who gave the Benedictine abbeys such extensive lands expected not only spiritual returns from their gifts but also a more tangible income from their investments.[1] Abbots, for example, were "enfeoffed with their lands," that is, they were officially given their extensive lands free-of-charge, but only in return for the feudal services they were then required, by law, to render to the king.

In their capacity as vassals, for example, they owed the king not only "suit of court" (the obligation to be present at the sessions of royal court and council), but they also owed him their military service. It was the Carolingians who first began the practice of requiring abbots to provide contingents of mounted soldiers, who were regular soldiers, not armed monks, for the royal army.

If an abbot himself was officially appointed as a "tenant-in-chief," i.e., holding his lands directly from the king and thus owing the king knight-service for them, he was also in effect the overlord of all the knights enfeoffed on the abbey's estates. As such, the abbot had to muster troops in case of need and to perform many other administrative duties for the king.

Important as these undertakings were, however, they ran directly contrary to the monastic rule of St. Benedict. To get around this problem, the French abbeys of the Carolingian age created some new and important lay officials known as "advocates." These men basically acted as the general managers of abbeys, thus permitting the abbots to focus chiefly on their own more important religious duties. The advocates also presided over the manorial courts and led the abbey's team of knights into battle if the knights were ever called out onto active duty.

The English counterparts of these advocates were the "lay stewards," who figure prominently in the chronicles and records of the Benedictine houses from the 11th century onward. Theirs was a position of considerable influence, patronage, and high social standing, too, but they lacked the much greater power and independence that their foreign counterparts enjoyed in northern France and Germany.

The downside of the state of affairs in those latter countries was that the advocate's role gradually rose higher and higher and became primarily a military assignment. His basic duty now was to protect the abbey and its lands against any invading soldiers or other predators. In many cases, however, the advocate gradually evolved into being a hereditary vassal who took full advantage of, and often exploited, his own high position. He could himself therefore, singlehandedly, come to dominate the monastery that he was supposed to protect.[2]

The first mention of armed monks *per se* occurred in 1095 as part of the preparations for the First Crusade of that year.[3] It is worth discussing this because to modern eyes there should be a major difference between a peaceful pilgrimage to Jerusalem on the one hand, and a military conquest of Jerusalem on the other.

This is not how popes and other contemporary European Christians saw the matter, however. To them, these were merely two different aspects of the same reality. They thus saw no contradiction whatsoever in waging a bloody war to gain permanent possession of Jerusalem, their most important and most longed-for religious site. Indeed, the 13th century Benedictine monk Matthew Paris (c. 1200–1259), who was one of Europe's most outstanding illustrators and chroniclers (and who is discussed again in later pages), often used the word *peregrinatio* (pilgrimage) to describe a Crusade.

The bottom line of the First Crusade was that the Crusaders captured Jerusalem in 1099 and made it the capital of a new state known as the Kingdom of Jerusalem. This was believed to stand on the Temple Mount, the reported site of King Solomon's temple. The Temple Mount also became the headquarters of the Knights Templar, an armed order of monastic knights who escorted and protected the pilgrims plying the dangerous roads between the Palestinian coastline and the city of Jerusalem.

These men were certainly the elite fighting force of their day. They were very carefully trained; well-disciplined; militarily well-equipped; backed up by a rich internationally-based infrastructure; and, above all, they were very highly-motivated. Not all of the Knights Templar, however, were combat troops: indeed, the assignment most of the order was simply to finance and otherwise support the combat troops.

One of the core beliefs of the combat troops was that they must never retreat in battle. There were only three exceptions to this rule: they could retreat if (1) they were outnumbered by at least three to one; (2) if their commanding officer ordered them to retreat; or (3) if the Templar flag itself went down. This combination of soldier-and-monk was an unusually powerful one, especially since these men believed that to die in battle against the "heathen," their non–Christian enemies, was the most glorious and the best possible way to die.

In the years 1127–1128, the first master of the order, a French knight from Champagne named Hugh of Payens, visited Western Europe to raise funds and recruits. At a church council held in Champagne at the city of Troyes, presided over by a papal legate, the new order received formal ecclesiastical approval.

At about the same time, Bernard of Clairvaux seized the opportunity to write a very influential public relations handout entitled *De Laude Novae Militiae* (*In Praise of the New Knighthood*). This explained to the literate public and, indirectly through them, to the illiterate masses as well, just why an order of armed monks was now so essential.[4]

Another armed monastic order, the Knights Hospitaller, would provide medical care for them. The Crusaders would in fact control Jerusalem until it was finally recaptured by the Muslims under Saladin, founder of the Ayyubid Dynasty, in 1187.

The First Crusade came about for two reasons. The first was that it was becoming ever more difficult because of the increasing dangers involved for European pilgrims to want to run the risk of making the long journey from Western Europe to Jerusalem.

The second reason was the growing threat posed to the Byzantine Empire itself, which controlled the access routes to Jerusalem, by the victorious Turkish armies. An armed escort was therefore needed to cross Turkey, where localized battles raged and where rapacious officials made life as expensive as possible for the pilgrims. Outside the biggest towns, moreover, outlaws roamed the land virtually unchecked. By the mid–1090s, conditions had deteriorated so much further that the roads to the Holy Land were now said to be closed entirely; it was thought to be quite impossible for pilgrims to reach Jerusalem at all.

The idea of launching a holy war to restore Jerusalem to Christian control appealed to both the Byzantine Emperor Alexius I Comnenus and Pope Urban II for strategic and political reasons. Alexius I probably thought that, if asked for help, the Europeans would probably offer only a few small detachments of Norman mercenaries. Pope Urban II, however, was very much in favor of a massive military intervention to provide long-term security. For this reason, he set in motion the first of the eight or nine mass movements that are now collectively known as the Crusades. They would last for 200 years and would involve many tens of thousands of men, women, and children in many different theaters of war.

In October 1095 at the Council of Clermont held in Auvergne, France, the Pope must have met some of the men who had first-hand knowledge of the problems facing Christian travelers to Palestine—namely, that the roads were now blocked and the Holy Land was therefore entirely off-limits to pilgrims. Perhaps it was as a result of these meetings that in

November 1095 he decided to "preach," that is, to stress officially, the great importance the Church attached to using military force to recapture the Holy Land.

There was no official transcript of what Pope Urban II actually said on this occasion, but he seems to have made five points:

1. Because Jerusalem was now in the hands of the Muslim infidels, Christians were running enormous risks trying to get there. As a result, he was convinced that a "holy pilgrimage" was definitely required to redress these wrongs.

2. The Eastern (Byzantine) Christians urgently needed the military support of European forces to stop the Turkish attacks on them.

3. The Pope stressed that Western Christians must therefore put aside their destructive civil wars and now rally to the support of their fellow Christians in the Middle East.

4. In the Pope's mind, there was no contradiction whatsoever between the Christian ideal of brotherly love, on the one hand, and the medieval ideal of knightly combat, on the other. In fact, he drew a very clear parallel between monks and knights.

The monks, he said, were *milites Christi* ("knights of Christ") who fought against evil by using spiritual weapons. By extension, in his mind, the Crusaders therefore became *milites Christi* who fought against evil with their swords, arrows, armor, war horses, and other temporal weapons of war. At Clermont, the Pope is famously said to have ordered the faithful: "*Nunc fiant [Christi] milites, qui dundum existerunt raptores*" ("Now let those become knights of Christ who had previously been nothing but robbers!")[5]

5. Any Crusader who died in battle during this Crusade would be absolved of all his sins and would go to heaven; those who survived would be considered by the church to be the "true friends of God and the heirs to the heavenly Jerusalem."

Regardless of the exact phrases the Pope used, however, his speech and his call for a crusade clearly met with a decisive, enthusiastic, and overwhelmingly positive public response. The crowd listening to him roared out, in their local French dialect: "*Deus le volt!*" ("God wills it!"). In the years to come, about 100,000 Europeans would be directly or indirectly involved in the First Crusade.

Even before the First Crusade began, however, some devout Italian merchants from Amalfi had established a hospital in Jerusalem to care for Western pilgrims coming to the Holy Land.[6] As the number of pilgrims rose, their medical needs increased, too, so in 1113 Pope Paschal II established the Hospital of St. John of Jerusalem as an independent nursing order staffed by priests as the chief officers and by male and female lay "hospitalers" in the ranks to take care of the pilgrims.

This nursing order became very rich, thanks to the many landed endowments it received in Western Europe, and it became increasingly militarized due to the very shaky military situation existing in and near Jerusalem. In 1142 the Knights Hospitaler also built the great fortress of Krak des Chevaliers (the "Castle of the Knights") in Syria near the northern border of what is now Lebanon. They held it until 1271, when it was finally captured by the Mamluk sultan Baybars I. In its heyday, it was manned by up to 2,000 regular troops.

After the First Crusaders had finished sacking Jerusalem in 1099, most of these men then went home to Western Europe. About 3,000 Franks (Frenchmen and other Europeans), however, stayed behind in Jerusalem, including about 300 knights and 1,000 infantrymen. This small but heavily-armed force was enough to deter the defeated Muslims from trying to recapture the city. Moreover, responding to a summons from the Patriarch of Jerusalem, these men also worked hard to establish some semblance of law and police order in the city itself.

Guillaume de Tyr (William of Tyre), who wrote a celebrated 13th-century work entitled *Historia rerum in partibus transmarinis gestarum* (*History of Deeds Done Beyond the Sea*), tells us that the Patriarch of Jerusalem had instructed the knights in these ringing words: "[They must] work with all their force and for the remission of their sins to protect the roads and paths, and dedicate themselves to defending the pilgrims against the attacks or ambushes of thieves and marauders."[7]

The net result of this order was that a handful of very zealous French knights, only numbering somewhere between eight and 14 men, decided to set up a new religious-military order. It would become officially known as the "Poor Knights of Christ and of the Temple of Solomon."

In about 1118, this handful of knights, reinforced by other knightly recruits, offered their services to Baldwin II, the king of the Kingdom of Jerusalem, to act as a police force to protect the pilgrims. The pilgrims were rarely if ever armed in any way, apart from their own daggers. If traveling on their own and unescorted, they would have been very easy prey for the many well-armed Arab bandits and other assailants who made the roads of Palestine potentially lethal for unarmed travelers.

Pleased by such a generous offer to protect the pilgrims, Baldwin gave the knights part of the former Aqsa Mosque, which the Crusader had renamed the "Lord's Temple" and which had now become a holy site for Christians on the pilgrimage trail. As a result, the new order became widely known simply as the "Templars." It received papal recognition and an official rule of monastic life in 1128. Templars soon became the dominant military force in the Holy Land, and their headquarters in Jerusalem soon reflected this fact. Theodoric, a German monk, wrote admiringly that

> The area is full of houses, dwellings and outbuildings for every purpose, and it is full of walking-places, lawns, council chambers, porches, consistories and supplies of water in splendid cisterns.
>
> Below it is equally full of wash-rooms, stores, grain rooms, stores for wood and other kinds of domestic stores. On the other side of the palace, that is on the west, the Templars have built a new house, whose height, length and breadth, and all its cellars and refectories, staircase and roof, are far beyond the custom of the land. Indeed, its roof is so high that, if I were to mention how high it is, those who listen would hardly believe me.[8]

It must be noted here in passing that the Templars and their brother orders were technically only *lay orders*, not formal religious orders. Because priests were forbidden to shed blood, very few of the members were ordained priests, and none of these are known to have had any active combat role in the Crusades.[9]

The Templars did take monastic vows of poverty, chastity, and obedience and they did follow the ascetic way of life outlined by Bernard of Clairvaux. He believed that a small but well-trained military force could, under the right conditions, defeat a much bigger force. One of the Templars' key battles showed that he was right. The proof came in the 1177 Battle of Montgisard, which took place in what is now Israel.

There the famous Muslim leader Saladin was trying to force his way toward Jerusalem from the south with a strong force of 26,000 soldiers. He had succeeded in surrounding, near the coast at Ascalon, some 500 knights and other forces of King Baldwin IV of Jerusalem. Eighty Templar knights and their entourage tried to stop Saladin and thus came into contact with his troops at Gaza. However, he considered this relative handful of Templars as too puny a force to be worth his time to fight, so he simply ignored them and continued to press on toward Jerusalem with his army.

Once Saladin and his forces had left, however, the Templars were able to join up with King Baldwin's men, and together they all moved north along the coast. But now Saladin made a serious mistake. Rather than holding his own men together in a disciplined manner, he permitted them to spread out and to pillage the villages that lay in their path toward Jerusalem.

The Templars quickly took advantage of the disorder of Saladin's army, and launched a surprise attack directly against Saladin and his bodyguard near Ramala at Montgisard. Saladin's forces were too widely dispersed to be able to stand their ground in the face of this fierce attack. They were forced instead to fight a losing battle as they retreated back toward the south. In the process, however, they lost 90 percent of their original number of men. This was certainly not Saladin's last battle, but it did usher in a year of relative peace for the Kingdom of Jerusalem. In addition, it did become a heroic achievement milestone in the minds of the Templars themselves.

Another military success of the Templars was the real effectiveness of their squadron charge. In this tactic, a small group of Templar knights, mounted on their specially-trained and heavily-armored warhorses, would gather together into one tight band and then gallop at full speed toward the enemy's battle line.

The enemy knew full well that these onrushing Templars would never stop unless they were killed, so this charge often had the desired effect of punching a hole through the enemy lines. Stand-by Crusader forces were then ready and eager to exploit this opening to launch their own attacks against the foe.

Though never large in their numbers, the Templars were also willing to play a key role supporting other armies in other battles. Their specialty was to ram through the front lines of an enemy at the onset of battle or, alternatively, to protect an allied army from any sudden attack from the rear. In various capacities, the Templars thus fought alongside King Louis VII of France, and King Richard I of England. In addition to combat in Palestine itself, the Templars also fought in the Spanish and Portuguese *Reconquista*, i.e., the series of campaigns launched by Christian states to recapture territory from the Muslims, who had occupied most of the Iberian Peninsula in the early 8th century.

In military terms, the Templars were organized into a hierarchy that consisted of four groups: knights, sergeants, chaplains, and servants. Most of the fighting men were sergeants, not knights. These sergeants were very skilled at arms, however, and were more numerous and could act more quickly than the knights, who wore heavy armor and rode very big warhorses.

At the head of the order itself was the Grand Master; each local branch of the order was led by an officer who had to obey the Grand Master's commands. In recognition of their high degree of organization and their fighting abilities, the Templars were put directly under the Pope's control in 1139, rather than remaining under the direction of the Patriarch of Jerusalem. Their future seemed fully assured, but this was certainly not to be the case.

Since they were now under papal authority and were thus no longer accountable to any local bishop, they greatly broadened the scope of their operations and soon became the defenders of every major town in the Holy Land. At the peak of their military power, the Templars could send about 20,000 armed men into the field. During their process of rapid growth, moreover, the order became extremely wealthy, thanks due both to the many deathbed-endowments it received from believers who wanted to thus assure their safe passage to heaven when they died, and to its own role as the Western European financial experts who invented the check.

The story of the Templars' dramatic fall from grace is too long to recount in any detail. Briefly: their immense wealth now seemed to be easily available simply for the taking. In 1303/1304, on behalf of King Philip of France, the Templars were charged, entirely falsely, with heresies, blasphemies, and homosexuality. Claiming to be appalled by their deplorably bad behavior, in 1307 Philip had every Templar in France arrested, and he then seized all of their property. Many Templars were jailed or were killed; the last Grand Master, Jacques de Molay, was publicly burned alive at the stake. A anti–Templar papal bull (a document issued by the pope) of 22 March 1312 ordered that all of the Templars' property be transferred to the Hospitallers, but a significant percentage of this booty was in fact kept by the king of France himself.

Well over a century earlier, the concept of another crusade against the "heathen" also had been very appealing to many Europeans. In the wake of the Third Crusade, a new military-religious order, known as the Knights of the Teutonic Order, had been created in the Holy Land in about 1192.

Founded in the wake of the Third Crusade and initially located in the city of Acre in the Kingdom of Jerusalem, this new order focused at first on the protection of Christians in the Holy Land. Later, however, as the Muslims became more powerful and began to reassert their control over the region, the order turned its attention to Eastern Europe, where it would became a major territorial power.

The military organization of this order was similar to that used in Poland and was based on a unit called a "Banner."[10] This consisted of smaller battlefield formations known as "lances," each of which consisted of one knight and up to seven other men, usually crossbowmen. The great advantage of the crossbow over the longbow was that although it could never be fired as rapidly as a longbow, new recruits could learn how to use it in only about one week. In contrast, mastering the longbow took years of constant practice. The best crossbows were composites made of goat horn, sinew, and wood. The order stockpiled about 4,500 crossbows and over a million bolts (arrows for crossbows) in Prussia alone. It could field hundreds of experienced crossbow-equipped infantrymen; the most skilled crossbowmen, such as the Genoese, were the most sought-after mercenaries.

The key element of the order consisted of both clergy and laymen, but not many of these men were actually ordained priests. Those that were, known as "priest-brothers," wore a characteristic white tunic with a black cross on it. A Teutonic lay brother was not an ordained priest but he lived as a monk and fought as a knight. The lower-ranking sergeants wore a grey rather than a white tunic; in their combat abilities, however, they were just as good as the knights themselves.

By 1400, a long-running disagreement between the Order of Teutonic Knights, on the one hand, and Poland and Lithuania, on the other, was coming to a head, partly as a result of the Order's meddling in the internal politics of its neighbors. In June 1410, the King of Poland therefore invaded the Order's lands with a powerful army that included all the enemies of the Teutonic Knights. These were the Poles, Lithuanians, Russians, Bohemians, Hungarians, Tartars, and Cossacks.

When the opposing armies clashed fiercely with each other in the wooded rolling hills near the small Polish village of Tannenberg, the Teutonic Knights suffered such a disastrous defeat that they would never recover from it. Their defeat was followed by decades of disorder as Polish armies ravaged Russia again and yet again.[11] Finally, during the Reformation, the Order of Teutonic Knights disappeared entirely.

One of the last appearances of any "armed monks" in England was along the southern coast of England from Cornwall to Kent, and was recorded in about 1380. In that year, the English monk and chronicler Thomas of Walsingham (died c. 1422) deplored the sea-borne attacks on the coast being launched by French raiders on the monasteries there. These institutions, of which there were about 18, were prime targets because they were prosperous and were virtually undefended. Thomas described the state of play as follows:

> Whenever the rogues on these boats perceived that a place lacked protection they disembarked and time after time took booty with impunity. Sometimes they even set fire to the towns and burnt them down, but if they saw an armed man [e.g., a knight, an archer, or a crossbowman] coming on to the scene, they left in great haste.[12]

At no point does Thomas or any other contemporary chronicler state that abbots or priors personally fought, man-to-man, against the pirates (in 1268 the Council of London had formally prohibited the clergy from bearing arms or shedding blood). However, when Abbot Hamro died in 1383, a notice in the Westminster Chronicle stated that "beneath his monkish habit he was a soldier of mark and a stout defender of home, neighbors, and coast against the attacks of pirates."[13]

9

Medieval Academic Life

In 1179, Pope Alexander III ordered that every cathedral must have a *magister* (literally, a "master" but "professor" is a better translation) who would teach Latin grammar, which was the cornerstone of academic knowledge in the Middle Ages, to bright but impoverished students—free of any charge.[1] This modest step marks the very beginning of the medieval university system. It was designed to instruct both undergraduates as young as 14, who could study the arts at Oxford or Paris, and mature students in their early 30s, who could study law in Bologna. This new academic institution turned out, over time, to be such a splendid idea that it would eventually become the chief centerpiece of medieval life that is still very much with us today. It arose—remarkably and uniquely—in medieval Europe, and chiefly for two unique reasons that existed only there at that time.

The first of these was the need to broaden the scope of higher education considerably in order to meet the rising educational demands and the employment needs of a more literate, more prosperous, and increasingly urbanizing society. This was one in which, moreover, for the first time in the history of Western Christianity, the Church itself was no longer the sole and unchallenged source of knowledge.

The second reason was the practical need of impoverished university students to organize themselves so that rapacious landlords and other townsmen could no longer exploit them so easily. The students needed to do this because there were never any "rent control" laws in force. They thus had no alternative but to pay whatever they were being charged if they wanted to stay in their lodgings and thus be able attend university lectures.

The monasteries were certainly the first and the only organized centers of learning, scholarship, and writing in the Middle Ages, but their achievements in these fields were still held in thrall to religion. During the 11th century, for example, a French monk stressed the great importance, for strictly religious reasons, of mastering these new skills. He wrote that "for every letter, line, and point [that are copied into the text of a manuscript] a sin is forgiven."

In the 12th century, an English monk even went one step further. He recounts the story of another monk who was very sinful but who was nevertheless a very devoted copyist and a very fine illustrator of the holy texts. When this latter monk died, we are told that God carefully weighed, as an asset, every word that monk had copied against the debit of his many sins. In the end (so the story runs), this monk was saved from the clutches of the Devil only because he had copied *one letter more than the number of his sins*. This tiny credit balance of one single letter was just enough to offset his sins: indeed, this happy fact was all that saved his soul from having to suffer the eternal fires of hell.

By about 1200, three truly excellent universities had come into being. These were Bologna, renowned for civil law and ecclesiastical law; Paris, celebrated for logic, philosophy, and theology in its famous faculty of the liberal arts; and Oxford, a leader in mathematics and in the laws of the natural order of the universe. (There were also ten or more less-famous but still competent medieval universities in Western Europe as well, but they are not discussed here.)

A "university college" is a college institution of modest size that provides advanced education for students but does not, by itself, have full or independent university status. A university college is therefore often part of a much larger independent university. The earliest university colleges appeared in Paris at the end of the 12th century. At first these were little more than pious charitable academic foundations designed to provide room and board for a handful of "poor clerics." The first genuine colleges were set up in Paris, and later in England, in the second half of the 13th century, at a time when the growth of the existing university system was beginning to face administrative problems.

In Paris, these schools included the colleges of the Sorbonne (1257), which in the Middle Ages had almost 10,000 students associated with it, and of Harcourt (1280). In Oxford, they included Merton (1263–1264), Balliol (1261–1266), and University College (c. 1280). In Cambridge, we find Peterhouse College (1284). All of these were organized along the lines of the mendicant monasteries, which had been established as early as the 1220s within the universities chiefly for the use of students belonging to those mendicant orders.

Once they were endowed with lands, properties, and rental incomes, the colleges considered it their assignment to accept a given number of students for a specified period of time. The first colleges had special units reserved for the use of the monks of a particular order or abbey and who were associated with certain priories. In Paris, such colleges included

Saint-Bernard (Cistercian, 1248), Cluny (c. 1260), and Saint-Denis (c. 1263). In England were the colleges of Gloucester (1283) and of Durham (1289). Most of these university colleges, however, were meant for secular rather than for religious students. During the years before 1300, a total of 26 such colleges were founded: 19 in Paris, six in Oxford, and one at Cambridge. Some of these colleges would later become the brilliant stars, as it were, of their respective universities.[2]

The friars, for their part, established religious schools in Paris, Oxford, and Cambridge, not only to take advantage of the excellent theological studies offered there but also to recruit students and teachers for their own orders. These schools, however, were not separate from the theological faculties of the universities themselves: secular masters as well as monastic masters taught at the friars' schools.[3]

During the 13th century, the University of Paris went from strength to strength and soon became the most important university in the world. Its recruiting area even extended far beyond the frontiers of France itself, stretching into the British Isles, Germany, Denmark, and the Low Countries as well. By the mid–13th century, however, the independence of the masters (i.e., the professors) at the University of Paris faced an unexpected but serious challenge from the friars of the two major mendicant orders—the Dominicans and the Franciscans.

The fundamental problem was that each order already had its own well-organized hierarchy of excellent schools, ranging from elementary to advanced levels, and each order wanted to retain full control of the monastic students it sent to the University. More precisely, the mendicant orders did not want their own students to integrate fully into the university. Only the most able friars were sent there to study theology, and their orders refused to let them take the mandatory introductory liberal arts course required for all entering students.

The orders argued that, thanks to their earlier studies, all of these very bright students had already totally mastered the substance of the liberal arts course. Therefore, said the orders, they need not risk being exposed to, and being tainted by, the secular learning that was the hallmark of the faculty of arts. At the University of Paris, the masters also strongly opposed the friars' efforts to "fish for novices" among the new and youngest university students. In 1385 they even tried (but failed) to forbid the friars from accepting any candidates who were under the age of 18.[4]

The following are some of the main points of what would become a long-running medieval academic quarrel.[5]

First, it is necessary to explain the important medieval academic term of "inception." As used at the University of Paris, this term meant the procedure by which the masters' guild could formally regulate the selection and the admission of all newly-arrived teachers into its own carefully-chosen and very prestigious ranks.

As part of their application process, the friars were expected to take the customary oath to comply with all the regulations of the university. They refused to take this oath, however, on the grounds that they were not now under, and did not ever intend to submit to, the authority of the masters' guild. Indeed, they wanted to be governed only by their own monastic superiors, not by any secular masters.

Second, the regular (non-mendicant) masters themselves became quite jealous of the concessions granted by the university to the friar-students. As the modern French scholar Jacques Verger has explained (translated into English):

> The Dominican and Franciscan schools enjoyed great success: filled with enthusiasm both by the quality of teaching and the evangelical lifestyle of the friars, many students rallied to the new orders. This success aroused the ire of other professors, who took note of the fact that the newcomers, while belonging to the university, continued as a priority to depend on their own respective orders [rather than following the procedures laid down by the university itself].
>
> Refusing to accept the constraints of university solidarity, they [also] made little effort to defend the university's privileges and autonomy. In the 1250s, the secular masters [even] went on the defensive against the mendicants—to try to drive them away from the university or at least to reduce significantly their influence....[6]

The papacy got caught up in this struggle. In 1254, for example, Pope Innocent IV had favored the masters' point of view, but in a bull of 1255 his successor, Alexander IV, decided to try to change this policy. He now wanted to use the University of Paris not as a fully independent advisory body of scholars but simply as a fully dependent tool of papal control.

It was not until long after he died (in 1261) that the masters would gain the upper hand. Finally, in 1318, they at last felt strong enough to demand that the friars swear an oath of obedience to the University of Paris. In the end, the friars yielded to this demand without too much opposition. The independence of the University of Paris—especially on the critically-important issue of the masters' and scholars' right to strike over academic issues that were vital to them, and even to leave university if their demands were not met—therefore survived intact.

The friars, for their part, now seemed to be content with the dominant place they had finally won for themselves in the teaching of theology, which for them was certainly by far the most important course in terms of their budding monastic careers.[7] It was also the most prestigious and most difficult path of university learning. Based on painstaking studies of the

Bible, during the Middle Ages theology was therefore hailed in French as "Madame la Haute Science" ("My Lady the High Science") and in English as "Lady Theology."[8]

The historian Barbara Tuchman noted that the sins of the monks and of the itinerant friars were very disturbing to lay citizens because the claims of the monks and friars to be "men of God" struck the secular community as much too pretentious. The monks and friars were in fact quite notorious for peddling furs and girdles to women, as well as small gentle dogs, simply "to get love of them."

We even learn from a 14th-century poem that a friar "came to our dame when the gode man is from home," and that

> He spares nauther for synne ne shame.
> For may he tyl a woman synne
> In priveyte, he will not blynne
> Er her a childe put hir withinne
> And perhaps two at ones.[9]

A rough translation of the above might be: "He came to the woman's house when her husband was away from home. He feels neither sin nor shame, for while in private he may lecture a woman about sin, he will feel no responsibility himself if he impregnates her—perhaps with twins!"

10

Scholasticism

Because of its great importance in medieval universities and thus, by extension, in medieval ecclesiastical life as a whole, we need to focus on scholasticism at this point. Scholasticism is a term that applies to both a method of thought, i.e., theology, and to a system of thought, i.e., philosophy. Used in this latter context, it also refers to the historical period between the end of the Patristic era of the 5th century, on the one hand, and the end of the Middle Ages and the beginning of the modern era in about 1450 on the other. A contemporary philosopher who adopted the method or the system of the medieval scholastics was said to have become a scholastic himself. The rise of scholasticism is closely associated with the flourishing of the monastic and other schools in Italy, France, Spain, and England during the Middle Ages.[1]

Scholasticism placed a very strong emphasis on dialectical reasoning to extend knowledge by inference and to resolve contradictions. Typically, in the classroom, a topic was raised in the form of a question; opposing arguments were given; a counterproposal was put forward; and all the arguments, pro and con, were then thoroughly debated. Because of the effectiveness of this rigorous dialectical method, scholasticism was applied to many other fields of study as well.

The academic subject of logic, which was taught in medieval universities as one of the three fundamental liberal arts, was defined to include dialectic, i.e., a reasoned discourse between two or more people holding different points of view about a subject but both wanting to establish the truth through reasoned argumentation. The other two liberal arts taught in the universities were rhetoric and grammar.

In university practice, the crux of the dialectical process was known in Latin as a *quaestio disputata* (a "disputed question") and was handled by six interrelated steps with a carefully-prescribed and highly-stylized format:

> The question first had to be formally defined, using the phrase "It is asked whether...."

A provisory answer then had to be given ("And it seems that …").

The principal arguments in favor of the provisory answer then had to be put forward.

An argument against the provisory answer had to be put forward, too, traditionally using only a single argument from some revered authority ("On the contrary…").

A conclusion had to be advanced, based on the evidence ("I answer that…").

Finally, replies to any objections were needed ("In reply to the first objection, to the second, etc., I answer that…)."

The *questio* method of reasoning was especially useful when two authoritative texts directly contradicted each other. In the *questio* process, the contradictory propositions would be consolidated into the format of one single either/or question. Since the absolute truth of Biblical and patristic sources could never legitimately be doubted, however, it often required some fancy intellectual footwork to show that such a contradiction was actually more apparent than real.

Each part of the question would have to be approved or rejected by a finding of either (*sic,* "yes") or (*non,* "no"). The most famous book on this subject was *Sic et non* by Peter Abelard. In his approach, arguments for the positive point of view are followed by the negative arguments against it. This method forced students to consider opposing viewpoints and to become willing and able to defend their own point of view.

Historically, much has been said both in praise and in blame of the use of scholastic terminology in philosophy.[2] It has also been noted, however, that whatever precision now exists in the modern languages of Western Europe is due chiefly to the endless dialectical disputations of 13th-century scholastics in the Middle Ages.

It is now added that their writing style in Latin, even when they had to translate from Greek sources not familiar to them, still has admirable qualities of clearness, conciseness, and richness of technical phrasing that is pleasing to modern readers. Moreover, the scholastics excelled most of all in their metaphysical ability, namely, being able to grasp complicated abstract general principles very quickly and then to apply them consistently and systematically in scholarly discussions.[3]

11

Medieval Heresy

A very short introduction to medieval heresy would run along the following lines. They are relevant here because of the central role that the canons and the Church played in this subject.

- One of the major questions of medieval European history was what, exactly, constituted a proper Christian life. This question would eventually rise to become a key issue, drawing the attention of popes, clergy, kings, aristocrats, and commoners alike.
- A Christian life inherently required both appropriate belief and behavior. By the year 1000, most of northern Europe had been converted to Christianity. Gradually, however, a new spirit of religious reform began to appear, holding that *the prospects for salvation for the world as a whole* would be very much better if all of its sinful inhabitants could somehow be reformed.'
- Moving in this direction, the Church would eventually opt for a much greater articulation of Christian beliefs and a much clearer set of systematic rules for what constituted appropriate Christian behavior. It was felt that such clarifications were badly needed: indeed, if the old sinful ways were allowed to continue unchecked, it was feared that the salvation of the whole world itself would thereby be imperiled.
- At first, the Church thought that any erring souls could be shepherded back into the fold simply by means of more effective ecclesiastical teaching and by better sermons. When both of these tools proved to have failed, however, ecclesiastical and lay leaders alike decided that they now had no choice but to resort to coercion.[1]

The Church's reasoning was that, to quote James Brundage, a modern expert on canon law,

Medieval churchmen claimed authority over virtually every aspect of human beliefs and actions. They believed that they not only had the right but also the duty to repress any religious or moral ideas that departed from orthodox norms. Deviant beliefs, they thought, not only endangered the salvation of those who entertained them, but *threatened to infect the rest of the community as well.*[2]

An opening gun in this campaign was probably the now little-remembered "heresy of Orleans," which took place in Orleans, France, in 1022 and which was reported by several texts and chronicles of the time. Although the major medieval heresy in France was the Cathar heresy, the smaller-scale Orleans heresy is worth reviewing here because it is not as well-known and is of interest on several medieval fronts.

In 1022 about a dozen of the most learned canons of the French cathedral of Orleans were burned alive, as heretics, in a wooden hut—on the direct orders of the Capetian king of France, Robert the Pious. These men were said be among the most famous clerics of the city of Orleans, and had been raised from childhood in the Catholic faith, almost certainly in monastery schools. Some of them may even have been tonsured monks.

This event was to be the first time in medieval France that a pyre was used to stamp out "scholarly heresy." Both the severity of the punishment and the very high intellectual and social quality of the victims made this a remarkable historical event. Basically, the "sins" of these heretics were that they had publicly called into question a whole litany of the key doctrines of medieval Christian life. These included, for example, refusal of baptism; doubts about the role of grace and of the sacraments held to confer it; doubts about transubstantiation in the Eucharist; doubts about the forgiveness of mortal sins; heretical views on the role of marriage; rejection of a bishop's spiritual authority; denial of the virginity of Mary; denial of any value to the laying-on of priestly hands; and a refusal to eat animal foods considered to be unclean.

Moreover, rather than relying on the well-established procedures of the Church itself to address some or all of their grievances, they advocated instead a *personal inner search for spiritual progress*, backed up by a rigorously ascetic way of life.

The anti-heresy forces feared that if some of these radical ideas became more widespread, they might well force significant changes in the social organization of medieval Western Christianity itself. Indeed, it was precisely for this reason that the very conservative ecclesiastical and lay authorities of the day wanted to inflict an exceptionally heavy judgment and harsh punishment on these highly intelligent and learned heretics, who certainly must have been well aware of how far they were getting out of line.

In addition, this event also took place during a major power struggle in Orleans between King Robert and Eudes II, the Count of Blois. Orleans was a royal city, but the counts of Blois had increased their own power by replacing the local bishop, who had been appointed by the king ten years earlier, with their own more pliant man who would now happily do their own bidding.

On Christmas Day in 1022, ten to 14 canons of the cathedral of Orleans were accused by Arafat, a Norman knight from Chartres, of disseminating heretical doctrines. King Robert immediately ordered his men to arrest them. He then convened a synod (a meeting designed to focus on a doctrinal issue) of his conservative supporters in Orleans, including the confessor of Queen Constance and the new bishop, to sit in judgment on them.

It is said that this synod lasted all day, and that while it was going on an angry crowd outside the meeting-room was demanding that the accused canons be executed. In the end, the canons admitted to having committed the religious offenses with which they were charged. On 28 December 1022, they were therefore led out of Orleans and locked up in a wooden hut, which was set on fire. All of them perished.

In a 1970 academic monograph, the French medievalist Robert-Henri Battier concluded that although the canons "had shown a certain audacity in doctrinal matters which left them open to a charge of heresy." An equally fatal failing on their part was ignoring the local political realities. These were twofold: first, rivalries over the prestigious office of the Bishop of Orleans and, second, the hostility of certain princes towards Queen Constance herself.

The most detailed document, however, on the heresy of Orleans was written about 60 years after the event by the Norman knight Arafat when he joined the Abbey of Saint-Pere de Chartres in 1027 as a monk. His account also includes a long passage on heresy that was drafted by a local monk, Paul de Chartres. Paul de Chartres justifies his account because, in his opinion, the testimony of Arafat and his behavior in the Orleans affair comprise an enlightening educational narrative that is very much *lignum memories* ("worthy of memory"). He concludes that these events reflect the triumph of "the true Catholic faith, the light of which shone more light on the whole earth, once the madness of the worst of the foolish [the heretical canons] has been extinguished." In this case, at least, heresy had been extinguished by force.

12

Monks in the Scriptorium

The scriptorium (literally, "a place for writing") was a room in a monastery where new works on history and canon law were written and where existing documents were copied or illuminated. Much of this painstaking work could be done by the monks themselves, but secular experts and illuminators hired from the wider world outside the monastery were often brought in to help them.

The earliest European monastic writing dates from around 517. As this process slowly evolved, the monks developed, preserved, and refined much of the literary history of Western Europe by copying Jerome's Latin Vulgate Bible and the commentaries and letters of the early Fathers of the Church. Monks saw their assignments not simply as slavishly copying these ancient texts but rather, in so doing, as being immediate and highly meritorious individual acts of meditation, prayer, and possibly even of personal salvation.

In the major monastic establishments such as Cluny or the cathedral priory of Canterbury, as many as 100 monks, that is, nearly half of the monastic community, were engaged not in manual labor but in administrative duties carried out inside or outside of the monastery's own grounds.[1] The work undertaken in the scriptorium was certainly the most difficult, the longest-lasting, and historically the most valuable of all their activities.

Copying manuscripts often called for a careful division of labor among the monks themselves. A scriptorium contained desks where the monks could sit and copy or correct the texts set upright in front of them, as well as the necessary ink wells, penknives, and quills. Some monks prepared the fine parchment (the premier writing material, made from the untanned skins of sheep, calves, or goats) by smoothing its surface and then by rubbing chalk onto it. Others ruled it, i.e., made lines in it, and copied the appropriate text onto it. The most artistically-gifted monks were given the final and most challenging task of illuminating the text.

Monasteries built in the later Middle Ages in cold or temperate climates often had their scriptorium installed near the heat of the kitchen or in a special "warming-room." Nevertheless, writing and illustrating manuscripts was still always a long, slow, tiring, cold process that was also very hard on the back and on the eyes. A 10th-century prior, Leo of Navora, recounts for us, in very informal terms, his own experiences in the scriptorium. He explained (lightly edited): "Just try to do it yourself, and you will soon find out how difficult a writer's task is! It dims your sight, makes your back ache from leaning forward so much, and knits your chest and belly together. It is really a terrible ordeal for your whole body!"[2]

A monastery built in southern Italy in the 6th century by the famous Roman monastic writer Cassidorus contained a scriptorium for the purpose of collecting, copying, and preserving texts. He also set up a library in which, at the end of the Roman Empire, he tried to bring Greek learning to Latin readers, and to preserve both sacred and secular texts for future generations. Cassidorus wrote treatises aimed at instructing his monks on the proper uses of these texts. Although later dispersed and lost, his library was still active around 630.

The German monastery of Reichenau was, around the year 1000, a very famous writing school, best known for the fine quality of its painted manuscripts. It produced some of the most beautiful illuminations of the Ottonian Renaissance, which began in about 1030. These monks (and the monks of other monasteries) also produced workaday copies of texts for much more utilitarian needs. It was not until the rise of the universities, and then the appearance of university stationers in the 13th century, however, that such inexpensive texts became more widely available for use in the schools.

Before that time, it was the monasteries themselves that continued to have monopolies on the production of books. After their heyday, however, the medieval literary baton passed to the *stationarii* (publishers), who hired scores of copyists. To speed book production, illuminations were eliminated, margins were reduced, cheaper parchment was used, and lettering was simplified.[3]

On the literary front, monastic authors were the prototypical writers of history in the Middle Ages. Their output embraced a very broad range of memorial practices over this entire period, namely, romances, lais (short poems on love and chivalry), sagas, letters, saints' lives, and cartularies (legal documents). The importance of the literary front to the monks themselves was highlighted by the modern historian James J. O'Donnell in these lightly-edited words:

> [In the monastery] each Psalm would have to be recited at least once a week all through the period of study. In turn, each Psalm studied separately would have to be read slowly and prayerfully, then gone through with the text in one

hand (or preferably committed to memory) and the commentary on the other; the process of study would have to continue until virtually everything in the commentary had been absorbed by the student and mnemonically keyed to the individual verses of scripture, so that when the verses were recited again the whole phalanx of Cassidorian erudition would spring up in support the content of the sacred text.[4]

Moreover, some monks were also very well-trained, well-informed, and highly literate writers on canon law (church law). Canon law was extremely popular and extremely complex. Indeed, there was such a great need for it in medieval society that it regularly attracted a large proportion of the very best minds of the six or seven generations between the mid–12th and mid–14th centuries. This was because of the very desirable administrative positions, wealth, and power so easily attained by skilled canonists, who were rarely confined to life in a single monastery.[5] As a modern expert reminds us,

> Canon law was extremely tough law indeed, not only in the sense that it was institutionally strong and sturdy, but also in the sense that it was very difficult and technical....
> It touched the lives of virtually every medieval man, woman, and child. Canonical courts had exclusive jurisdiction over marriage, divorce, and sexual conduct outside marriage. They also dealt with wills, testaments, probate, for laymen and clerics alike, as well as church property, its tax system, loans, bankruptcy, and a wide range of other financial and economic issues.
> Medieval canon law ... constituted a fundamental force in the creation of some of the most elemental ideas and assumptions that continue to this day to characterize Western societies.[6]

Canon law comprised not only the large body of papal decretals, i.e., decrees from the pope, and official promulgations from the Church, but also drew very heavily on the Roman civil law tradition itself. This combination provided a flexible if complicated network of traditional and legal procedures.

Despite its complexities, however, canon law was more lenient and more rational than the prevailing secular law. For example, it did not permit the torture of defendants or witnesses in order to get at the "truth" of a matter. Canon law was specifically not allowed to inflict the death penalty itself; instead, any "criminous clerks" (i.e., clerics who were accused of committing a major criminal act) had to be handed over by the Church to face civil sentencing, e.g., up to and including their execution. Ironically, some members of the public thought that the Church was simply coddling its cleric by insisting on trying them only under the relatively benign proceedings of canon law.[7]

Canon law was sometimes confusingly referred to in the Middle Ages as the customary *ius commune,* or "common law," but this was technically incorrect. Common law was based on traditional and current city and rural practices that were interpreted and understood, as need be, in the light of their "customary usages," rather than by any formal reference to a fixed body of Roman or other law.[8]

A volume on canon law, arranged by themes and used from the 11th century onwards, was known as a *Decretum* (meaning a Decree), as in *Gratian's Decretum,* which was written by the monk Gratian. This latter book remained a fundamental work on canon law throughout and even beyond the Middle Ages. Its dialectical argumentation strongly appealed to teachers of canon law because its complex and sometimes subtle reasoning showed how abstract legal principles could be applied to resolve the complicated and the very messy disputes that so often arise between real people living in the real world.[9]

During the Middle Ages, religion would always have a major impact both on substantive legal principles and on the interface between law and Christian morality.[10] For example, maxims of canon law such as *volunti non fit* ("to a willing person no injury is done") and *nemo obligatus ad impossibile* ("no one is obliged to do what is impossible") became firmly established in the English law of tort by about 1310. (A tort is a civil wrong that causes a claimant to suffer loss or harm, resulting in legal liability for the person who commits the tortious act.)

Moreover, under medieval English law, "Leaving matters to the conscience"—a policy drawn chiefly from the ecclesiastical courts—was increasingly used to encourage reconciliation among the many litigants who were appearing in the civil courts. An additional Church-backed belief was that the important medieval concepts of "right" and of "law" could never be overlooked without endangering the souls of the litigants. In essence, then, all these religion-based concepts formed the basis for a more discretionary and more morality-based style of justice.

During the first five centuries of the Christian era, the clerics who were known as canons (their title comes from the Greek word for "rule") defined the norms for the religious life of members of the early Christian communities. Most importantly, they laid out the key elements of Christian doctrines and drew increasingly sharp lines between the authentic Christians, on the one hand, and those whom they considered to be heretics or unbelievers, on the other.

Canon law in the early Church defined the powers and qualifications of bishops and other clerics, setting out their obligations and enacting disciplinary measures for clergy who were either too aggressive or too sluggish in discharging their duties. As monasticism became an increasingly important part of medieval religious life after the 4th century, canon law also had to define and to take account of the official status of monks and nuns.

Moreover, as the Church itself increasingly became a major property owner (due to the many pious bequests from the faithful, who hoped that giving generously to the Church now would improve their own prospects for a heavenly life after death), canons also prescribed detailed rules for the management of monastic lands and other earthly goods.[11]

Writing on history and on canon law was a very popular medieval activity. Between 570 and 1338, for example, there were approximately 24 significant English, Norman, or Welsh authors (not all of whom were monks) who wrote about the history of England. This chapter introduces three monks who were also good historians: William of Jumièges, Oderic Vital, and Robert de Torigni, and one monk, namely, Gratian, who was an early expert on canon law.[12]

The first author, William of Jumièges (c.1000–after 1070), was a French monk and was one of the earliest writers on the Norman conquest of England in 1066. Not much is known about him on a personal level, possibly because, at that time, monasticism in England itself was not very widespread: indeed, there were probably only six houses that had more than 40 monks in them.[13] The *New York Times* journalist Elaine Sciolino has given us a short (see below) but very clear description of the monks' way of life at the Benedictine abbey in Jumièges in Normandy.

Founded in 654 by Saint Philibert, this became the largest and most influential Benedictine abbey in Normandy. By the time of the second abbot, about 1,000 monks were living, working, and praying there. During the Viking raids along the Seine River as far upstream as Paris, however, by the end of the 9th century the abbey had been pillaged and burned to the ground.

A new and much bigger abbey arose on its site in 1067, thanks to the support of William the Conqueror. This became such an important religious and educational institution that its abbots played important roles in both the Church and the French state. For this reason, however, it also attracted the ire of anti–Church revolutionaries in the late 18th century, who destroyed it. The abbey's imposing ruins were described by 19th-century French historians as "the most beautiful ruins in France."

Lightly edited, Sciolino's account runs along the following lines:

> The Seine Valley from Rouen to the sea was once the domain of monks. They organized the construction of their own harbors and ports, collected taxes from the local farmers, sold the right to fish, and managed commerce through a centralized string of abbeys built along the Seine. Jumièges, a grand Benedictine abbey founded in the seventh century by Saint Philibert, was the most powerful of them all.

With control of the valley, a place of fertile land and forests filled with wild game, the monks were rich—until the Vikings raided, plundered, torched, and destroyed abbeys and towns. Afterward, Jumièges was rebuilt on a grander scale, and William the Conqueror consecrated it in 1067. It became a great center of religion and learning, and a haven where the poor could find food and shelter.[14]

Educated at the abbey, William of Jumièges was given the nickname "Calculus," which suggests that he had some facility with facts and figures. Although as a monk he had no military training whatever, he was very bright and was able to write, with considerable pride and facility, about the military exploits of the Normans.

William of Jumièges was the original compiler of a famous history known as the *Gesta Normannorum Ducum* ("Deeds of the Dukes of the Normans"). He dedicated it to William the Conqueror; finished it in about 1060; and then extended it later, after William the Conqueror had become king of England, by carrying the story up to 1070. His own work was later expanded by two 12th-century monks, namely, the chroniclers Orderic Vital (d. c. 1142) and Robert Torigni (d. 1186), to include the reign of Henry Beauclerc of Normandy, who was also King Henry I of England and the son of William the Conqueror.

During the Middle Ages, this revised work was very widely distributed and was read in many monasteries. Its great popularity is shown by the fact it still survives in 47 manuscript copies. The only noteworthy errors in the book are, first, that William of Jumièges wrote King Harold was killed at the *beginning* rather than at the *end* of the fighting, as was in fact the case; and, second, Orderic Vital's factual errors and his strong desire to write a *theological* history, rather than an objective secular history, tended to mar his work.

The best and most recent version of this book was edited and translated by Elisabeth M.C. van Houts in two volumes, published by the Clarendon Press of Oxford in 1992 and in 1995. A British medievalist, the late Marjorie Chibnall, praised these texts very warmly as "an event of capital importance in the history of Normandy."

Perhaps the most dramatic part of this book deals with Prince William the Conqueror's successful assault on the English coastline in 1066. Some of its death-or-glory highlights can profitably be quoted here:

[From his own vantage point, i.e., while standing on the French coast of the English Channel], Prince William was thus compelled to watch the strength of Harold [the English king] increasing daily at a time when it was the duke [i.e., William himself] who should have been crowned with a royal diadem.

He therefore hastily built a fleet of three thousand ships [a modern guess is 726 ships, but this estimate, too, may well be inflated]. At length he brought this fleet to anchor at St. Valery in Ponthieu [France] where he filled it with mighty horses and most valiant men with hauberks [i.e., war-shirts made of mail] and helmets. When a favorable wind began to blow, he set sail and, crossing the sea [the English Channel], he landed at Pevensey [England]....

[Before dawn on the next day], William advanced undaunted against the terrible enemy. The battle began at the third hour of the day, and continued amid a welter of carnage until nightfall. Harold himself, fighting in the front rank of his army, fell covered with deadly wounds. And the English, seeing their king dead, lost confidence in their own safety, and as night was approaching they turned and fled.

The most valiant duke, returning from the pursuit and slaughter of his enemies, came back to the field of battle in the middle of the night. At first dawn, having despoiled [looted] the corpses of his enemies and buried the bodies of his dear comrades, he took the road which leads to London.[15]

The second monastic author of note here is Oderic Vital, who was probably the best Norman historian of the era.[16] The son of one of the many French mercenaries who had been hired by Duke William for the 1066 conquest of England, Oderic Vital remained a member of the Saint-Evroult monastery in Normandy until his death in about 1142.

At the monastery, he quickly proved himself to be a most gifted copyist and a very able author. His masterpiece is the *Historia ecclesiastica* (its English title is the "History of Normandy"), to which he devoted 30 years of his life. Initially, Oderic began, at the request of his abbot Roger, to write about the founders and benefactors of the abbey so that future generations would never forget them. However, Pierre Bouet, a modern French historian working in the University of Caen's Office of Norman Studies, tells us that the temporal and geographical perspective of this work gradually widened:

The Normans, who no longer gave geographical limits to their political ambitions and the Church, which by nature had a Catholic [i.e., in this context, a *universal*] vocation, encouraged the historian to adopt an ever-broader perspective. The title of the work, borrowed from Bede the Venerable [a monk and an Anglo-Saxon historian] could just as well have been *Gesta Die per Normannos* ("Deeds of the Normans").[17]

This work is divided into 13 books. The first two books chronicle the years 1 to 1142. Books 3 to 5, covering 1114–1129, recount the Norman expeditions to England and Italy. Book 6 addresses the history of the Saint-Evroult monastery, while the next seven are presented as a history of the Christian world of 1080–1140, still centered on the Anglo-Norman world and the monastery as the major centers of interest.

The *Historia ecclesiastica* offers the reader a varied and exciting range of subjects. These include wars, marriages, storms, monastic foundations, shipwrecks, miracles, fashions, lives and deaths of princes, unusual customs, and even rumors. Orderic's great achievement was submitting to posterity a broad, if imperfect, history that is, at the same time, religious, social, economic, administrative, intellectual, and genealogical.

The third monastic historian is Robert de Torigni (c. 1142–1180). He entered the Normandy monastery of Bec-Hellouin in 1128, where his passion for letters and books encouraged Abbot Boson to put him in charge of the library. He must have handled this assignment very well because he was then elected abbot of the monastery of Mont-Saint-Michel in 1154. There he cultivated a friendship with the Anglo-Norman king Henry II Plantagenet. Robert made himself best known to posterity, however, through his continued writings and his love of books.

His works include additions, after 1139, to the *Gesta Normannorum Ducum* of William of Jumiéges; a *Chronicle* that relates the main events of the abbey of Mont-Saint-Michel and provides a historical panorama of the Anglo-Norman kingdom from 1100 to 1182; and a treatise on the monastic orders of Normandy. Under Robert's leadership, his monastery became known as the "city of books." Alas, a collapse in the 12th century of the north tower of the abbey church, where many of these books were stored, caused the permanent loss of an important part of the monastery's library.

Finally, one must consider the early canon law expert known as Gratian, who was believed to have been a monk who taught canon law in Bologna in about 1140. Although very little is clear about his life, it is clear that he wrote or at least compiled the definitive textbook of canon law entitled *A harmony of conflicting canons* (*Concordia discordantium canonum*). The tile of this work, while entirely accurate, is too cumbersome for daily use, so his book has always been known simply as *Gratian's Decree* (*Decrehistum Gratiani*). This book was such a departure from earlier works on canon law that it is now cited as marking the beginning of what is termed "the classical period" of this body of law; namely, for its final definitive shape and its lasting characteristics.[18]

Perhaps the best way to approach it here is simply to follow one of Gratian's more than 36 fictitious legal cases. The following is a good example of Gratian as a law professor who raises some very difficult and intertwined legal questions for his students to answer. He himself does not answer them. Gratian asks the following eight questions:

Since he did not have a wife, a man joined a prostitute to himself in marriage. She was infertile and the daughter of a serf and the granddaughter of a freeman. Although her father wanted to give her to another, her grandfather joined her to this man, for the reason of incontinence [i.e., sexual restraint] only. Thereafter this man, led by regret, began to attempt to conceive children with his own maid. Afterwards, when he had been convicted of adultery and punished, he asked a man to take his wife by violence [i.e., to rape her], so that he would be able to divorce her. When this had been done, he married an infidel woman, but on the condition that she convert to the Christian religion.

Now it is first asked if it is licit to take a prostitute as a wife? Second, if she who is taken [as a wife] for the reason of incontinence is to be called "wife"? Third, whose judgement would she follow, the free grandfather or the servile father? Fourth, if he is allowed to conceive children with a maid while his wife is alive? Fifth, if she who suffers violence is proven to have lost her virtue? Sixth, if an adulterous man can divorce his adulterous wife? Seventh, if a man may marry another while his divorced wife is alive? Eighth, if a Christian man may take in marriage an infidel under the aforementioned condition?[19]

Gratian's approach to this kind of problem-solving was to present all the different sides of a question, with the expectation that an acceptable solution would inevitably emerge from careful discussions of the process. This was not always the case, however, as the following example will show.

Sometimes Gratian simply failed. Consider the difficult and tricky question of "Shall priests be acquainted with profane [i.e., non–Christian] knowledge?" This was, in effect, to ask whether priests and monks should be allowed to read the pre–Christian works of the Greek authors. Gratian first addresses and dismisses, in one brief sentence, the option that they *should not* be allowed to read them. It therefore follows that Gratian believes they *should be allowed* to read such works. He then goes on, moreover, in four long sentences, to cite many cases in which revered Biblical figures *did indeed profit*, in a moral sense, from receiving such profane knowledge. In the end of his argument, however, Gratian draws only the very colorless, unclear, and logically-unsupported conclusion that "priests must not be ignorant." What this implies is that for Gratian there is no religious objection to their reading the Greek authors.

Writing in 1927, the great medievalist Charles Homer Haskins speculated that Gratian had arrived at this remarkably unsatisfactory answer simply because "Plainly the problem was too much for the canonists, and it was never wholly solved, for there was a strong current of sheer paganism in the Italian Renaissance" of that time.[20]

13

Monks and Medicine

During the Middle Ages, a rudimentary medical system was set up and was chiefly administered at the hands-on level by the monks.

It is certainly true there were more formal medical schools in existence throughout Europe at that time. One of the most famous, for example, was the school of Salerno in southern Italy, set up in the 9th century, which was reputedly cofounded by a Christian, an Arab, and a Jew. In 1140, Roger of Sicily forbade any one from practicing medicine without a license, which shows that doctors were clearly under some form of regulation there. By 1340, the French university at Montpellier even included a school of anatomy.

The major involvement of the monks in medicine began at a time when the physical aspects of medicine itself and the importance of spiritual (religious) healing were both valued very highly and thus could coexist harmoniously.[1]

Due to widespread poverty and to a profound lack of knowledge about the real causes of disease, it was omnipresent and widely feared. As a result, the study and practice of medicine became extremely important and embraced a wide range of curative theories. These ranged from physically-based perceptions of illness to religious, magical, and herbal remedies. Perhaps the best result was the appearance of the medieval monastic hospitals, which became a major source of medical care in the Middle Ages.

The monks got involved in health care for a variety of reasons. These included the simple fact there was often no one else around who was willing and able to help the diseased. Monks were in fact a very good choice for this assignment because they were literate, relatively well-educated, highly motivated to serve God by helping the poor and the sick, and had access to some historical documents on how to treat diseases.

Being primary care-givers, the monks usually stuck to the tried and true medieval medical practices that were already well-known and often-used, such as general cleanliness, including baths for patients;

treating the sick with love and care; bloodletting; and using a wide range of herbal remedies.

A unique feature of monastic medical care was that almost all of the treatments they were able to use flowed from religious rather than from what we would call scientifically valid considerations. The bottom line was that monastic health care was always the handmaid of religion. Monks focused on treating a patient's soul, in addition to his or her body, being confident in their belief that, at the end of the day, it was God alone who had the final word on an individual's health and recovery.

A good example of this state of affairs can be seen in what is known as "The Plan of St. Gall." This plan was a historical document drawn up to help Abbot Gozbert rebuild the monastery of St. Gall in Switzerland in 820. Although it was never actually used for this purpose, it does show two important things: (1) the rise of monastic hospitals as part of the alms-houses and hospitality centers traditionally provided for pilgrims and paupers, and (2) the medieval health care system under the monastic rule of St. Benedict. The first point is probably self-evident. On the second point, Benedict himself explained that "Before others and above all, special care must taken of the ill so that they may be looked after, as Christ [directed] … The sick must remember they are being taken care of for the honor of God."[2]

An important part of the plan for the monastery was the medicinal herb garden, which furnished physicians and monks with the pharmaceutical products used in their treatment of patients. Taking good care of this garden was an expected part of the monks' daily life.

In addition, physicians and monks were familiar with the ancient Greek medical theory that the human body consisted of four "humors," namely, blood, phlegm, black bile, and yellow bile, and that these were controlled by the "four elements"—fire, water, earth, and air. A person was healthy only when all of the humors were in perfect balance; disease was explained as an imbalance or a poor mixture of them.

To summarize this brief discussion of monks and medicine, the following points can usefully be made[3]:

- The monastic medical program was a transitional period in the history of medicine. In it, physical medicine, on the one hand, and spiritual healing, on the other, worked side-by-side. Of these two factors, spiritual healing was always held to be by far the most important.
- As the practice of medicine gradually became more secular, however, this also involved the need to pay for medical treatment. Some monks even began to use their medical skills and knowledge

of medicine more on a for-profit basis rather than a purely religious basis.

- Although this trend is not known to have enriched any them personally, it did run directly counter to the monks' own vows of poverty and obedience, and to the Church's core belief in the greater importance of purely spiritual healing. As a result, the Church took steps to discourage any for-profit medical practice by the monks.

14

Alchemy and the Mendicant Orders

The never-achieved goal of alchemy was to be able to transmute "base" metals of little or no value, such as lead, into very valuable "noble" metals, such as silver or gold. This effort was based on the idea that metals were compounds, e.g., of sulfur and mercury. It was believed that, through some as-yet-undiscovered secrets of alchemy, they could yield a "universal medicine" (a panacea) or perhaps an elixir to promote long life. Not surprisingly, the study and practice of alchemy in the Middle Ages and in the Renaissance was often accompanied by philosophical, mystical, or religious speculation.

The rise of alchemy in Western Europe itself dates from 1144, when Robert of Chester translated the Arabic *Book of the Composition of Alchemy*. During most of the 12th and 13th centuries, alchemical thought there was centered on old translations, and new translations of Arabic texts were not made. Later, however, some monks of the mendicant orders (and other thinkers as well) did play important roles in the development of alchemy as a more respectable undertaking.[1]

Many English alchemists were monks and friars who traveled abroad to track down parchments relating to geometry, magic, theology, medicine, and alchemy. In the 13th century, for example, Albertus Magnus, a Dominican friar, wrote *The Book of Minerals*, in which he presented and commented on the theories of Greek and more recent alchemical authorities. From the time shortly after his death through to the 15th century, more than 28 alchemical texts were incorrectly attributed to him. This kind of misattribution was a common practice of the time and it burnished his reputation as a skillful alchemist. By the same token, alchemical texts were also mistakenly attributed to the great philosopher Thomas Aquinas, a student of Albertus Magnus.

In the 13th century, Roger Bacon, a Franciscan friar, composed his *Opus Majus* ("Great Work") for Pope Clement IV as part of a project to restructure university education in order to include the new Arabic-based learning of his time. Bacon thought that alchemy would help human beings to prolong their lives and to get ready for the expected, soon-to-arrive, Apocalypse marking the end of time.

While Bacon did not single out alchemy for any special treatment, he did consider both this and astrology to be significant parts of natural philosophy (the philosophical study of nature that was a precursor of modern science) and of medieval theology. In later European folk-belief, Bacon himself even became an archmage (a man believed to have magical powers) and was credited with forging, along with Albertus Magnus, the brazen head of a magical mythical creature that was able to answer all of its owner's questions.

15

Nuns

Earlier pages of this book have discussed nuns, who were sometimes known as "religious sisters," in general terms. This chapter looks at some of them in much greater detail. The next chapter focuses on the Beguines, who were religious women similar to but not identical with nuns.

During the Middle Ages very few women wrote anything about their own religious experiences. This makes the hidden "mental world" of the convent very hard for outsiders, male or female, to penetrate. This is especially true today since we are all now so far removed from the realities of daily life in the Middle Ages, both in terms of time and our far more secular lives. For the most part, the feelings of these medieval religious women are usually presented to us only through the writings of monks, who were perhaps not the ideal ambassadors for such a task, since as the Austrian historian Friedrich Heer notes in *The Medieval World*, religious communities continued to be ordered along the lines laid down for men.[1]

Women were therefore confronted with the closed ranks of a masculine society, governed by a thoroughly masculine theology and by a morality made by men for men. A handbook for nuns—the *Speculum Virginum*, composed about the year 1100 and still extant in versions in Latin, Middle Low German, and Swedish—has no section devoted to love, nor to any private prayer or any hint of concern for the soul of the individual nun. In fact, the spiritual regime prescribed for the nuns is singularly harsh and unyielding. No penance could be accepted from a fallen nun, even though as Heer notes, "all the world knew how easy it was for young nuns to fall from grace—seduced as often as not—by clerks."

The 12th century, i.e., the 1100s, wrought a sea change. Characterized as the age of feminine spiritual energy, this was a time when women learned both to "sing and say," that is, to use their minds and their imaginations to conduct their religious lives on a highly civilized plane. The most formidable religious woman of that age was Hildegard von Bingen (1098–1179), whose fame in the 12th century extended beyond Germany and reached England and even Iceland.

Often referred to as the Sybil, or prophetess, of the Rhine because of her prophecies and visions, Hildegard has been lauded since her own day as a Benedictine abbess, the founder of two monasteries, and the composer of sacred monophony, i.e., the melody (or "tune") of a piece of music. Most notably, she also wrote the words as well as the melody, which was sung by a single singer or played by a single instrument player, e.g., a flute player, without any accompanying harmony or chords.

Skilled, too, in the traditional medieval rhetorical arts practiced primarily by men, she preached publicly in 1160 in Germany to both clergy and laity in chapter houses and in public. She contended that the decadence of Church, state, and society was chiefly caused by masculine weakness. Therefore, she asserted, women needed to act where men had failed take charge. Since the clergy would not do so, however, Hildegarde was convinced that it was therefore up to the women to go out to preach against heretics and to make missionary journeys up and down the Rhine and the Nahe. With considerable wit, this was her rejoinder to the biblical assertion that woman comes from a man's rib: "Women may be made from man, but no man can be made without a woman!"[2]

Multi-talented, Hildegard was a polymath. She had a thorough knowledge of many different and often-unrelated subjects. Well-versed in reading and writing Latin (the common language of educated people in the Middle Ages), she wrote a multi-volume work, entitled *Physica*, on the scientific and medicinal properties of plants, fish, reptiles, and animals.

In her two-volume *Causa et Curae* ("Causes and Cures"), she also explored the human body, its connections to the rest of the natural world, and—most importantly—included the causes and cures of various diseases. These two latter books are historically significant: they reveal areas of medieval medicine that were not well-documented in their day because their practitioners (generally women) were rarely able to write in Latin.

Hildegard was the tenth child of a minor-nobility family and, as was the custom at the time, her parents dedicated her to the church at birth because they could not afford the expense of bringing her up. At the age of three she began having visions of luminous objects, but soon realized that she was unique in this ability and so concealed it for many years. Her family eventually sent this strange child to an anchoress (a female hermit) named Jutta, who was to give her a religious education. With Jutta, Hildegard learned to read the Psalter in Latin. Because the anchorage was physically attached to the church of the Benedictine monastery at Disibodenberg in what is now Germany, she was probably also exposed there to the musical services which would become the basis of her own later musical compositions. Other devout women were attracted to the anchorage, and after Jutta's death when Hildegard was 38 years old, Hildegard was elected by her colleagues to be the abbess of this budding convent.

During all these years, Hildegard had confided her visions only to Jutta and to a monk named Volmar, who was to become her lifelong secretary. In 1141, however, Hildegard experienced a powerful new vision that radically changed the course of her life. It was an insight, she said later, that gave her an instant understanding of the meaning of all the religious texts she had read, and that commanded her to write down, in the future, everything she saw in her visions. She tells us:

> And it came to pass ... when I was 42 years and 7 months old, that the heavens were opened and a blinding light of exceptional brilliance flowed through my entire brain. And so it kindled my whole heart and breast like a flame, not burning but warming ... and suddenly I understood the meaning of expositions of the books....[3]

In 2012 Pope Benedict XVI named her a Doctor of the Church in recognition of "her holiness of life and the originality of her teaching." Modern medical knowledge suggests Hildegard suffered from migraine, and that the intensity of her visions was affected by this.

What set Hildegard and a small number of other nuns apart from the vast majority of nuns, who served in quiet good works and in total obscurity, was their level of education. As the medieval scholar Eileen Power tells us, "the whole trend of medieval thought was against learned women." This was the case even in the Benedictine nunneries, where the monastic rule they lived under clearly mandated only prayer, study, and labor. It was evidently considered to be too far outside the scope of appropriate womanly activities for nuns to be allowed to write anything of substance. Thus, as a result, while medieval monks composed chronicles, medieval nuns simply embroidered.[4]

If English nuns were not noted for their learning at the time of Hildegard, they certainly had been during the earlier Anglo-Saxon period. Perhaps the best known of these nuns was Lioba (710–782), who had been educated by the nuns of Wimborne. Her biographer describes her as having been "so bent on reading that she never laid aside her book except to pray or strengthen her slight frame with food and sleep." She had studied grammar and other liberal arts since childhood and was skilled at composing verses in Latin. Even after she became Abbess of Bischofshein in Germany, Lioba pursued learning. An avid reader of canonical decrees and the laws of the Church, she also corresponded in Latin with St. Boniface, begging him to "correct the rusticity of her [literary] style."[5]

Judging from the available documents, learning throughout the medieval period was also a consistent priority for nuns in Germany.

During the 10th century, for example, Roswitha, a nun at the Abbey of Gandersheim, was acclaimed for the religious legends she wrote in Latin verse; for the composition of seven dramas; for a poem on Emperor Otto the Great; and for a history of her own nunnery. An assessment of her work has led scholars to conclude that she was familiar with all the classic Latin writers: Virgil, Lucan, Horace, Ovid, Terence, and others. Although perhaps not as well known today as Hildegarde, Roswitha has nevertheless been judged a woman of originality and some genius.

Yet another notable nun in Germany was the 12th-century Abbess Herrad. Located at the Hohenburg Abbey, she compiled and decorated a massive 324-folio volume with more than 600 exquisite illuminations in the great encyclopedia *Hortus Deliciarum* ("Garden of Delights"). It contained invaluable information on the manners and appearance of the people of her day. Sadly, this historic, socially significant work was destroyed in 1870 by the bombing of Strasburg during the Franco-Prussian War. Yet another nun of the period—St. Elizabeth of Schonau in the Rhineland-Platinate section of Germany, was a Benedictine nun-mystic who saw visions and dreamed dreams, all of which she wrote down on wax tablets.

Subsequently, from the 13th to the early 16th century in Germany, in Saxony, and later in Nuremberg, nuns continued to make their mark, not only by collecting, copying, and illuminating books but also by learning and writing in Latin. All this was to change throughout Western Europe, however, as schools and universities gradually began to flourish and as the learning which had previously been a monopoly of the monasteries gradually became more widely available. This had a domino effect on the nunneries, where the final repercussions were suffered by the children the nuns were required to teach. Not surprisingly, most nunnery libraries fell into poverty, and it is probable that by the 14th, 15th, and 16th centuries the majority of nuns knew no Latin at all, and not much French, either.

Because Latin was the learned and ecclesiastical language, all communications from bishops to monasteries—that is, notices of visitations, mandates, and injunctions—were in Latin. Since nuns were no longer proficient in Latin, however, communication with them became much more difficult. Indeed, the contemporary Scottish poet Sir David Lyndsey lamented that, very often, the nuns did not understand any of the Latin words in the services that they sang, but simply repeated them "like parrots."

16

Beguines

Beguines were groups of deeply pious urban lay-women, usually unmarried, celibate, or widowed, who lived under a semi-monastic rule. However, they were not required to take perpetual vows; were allowed to manage their own finances; and were not part of any officially-sanctioned religious order. Living together, often in the Low Countries of Western Europe (in parts of present-day northern France, Belgium, and the Netherlands), they practiced an entirely new form of collective religious life.[1]

Their name is now thought to derive from the root *begg* ("to murmur"). It may have been sardonically to mock someone who was thought to be much too pious in public and who frequently murmured her prayers. Much like the Cistercian nuns, however, the Beguines were part of the tidal wave of religious fervor that swept through some Western European societies during the 12th and 13th centuries. Not members of any established religious order or followers of any given monastic rule, the Beguines voluntarily embraced poverty and followed what they considered to be a truly apostolic way of life.

According to the medieval cleric and historian Jacques de Vitry, a lady named Marie d'Oignies (1177–1213) was a mystic who became the head of the Flemish Beguines. She was "consumed with the desire to follow the Gospel and to make herself a beggar, 'so as [to be] naked to follow the naked Christ.'"[2] Marie is now considered to be the prototype and the very model of Beguine status. Marie became so famous entirely thanks to the efforts of Jacques, who upon hearing of Marie's saintly reputation, had left his own studies in Paris and had settled in the town of Oignies to be near her. He petitioned the papacy to support the Beguines of the region and he appreciated the religious inspiration that Marie gave him in return. He said that she also helped him to become a more effective preacher.

The Beguines took no irrevocable vows of any kind but simply promised to remain celibate while they lived together. To become a member of their community, an applicant did not have to surrender her personal wealth but did have to agree to help the poor and the ill. Some Beguines were wealthy and therefore did not have to work. Others, however, had to support themselves by weaving, sewing, and embroidery so that they would not be a burden on the community.

As the Beguines gradually won wide recognition from the Church and the state alike, Beguinages (the buildings in which they lived) sprang up rapidly in northern European towns. By the end of the 13th century, for example, Namur, in what is now Belgium, had five of them; Cologne, the largest and most populous of the north German cities, had no fewer than 54. In Brussels, the Beguines were supported by the dukes of Brabant, and had their own enclaves in the towns of the Low Countries.

There are a number of interrelated reasons why medieval women were so strongly attracted to this self-directed and relatively independent religious life-style. Listed in random order, they probably included the following:

- A lack of space in the conventional convents.
- An acute shortage of acceptable marriage options for relatively prosperous women—to the extent that "taking the veil," becoming a nun, was one the very few respectable options open to them once they had become adults.
- The number of marriageable-age women is thought to have significantly exceeded the number of available men due to normal female longevity; to the frequent warfare between men that was endemic to medieval life; to the physical and health dangers of medieval travel (most travelers were men); and, last but by no means least, to widespread clerical celibacy.[3]
- A strong emotional desire to emulate Jesus and his apostles.
- An increasingly evident gap between the haves and the have-nots in European cities. This inspired charismatic priests and preacher-monks to call for reforms within the Church itself, on the one hand, and to stress the importance of more charity and public service by the laity, on the other.

In terms of the social status of their members, Beguine communities ranged from aristocratic ladies to poor women, but they generally welcomed applicants from many walks of life and tried to treat all of them equally.

The very favorable publicity that Jacques de Vitry gave to the life of Marie d'Oignies probably inspired other pious women who were also living in the diocese of Liège to congregate in communities in order to work and to pray together. The facts that at first these women had no official religious standing whatsoever and had no papally-approved privileges, special protections, or physical enclosures such as convents, did generate some initial concerns about their reputations and their personal safety while "out in the world."

Supporters of the Beguines, however, then agreed to work to obtain special papal privileges so that these women could meet together in their own communities and could continue to devote themselves to good works and to prayers. In 1216, Jacques de Vitry therefore wrote to his friends with the welcome news that he had been able to get approval from Pope Honorius III for the Beguines of Liège, as well as those in France and in the Holy Roman Empire, to live in common and to support one another in their spiritual quests.

Official papal approval arrived in 1233, when Pope Gregory IX issued the bull *Gloriam virginalem* that offered religious protection to virgins in Germany. This was followed five days later by the pope extending the same protection to the virgins of the French diocese of Cambrai. This bull failed to use the term "beguine" but it did emphasize the women's promise to practice chastity. However, it also failed to define the complexities of what would later become known as "the beguine status," which would attract widows and never-married women alike. Most critically, it did not define the women's canonical status, i.e., whether they were lay or religious, which was a key legal distinction.

The good news was that *Gloriam virginalem* did give religious and secular authorities in cities throughout northern France, Belgium, and the Netherlands the green light they needed to issue formal approvals for local communities of devout laywomen. Many such communities already existed, and it was around this time that the term "beguines" begins to appear in charters and other legal documents.

The downside, however, was while the supporters of the Beguines continued to praise their reputations for prayer and mutual support, some medieval critics feared that their activities, which were being undertaken without any daily hands-on supervision of the church, would inevitably lead to heresy and to doctrinal errors.

Indeed, in 1317 the Council of Vienne, where church officials condemned the Beguine status, issued two anti–Beguine decrees, and many similar decrees would follow in the years come. In the end, however, the ups-and-downs of the Beguines would quietly continue in one form or another for many, many years—until Marcella Pattyn, the last Beguine still living in one of the 13 beguinages on UNESCO's World Heritage List, died in 2013 at the age of 92.[4]

The modern scholar Tanya Stabler Miller offers us this balanced summary of Beguines' experiences, writing as follows:

... on the local level, beguines found a great deal of support from clerics, urban authorities, and the broader public. Beguines were significant, valued members of their communities. Even as they were frequently swept into debates about religious poverty, enclosure, and clerical authority, beguine communities adjusted and adopted to shifting expectations about female spirituality, often changing their names, modifying house rules, or seeking politically powerful affiliations or patrons in order to continue to live lives of prayer and service.[5]

17

Early Irish Beliefs and Irish Monasticism

Christianity was probably introduced into Ireland from Roman Britain or from Gaul in the 4th century. As it spread into Ireland and nearby parts of England, small monastic communities emerged in such far-flung locations as Iona, Lindisfarne, and Kildare. Several early Irish monks also became famous missionaries, traveling extensively into England and continental Europe in order to convert the pagan locals to Christianity.

The semi-legendary Patrick of Ireland, who was born between 373 and 390 and who died at some point between 460 and 496, is traditionally considered to have been the man who brought Christianity to Ireland, although in fact some Christians were already living there.[1]

The first firm date in Irish history is actually 431, when, we learn, "To the Irish believing in Christ: Palladus, having been ordained by Pope Celestine, is sent as first bishop." Irish folk tradition, on the other hand, strongly asserts that the man responsible for founding the Irish church was actually a Briton named Patrick. This profound disagreement, traditionally known to historians as "The Problem of Saint Patrick," has lain unresolved for some seventeen hundred years, and we will not try to resolve it here.[2]

The total number of early monastic sites in Ireland is difficult to establish accurately. Estimates have ranged from a low of about 145 in a 1931 study; to over 800 in a 1970 paper; and to over 2000 in an estimate done in the late 1980s.

Leo Swan, a modern Irish scholar, has summarized the situation in the following terms. At the end of the 8th century the great Irish monastic houses had achieved almost complete spiritual dominance, had acquired a great measure of political influence, and had established themselves as a major factor in the economic life of the country as a whole. Swan tells us that

The [impression] that emerges is one of a populous community of religious
foundations showing considerable diversity in origin and form, but with a
striking unity in function, organization, and plan, which evolved in a manner unique in Christendom, and which survived many vicissitudes until by the
changing circumstances of the 11th and 12th centuries in Ireland.[3]

Long before either Palladus or Patrick arrived in Ireland, however,
and certainly for a long period of time after their deaths, it was a vibrant
pre–Christian mythology that flourished in Ireland and attracted many
believers. Interestingly there is a unique historical counterpoint to conventional Irish Christian thought. From pre–Christian times in Ireland
down to about the early 19th century, it was believed by many rural folk
that a supernatural race of beings lived—always unseen by humans—in
the hills, tombs, beneath the sea, in the lakes, or on the far-away islands
of Ireland. Today, "*aos sí*" is the term in Irish for this supernatural race,
which is comparable to the fairies or the elves of other cultures. In his
book *The Mysterious Republic: Elves, fauns, fairies and similar,* published around 1692, the Scottish pastor and scholar had this to say about
them:

> These *Siths* or *Faeries*, which they call *Sleagh Maith* or the Good People, pre-
> sumably to avoid attracting their nefarious attentions (according to the
> Irish custom of blessing whatever they fear) are said to be of an indetermi-
> nate nature between man and angels, identical to the old considerations on
> demons. They are intelligent minds with changing light body, sort of a nature
> of a cloud, rather visible at dusk.[4]

It is notable that a unique form of monasticism flourished in Ireland in the 5th through the 7th centuries. It is now often known as Celtic
Monasticism. In it, and over time, some Irish monasteries grew into
local centers of a unique highly literate, self-confident, and expansionist
missionary-oriented monastic way of life.[5] Its differences from the standard continental Benedictine monastic practice were notable.

It is not certain now how or when monasticism itself first reached Ireland: it may have come from Britain, France, or possibly even from the
Mediterranean. All that is evident is that the early monks in Ireland lived
either alone as hermits or in little monastic communities dotted with
stone-piled-upon-stone "beehive cells." These cells, erected on uninhab-
ited, cold, windswept rocky islands off the Irish coasts, permitted a few
hardy monks to pursue their ascetic lifestyles and to isolate themselves,
to the maximum extent possible, from any wider and corrupting contacts
with other human beings outside their closed monastic world.

The practice of "monastic peregrination," i.e., the wanderings of
Irish monks over waters and lands without much advance planning and

without any clear sense of the best direction to take, was also distinctly Irish. These monks relied blindly on God's will to reach whatever new destinations and to begin any new assignments there that God might have in mind for them. In practice, however, their new assignments would often involve teaching Christianity to the locals.

One of the most charming legends about Irish missionary monks during Ireland's "Golden Age" (c. 660–c. 800) is one that—to quote from the Venerable Bede's *Ecclesiastical History of the English People*, which he wrote in the 730s and which required, in its hand-lettered form, sheets of fine parchment made from the skins of about 30 calves—"The Irish welcomed [all religious students from abroad] gladly, gave them their daily food, and also provided them with books to read and with instruction, without asking for any payment."[6]

Although Bede almost certainly overstates, for public relations purposes, both the academic quality of Irish learning and the generosity of the Irish scholars, what is clear is that the Irish monastery itself was the political and emotional focal-point of the island's most important early dynasty. Ireland then was a very rural society, with a countryside ruled and dominated only by local hereditary chieftains. When a clan chieftain accepted Christianity, his followers were therefore, as a practical matter, obliged to do so as well. Irish monasteries were usually initiated by a grant of land to an abbot or an abbess who was a member of a local noble family.

A monastery became the spiritual focus of the tribe or the kinship group. Successive abbots and abbesses, who had great prestige but only a limited amount of real power on their own, were all members of the founder's extended family—a policy which kept monastic lands firmly under the control of the family group. The abbot was one of the dynasty's most senior members: indeed, he was known by an Irish term (*coarb*) that indicated he was the heir or successor of the founder himself.

The Irish founder of the famous monastery of Iona, located on a Scottish island, was St. Columba (also known as Colm Cille), a prince of Ireland's ruling Uí Néill dynasty, the most powerful group in the northern half of Ireland. Such a monastery, always the most important possession of the tribe or the kindred group, was given enough land to keep it in operation and to retain *de facto* control of it over many years. Irish monasticism was so successful that it would eventually spread rather widely, into Scotland, Northern England, France, and Italy.

Irish monastic leaders periodically liked to spend some time alone, as hermits, in order to re-center themselves on holy matters without the endless distractions of communal life. An unknown Irish author, writing in the 12th century, has this to tell us about "St. Columba's Island Heritage." His piece has been shortened and lightly edited here:

Delighted I think it to be in the bosom of an isle, on the peak of a rock, that I might often see there the calm of the sea.

That I might see its heavy waves over the glittering ocean, as they chant a melody to their Father on their eternal course.

That I might see its smooth strand of clear headlands, no gloomy thing; that I might hear the voice of the wondrous birds, a joyful thing....

That I might bless the Lord who has power over all, Heaven with its pure host of angels, earth, ebb, flood-tide.

That I might pore over one of my books, good for my soul; a while at psalms.

A while gathering dulse [edible seaweed] from the rock, a while fishing, a while giving food to the poor, a while in my cell....[7]

Irish monks used a different calendar date for Easter (the most important event in the Christian year) rather than the official date set by Rome.[8] They also practiced an ascetic exercise known as "crossfigill." This involved standing upright in prayer, with arms outstretched in the form of a cross, for very long periods of time. In some folk-legends, a monk might stand, motionless, in this position for so long that that seabirds would even perch on his arms!

On the more productive side of their lives, Irish monasteries also produced lovely hand-crafted and hand-illustrated books that are still treasured today. The most famous of these is the Book of Kells, which was a unique copy of the New Testament of the Bible and which used artistic knotwork patterns and designs in a dramatic range of colors: violet, brown, yellow, and green. This stunning book was created by Columban monks, who originally lived on the Scottish island of Iona but later moved to the nearby island of Kells in the early 9th century. This is when the Book of Kells was known to have first appeared. It is now on permanent display at Trinity College Library in Dublin.[9]

Irish missionaries were exceptionally energetic travelers as well. Most famously, they included both Patrick (c. 390–461) who is the patron saint of Ireland, and the Irish monk Columbanus, who founded monasteries at Annegray, Luxeuil, St. Gall, Bregenz, and Bobbio. In about 591, for example, Columbanus and a handful of his followers landed in King Childebert's kingdom in Burgundy, France. Remarkably, he quickly won this ruler's permission to set up monasteries in his kingdom. He then wrote two sets of monastic rules for use in the three monasteries he himself had just founded in Burgundy.

Today, much of Patrick's own story appears to be pious legend. Columbanus, however, has left us some real-life and very chilling advice on the workings of the ideal monastery. He tells the reader:

The chief part of the monk's rule is mortification.... Let the monk live in a community under the discipline of one father [the abbot] and in the company of many ... let him not do as he wishes, let him eat what he is bidden, keep as much as he has received, complete the [work he has been assigned], be subject to him whom he does not like.

Let him come weary and as if sleep-walking to his bed, and let him be forced to rise while his sleep is not yet finished. Let him keep silence when he has suffered wrong. Let him fear the superior of his community as a lord, love him as a father, believe whatever he commands is salutary for himself.[10]

Columbanus lists these features of Irish monasticism, but there is even more to be said.[11] From about 600 onward, for example, the Irish churches were organized along lines that were then quite new and unique when compared with the familiar and classic structure of the churches in Gaul and elsewhere in Western Europe. This new approach, however, was apparently a much better match for the tribal conditions of early Irish society.

In the classic Church structure, bishops ruled over dioceses that had very clearly-defined boundaries. The Irish approach to this issue, on the other hand, was simply to treat the many scattered small churches of the Irish countryside as "daughter houses" of the larger monastic houses. This procedure united these smaller houses into one large confederation which was known as the *paruchia*. Under this unique system, all of the administrative power now lay in the hands of the abbots of the monasteries, not in the hands of the bishops, as was invariably the case in Gaul and in other parts of Western Europe. Perhaps the best account of this radical change was given by the great Anglo-Saxon historian and monk Bede in his famous *Ecclesiastical History of the English People*. He wrote:

This island [Ireland] always had an abbot for its ruler, who is a priest to whose authority the whole province, including its bishops, are subject—an unusual order of things in which they follow the example of their first teacher [Columba], who was not a bishop, but a priest and a monk.[12]

The monk Columbanus, for his part, was the first great "man of letters" of Ireland. His fame rests chiefly on the letters and poems attributed to him. Perhaps the best of these is the *Carmen naule, or* "Boating Song," which he composed to encourage his crew of monks as they rowed up the River Rhine towards Switzerland in 611.

The sweeping rhythms of this poem in the original Irish are said to give the reader such a good feel for the traditional Irish wood-and-canvas rowboat, known as a currach, when it is underway in a choppy sea, that they are worth quoting here in full in English:

See, cut in woods, through flood of twin-horned Rhine
passes the keel, and greased slips over sea—
Heave, men! And let resounding eco sound our "heave."

The winds raise blasts, wild rainstorms wreak their spite
but ready strength of men subdues it all—
Heave, men! And let resounding echo sound our "heave."

Clouds melt away and the harsh tempest stills,
effort tames all, great toil is conqueror—
Heave, men! And let resounding echo sound our "heave."

Endure and keep yourselves for happy things;
you suffered worse, and these too God shall end—
Heave, men! And let resounding echo sound our "heave."

Thus acts the foul fiend: wearing out the heart
and with temptation shaking inmost parts—
You men, remember Christ with mind still sounding "heave."

Stand firm in soul and spurn the foul fiend's tricks
and seek defense in virtue's armory—
You men, remember Christ with mind still sounding "heave."

Firm faith will conquer all and blessed zeal
and the old fiend yielding breaks at last his darts—
You men, remember Christ with mind still sounding "heave."

Supreme of virtues, King, and fount of things,
He promises in strife, gives prize in victory—
You men, remember Christ with mind still sounding "heave."[13]

Teamwork and close cooperation were always essential, not only on the rivers but also on the land. In early Ireland, high offices in the Church were usually inherited, and many clerical lineages were in fact only the branches of royal dynasties. Such close kinship ties were widely accepted and, indeed, were *expected* as a matter of course.

The heads of the great monasteries such as Cork and Emly rivaled the king of Munster in terms of high social status, while the leaders of other major Irish monasteries were all well-born and politically well-connected. Indeed, by the late 7th and 8th centuries, the monasteries had even formed federations of their own because of the unsettled security conditions they faced. Defensive preparations were necessary because no attacker could afford to ignore the monasteries, which, if undefended, were very easy-to-plunder lucrative targets indeed. Peace-oriented Irish congregations, however, could thus find themselves pulled into preparing for civil strife, very much against their own will.[14]

As noted earlier, in an unusual evolution, the tribally-based Irish Church gradually changed into a monastic structure that was ruled not by bishops appointed by the church but instead by the members of a given clan, i.e., by a hereditary series of abbots from that particular clan. This unique development has been called "an Irish solution to an Irish problem." Bishops were of course still necessary for religious reasons, but the real ruler of the Irish Church always was a tribal abbot.[15]

Finally, it is noteworthy that the arrival in Ireland of the mendicant Franciscans and Dominicans brought with them both a refocus on material poverty for the monks and a new emphasis on spiritual growth for the faithful that won the mendicants many new supporters. Because they were not tethered to any mother house, these mendicants were very mobile and were keen to spread their missionary message to even the most remote parts of Ireland. Their extensive travels gave them an excellent firsthand knowledge of the many hardships and great poverty of rural Irish life. It is even said that the unofficial motto of the Irish mendicants, derived from the teachings of St. Francis, was that "the world was their cloister."[16]

One of the unique historical artifacts from this era is that of a "moralized hand," a life-sized line drawing, on paper, of the outstretched palm of a man's hand. One of these drawings is now in the collection of Trinity College Dublin. A Franciscan preacher could readily use it as a template or aide-memoire when delivering his sermon to a local congregation. For example:

- The depiction of the thumb also contains written words which, run together, read: "You don't know how greatly, nor how often, you have offended God."
- The message of the words on the index finger is: "Your ending is bitter, your life brief, and you have entered the world in sin."
- The middle finger says: "You will take nothing hence other than your deeds, nor can you prolong your life nor evade death."
- The fourth finger conveys this message: "You don't know whence you came, nor how nor when you will die."
- The little finger warns that "You will soon be forgotten by those dear to you, your heir will seldom make provision for you, nor [will] those do any differently to whom you leave your wealth."[17]

18

The Monk Raoul Glaber
Meets the Devil

Raoul Glaber (c. 985–c. 1047) was a Benedictine monk who in about the year 1000 chronicled the events of his era. His accounts constitute some of the most important sources on France during this period. Moreover, his story is intrinsically interesting.

Probably the illegitimate child of a cleric or a monk, Glaber was put into a monastery as an oblate (a young person given to a monastic community by his parents or guardian) at the age of 12 by his uncle, who was a monk. He was later expelled from it, however, because he was so independent-minded that he resisted monastic discipline, disobeyed his superiors, and argued with the other monks. He then spent time in four other monasteries, where, on a more positive note, he developed his skills as a writer and a historian.

His justly-famous phrase about the "white mantle of churches" covering the medieval countryside has been used as the opening quote in the present book. His chief work was the *Historiarum libri quinque ab anno incarnationis DCCCC usque ad annum MXLIV* ("*Five books of stories from the year 900 after the Incarnation until the year 1044*"), part of which he wrote at the abbey of Cluny.

Glaber thought of this book as a "universal ecclesiastical history" of events in central France, and it does give the reader some historically-valuable insights into contemporary life then. For example, he sees the year 1033 as an occasion to celebrate the thousandth anniversary of the death and resurrection of Christ, treating it symbolically as marking the end of time. In so doing, he was echoing other medieval chroniclers, who also liked to use the year 1000 to herald a symbolic but major turning point in human affairs. As Glaber put it in his book, "It was believed that the order of the seasons and the elements' laws which had hitherto ruled the world had [now] fallen into chaos eternal, and the end of mankind [was therefore] feared." Indeed, some local conditions were so bad then

113

that even cannibalism was reported. To quote Glaber again, "Alas! O pain! Something seldom heard of over the ages: a raging hunger caused men to devour human flesh. Travelers were kidnapped by [those] more robust than them, their limbs cut off, cooked in the fire and devoured...."[1]

It is rather amazing that, despite his many failings as a monk, Glaber managed to win the support and protection of the monk-reformer Guillaume de Volpano, who was the abbot of a monastery in Dijon, France. This very pious and austere abbot overlooked all of Glaber's shortcomings as a monk because the abbot valued men who could write well and who shared his strong commitment to monastic reform. Glaber was also gifted with a very lively imagination on religious matters. Here, for example, is his account of his meeting with the Devil:

> One night stands before me a sort of terrible monster to see. Small in stature, he had a slender neck, thin face, very dark eyes, a rough wrinkled forehead, pinched nostrils, a huge mouth, swollen lips, a receding chin, a goatee beard, hairy ears, and pointed, spiky hair and doggy teeth, flattened skull, swollen chest, hunchbacked back.[2]

Inspired by Glaber's "white mantle of churches" and using a lovely photo of the nave of the Gothic cathedral of Notre Dame de Laon in Aisne, France, to illustrate Glaber's dramatic metaphor, the late photographer Dennis Aubrey offered this personal opinion on the "white mantle":

> The Christian monastic orders were the mortar of society, the bond that kept it together. Through these orders, Christian Europe began to defend itself, not just in arms but also in terms of philosophy. The Church needed to restate its very identity. That restatement was powerful and profound.
>
> The Christian identity was *re-imagined completely*, not merely rediscovered. The Church incorporated the new learning of the day—the sciences of logic and philosophy. In doing so, Christian Europe managed to achieve two monumental feats: it united faith and intellect, and [by building all the medieval cathedrals] it transmuted stone into an expression of faith.[3]

19

Robert d'Arbrissel

Controversial Breton Hermit and Monk

Born in about 1047 in Brittany, Robert is remembered today both because he founded the abbey of Fontevraud in what is now Maine-et-Loire, France, and—much more interestingly—because he was also a practitioner of "syneisaktism."

This unfamiliar "ism" can best be defined as *a chaste cohabitation with a member of the opposite sex*. Syneisaktism was also known as the practice of "spiritual marriage," in which a man and a women, both of whom have taken vows of chastity, live together in the same dwelling in a friendly, chaste, but unofficial relationship. The term itself comes from a Greek word that refers to "those brought into the house together."

This practice, designed for companionship and to help both men and women overcome their carnal temptations (presumably by seeing each other very frequently but never by making love together), began in about the 2nd century. Although it was roundly and repeatedly denounced by numerous Church leaders, writers, and religious councils, it nevertheless continued to be practiced well into the Middle Ages.

A New Testament verse often advanced by many as proof that spiritual marriage was never endorsed by Christ himself is the Biblical passage of John 20:17. There are many slightly different Biblical translations of this text from the original Greek, but perhaps the best for present purposes is the Literal Standard Version. This translation, with some nearly-Irish lilting overtones in its cadences, reads as follows:

> Jesus says to Mary Magdalen, "Do not be touching Me, for I have not yet ascended to My Father; and [you] be going on to My brothers and say to them, I ascend to My Father and your Father, and [to] My God and your God."

Robert d'Arbrissel's own practice of spiritual marriage created very severe problems for him throughout his life up to his death in about 1117, and eventually prevented his canonization.[1] Historians have long argued over whether he was in fact a precursor of feminism, or whether he simply used his sex appeal as a holy hermit and his skill as a charismatic speaker in order to spend a great deal time, as a single man, with a variety of willing women.

He certainly was an arresting figure. A contemporary account tells us that in his hut in the forest of Craon in Brittany, he wore only a very rough hair shirt; slept on the bare earth; renounced "wine, delicate meats, and almost sleep"; and so persuasively addressed the crowds that flocked around him in large numbers that "most of them stayed with him and tried to imitate the austerities of which he gave the example."

Pope Urban II even appointed him to be a preacher, and in that official capacity he was followed by large crowds of men and women from very different social classes. It was said of Robert that "His words had the sweetness of honey, a divine charm issued from his lips and captivated souls." Listeners therefore began to follow him in large numbers in his wanderings as an itinerant preacher. He settled between 1099 and 1101 in a local valley and set up a monastic community, founding a "mixed house" of both men and women, thereby totally breaking the normal and long-established rules of monasticism. Robert scandalized the religious hierarchy by sleeping as the only man in the midst of a group of women, who ranged in social status from prostitutes to noble ladies. His monastery, known as Fontevraud and located in the woods near Saumur in the Maine-et-Loire region of France, was very successful, and would grow to have as many as 300 "choir nuns."

As monastics, the nuns living within an enclosure were committed to reciting the full Liturgy of the Divine Hours throughout the day in church, usually in a very solemn manner. They were known as choir nuns, to distinguish them from the lower-ranking lay sisters who performed housekeeping tasks for the monastery or who ran errands outside the cloister itself.

Robert refused to use the official too-limiting title of abbot, preferring instead to visit different parts of the monastery on his own and to meet privately with the women there. He was always a very controversial figure. The bishop of Rennes, for example, reproached him wandering around "hair to the winds, shaggy beard, in rags, knees in the air [i.e., his tunic was so short that it did not cover his knees], and bare feet." He was also criticized for preaching ideas contrary to the teachings of the Church and for doing so "in front of a vulgar crowd and ignorant men."

Suspecting in 1115 that he would die soon, Robert appointed a woman—Pétronille de Chemillé—to be the abbess of his monastery. He died there in about 1117. When trying to evaluate his life today, scholars are left with more questions than answers. For some modern French commentators, Robert was the champion of the poor against their exploitation by the rich; his life was, they claimed, a clear challenge to the established social order.

For other modern French observers, however, he was instead a "rising wind" (i.e., a precursor) who defended women and the practices of his own monastery at Fontevraud, where, very notably, the men were placed under the supervision of a woman (the abbess). These latter writers believed that Robert demonstrated "the restoration of feminine dignity in the 12th century" and that his work testified to the greater social equality which the medieval era, formerly known pejoratively as the Dark Ages, had in fact accorded to the "weaker sex," namely, to women. A modern French medievalist, the late Régine Pernoud, wrote that Robert's abbey was "the most perfect and most convincing illustration of the new power of women that flourished between the 11th and 12th centuries."[2]

It is important, however, to focus on a long letter that Bishop Marbode of Rennes sent to Robert at some point after 1098. In it, the Bishop vehemently reproached Robert for his lack of prudence and for his *de facto* attacks on the current social and moral order, i.e., by allowing men and women to travel together and live and probably sleep together as a troop of itinerant and undisciplined disciples.

Later, in around 1106–1107, Geoffrey, abbot of the Trinity of Vendôme, also tried to bring Robert back into line by pointing out two of his most significant failures in his relations with the women he had undertaken to lead. First, Geoffrey said, Robert was much too gentle with some of them and, indeed, even shared their beds. Second, he was much too hard on others, punishing them by keeping them hungry, thirsty, or nude. Geoffrey therefore urged Robert to find a middle way between these two excesses.

20

Chaucer's Literary Sketches

The Canterbury Tales is a remarkable collection of 24 stories written in Middle English, and mostly in verse, by Geoffrey Chaucer between 1387 and 1400. He was variously a poet, translator, courtier, diplomat, and civil servant. This book, the best-surviving and most illustrated manuscript of which is now housed at the Huntington Library in San Marino, California, is one of the first great works of English literature. Its cast of characters (about 30 pilgrims) offers a very good snapshot of medieval English society in the 14th century.

Chaucer introduces us to some very memorable figures—for example, the bawdy Wife of Bath, the gallant Knight, the fastidious Prioress, and the burly drunken Miller. The many tales in the book are told by these and by other pilgrims, who are all en route from the Tabard Inn in Southwark in south London to Canterbury in order to visit the shrine of Thomas Becket in the cathedral there.

To make their travels more enjoyable, one of these characters—the jolly innkeeper of the Tabard Inn, which was also a hostel where travelers could spend the night—arranges a friendly competition. Each pilgrim must tell four stories to the others (two stories on the way out, and two on the way back); the best story will earn its narrator a free meal at the Tabard.

These stories are too many, too long, and too complicated to recount. Suffice it to say that they cover a very extensive range of genres, including romances of chivalry; fairy tales; Breton lais (stories with Celtic motifs); fabliau (simple, funny stories); animal fables; mythology; short stories; life of a saint; and allegories.

The present work looks at the stories that focus, one at a time, on five characters, a prioress, a monk, a friar, a rooster, and a pardoner (i.e., a man licensed to sell papal pardons or indulgences). The accounts used here have all been chosen for their medieval color and have been edited, shortened, and translated from Middle English into modern English.[1] A later chapter will discuss other medieval pilgrims in more detail. The following descriptions all have been adapted, nearly verbatim, from contemporary sources.

Our first notable character in Chaucer's book is the prioress, who is a nun named Madame Eglentine (her name means "sweetbriar" in English), and who is one of Chaucer's most memorable and most enduring creations. (The best modern account of her fictional but historically accurate life and times can be found in Eileen Power's splendid book on *Medieval People*, see the Bibliography, and will repay careful reading.) In *The Canterbury Tales*, Chaucer says of Madame Eglentine:

> She certainly was an affable lady, very pleasant in her conduct, and took great pains to emulate the refined manners of the court. Her behavior was dignified and worthy of high praise....
>
> She wears a rosary made of small bits of coral, the larger beads of which are green, and she also wears a shiny gold brooch [a piece of jewelry] on which is written, in Latin, the motto "Amor vincit omnia" ["Love conquers all"].[2]

Being a prioress in medieval times, however, was not always a bed of roses, and she had to be ready to face a good deal of in-house criticism. For example, there was usually an annual "visitation" (inspection tour) by the local bishop, who was required to find out, by meeting privately with the nuns one-by-one and one-on-one, whether they believed that their prioress was in fact doing a good job.

Eileen Power tells us that at one such convent the nuns strongly complained to the bishop that their house was already £20 pounds in debt, a very large sum at the time. They claimed that

> this was principally due to the costly expenses of the prioress, because she frequently rides abroad [travels far outside the convent] and pretends that she does so only on the [official] business of the house, although it is not so, with a train of attendants much too large and tarries too long abroad and she feasts sumptuously, both when abroad and at home and she is very choice in dress, so that the fur trimmings of her mantle are worth 100 shillings [a hefty sum].[3]

On a more humorous note, Eileen Power also strings together some of the many other things the nuns must have so breathlessly told the bishop about their prioress:

> "She-is-a-very-bad-business-woman-and-she-has-let-the-house-get-into-debt-and-the-church-is-falling-about-our-ears-and-we-don't-get-enough-food-and-she-hasn't-given-us-any-clothes-for-two-years-and-she-has-sold-woods-and-farms-without-your-license-and-she-has-pawned-our-best-set-of-spoons...."[4]

The next character is the monk. Chaucer has a good deal to say about him. For example:

- This monk was really a "manly man," excellent in his calling. His job as a Benedictine monk was to ride all over the extensive monastic property on horseback to make sure that everything was always in tip-top condition. He especially enjoyed hunting for game and, probably, also liked hunting for ladies as well.

- He was the prior of a smaller monastery that was subordinate to a great abbey. He preferred to ignore all the old and annoying customs, however, such as obeying the strict Benedictine rule that governed his order, and preferred to focus instead only on the most interesting daily events. For example, he paid no attention whatsoever to the admonitions that "hunters are not holy men," and that a monk who is careless in discharging his duties in the cloister is like "a fish out of water."

- He was skilled at "hare pricking"—tracking a rabbit by his "pricks" (paw-prints)—another sexual pun is certainly intended here. He was handsome and was dressed expensively in the very best of taste. Chaucer also tells us that he was "a lord full fat" (quite prosperous in appearance) and was in very good physical condition. His favorite roast was a fat swan, and his well-trained "brown as a berry" saddle horse was also in tip-top condition.

The third character is the friar. He is a most engaging personality and is named Huberd. Chaucer says of him:

- He was a wanton and a merry "limitour" (that is, a friar with the right to beg within a given district). Of all the monks in the four orders of monks, Huberd was the man most full of flirtatious chitchat and pleasant language. He had arranged many marriages of young women at his own expense [Chaucer also implies that he had seduced all these girls first] and was an important figure in his own order.

- He was a friend of all the wealthy landowners of the region and of all the important ladies of the town. He was very popular with them because although he had the power to hear their confessions and to forgive all their sins, he never demanded any heavy penance from them. Instead, he believed that his parishioners should repay him not with "weeping and prayers" but rather with silver coins.

- His "tippet" (the monastic hood covering his head) was always full of trinkets, which he freely handed out to pretty wives, and he also had a fine voice for singing. His neck was as white as a white flower [this point traditionally suggests lechery]. He knew well the taverns of every town, and every innkeeper and barmaid who worked there.

- In addition to being able "to live it up just like a puppy," Chaucer tells us, Huberd was intelligent and was very good at serving as an arbiter in court; was always well-dressed; and carried himself like a highly-educated scholar, or even like a pope. He affected a charming lisp "to make his English sweet upon his tongue," both when he spoke and when he sang. His eyes twinkled in his head just like stars do on a frosty night.

We can note in passing that Chaucer's observations on many of the religious figures he discusses are mirrors of and commentaries on some of the negative consequences of pilgrimage. Medieval moralists, for example, often believed that such a heady "away-from-home" involvement with travelers of the secular world could only be a constant temptation to frivolity and sinful behavior.

Chaucer's fourth character, starring in the tale told by a priest in the cavalcade of pilgrims, is a rooster. To make his religious point, the priest uses a story about a very handsome rooster named Chauntecleer, who has an enormous ego but is also quite intelligent. The purpose of this tale is to warn the listener that excessive pride can only lead to failure.

When a clever fox meets Chanticleer, the fox capitalizes on the rooster's inflated ego and overcomes the rooster's instinct to run away by assuring him how much he (the fox) would love to hear him crow loudly and to watch him strut around proudly, just as his impressive father had done. As soon as Chauntecleer complies with this very flattering request, however, the fox seizes him in his jaws and dashes off with him into the forest in order to eat him. All the other animals in the barnyard immediately give chase to try to save the rooster.

Chauntecleer, however, now suggests to the fox what a wonderful idea it would be for the fox to stop unexpectedly, to turn around, and to boast to his pursuers that they should give up immediately because he can run so fast that they will never be able to catch him. The fox's excessive pride leads him to abject failure. As soon as the fox stops and opens his mouth to taunt his pursuers, Chauntecleer flaps away from his jaws and flies up into the safety of the nearest tree. Although the fox tries hard to persuade him to come down again and to brag some more, Chanticleer now prefers the safety of the tree and refuses to fall for the same trick a second time.

Chaucer's fifth character is a pardoner, who shamelessly uses no end of verbal tricks and outright lies in order to sell his worthless papal pardons and indulgences to the naïve, ignorant buyers he meets on the street. Pardoners may have been distrusted or even hated, but the common people accepted them, warts and all, as a possible and affordable pathway to spiritual salvation.

The best news is that, thanks to Richard Scott-Robinson's excellent translation (see the Bibliography) into modern English of what a pardoner says in Middle English, we can get a good understanding of this unique way of medieval life.

The pardoner begins by addressing his fellow-pilgrims in these words:

My most esteemed fellow travelers:

When I preach in churches I try my best to cry my words out with clarity and resonance, like a peel of bells, for I know them all by heart and it is good to sound authoritative. And it helps to speak on only one subject. Mine is *radix malorum est cupiditas*, which is to say, "money is the root of all evil"....

I tell everybody where I have come from, and set out all my papal indulgences and show off my seal of authority, so that nobody will have the courage to interfere with me. After this, I will deliver my address, drawing attention to all the papal bulls that I have, the signatures of cardinals, of bishops, and of the [long-dead] patriarchs of the Church in the east. I speak a few words of Latin, just to impress everybody and to encourage thoughts of devotion....

I address congregations far and wide—no manual labor for me! You will not find me trying to scratch a living by weaving baskets! I will emulate none of the apostles by embracing poverty.... I will drink wine and have a jolly wench in every town.... Now that I have finished this pint of good ale, I hope I may be able to deliver something for you that you will like, for though I may be a nasty piece of work [i.e., a disreputable person], I can tell a moral tale if I want to, and here is one that I often repeat for a fee. So be quiet and I will begin.[5]

21

Peter Abelard

Pre-Eminent Theologian
and Ill-Fated Lover

This chapter consists of three interrelated parts: a short general summary of the life of the high-achiever Peter Abelard (1079–1142); his torrid but disastrous love affair with a young woman named Heloise; and his philosophical and theological works.[1] There are no accurate portraits of either Abelard or Heloise, but a fanciful illustration by Jean de Meung (1250–1305), now in the Musée de Chantilly in France, depicts them as a very appealing young couple in, say, their mid–20s.

Abelard was born into a family of the lesser French nobility in about 1079. He was a brilliant student from an early age, to such an extent that he renounced his inheritance, including knighthood, simply in order to be free to study philosophy with famous experts. A polymath, he would also become a gifted poet, a musician, and a monk. In fact, his genius was visible in everything he did. Both his supporters and his opponents agreed that his quick wit, perfect memory, sharp tongue, and unbridled arrogance made him quite unbeatable in debate. Indeed, it was even said of him that he had never once lost an argument.

His many opponents, however, believed that he was simply too full of himself and too arrogant; what is certain, in any case, is that he was very quick to provoke arguments with them, which, of course, they invariably lost. Perhaps because of his unbroken string of intellectual successes, Abelard began to think of himself as the only undefeated philosopher in the world.

He was the greatest logician of the Middle Ages and was the founder of scholastic theology. Moreover, he was also the intellectual progenitor of the University of Paris and the first great Nominalist philosopher. (Nominalism is a philosophical doctrine holding that concepts are merely human constructions and that the names given to them are only language conventions.) Equally importantly, Abelard was also a gifted writer. Here, for example, is what is certainly the shortest but the most moving poem he wrote on a Biblical theme:

> Est in Rama
> Vox audita
> Rachel flentis,
> Super natos
> Interfectos
> Eiulantis.[2]
> [A cry was heard in Rama:
> it is Rachel weeping for her children,
> and she refuses to be comforted,
> because they are no more.]

Rachel's children, along with many other children, were murdered by King Herod in an effort to get rid of the newborn Jesus of Nazareth, whom he considered a rival.

Abelard was a very strong advocate of the use of reason, rather than thoughtless obedience, in matters of faith. He was such a splendid and inspiring teacher that crowds of students flocked to him from faraway parts of Europe. Twenty of his students became cardinals and more than 50 of them became bishops. Distilled to its essence, the best single evaluation of Abelard's work can arguably be found in the medievalist Hastings Rashdall's 1895 definitive three-volume study of the universities of Europe.

In his comments on Abelard, Rashdall makes the fundamental point that the real grievance against Abelard that was put forward by his many opponents, i.e., the conservative "old guard" theologians, was not about any single failing of his but rather the whole radical tone, spirit, and method of his theological teaching. Rashdall summarizes this as follows with a nice turn of phrase:

> [Abelard] had presumed to endeavor to understand, to explain the mystery of the Trinity: he had dared to bring all things in heaven and earth to the test of reason. *For his conservative opponents that was heresy enough: to accept the doctrine of the Church because they were rational was hardly less offensive than to reject them as irrational.*[3]

Abelard's torrid love affair with Heloise, which led to his being castrated by his enemies, is the stuff of legend and quickly transformed him from a brilliant, if very arrogant and vain scholar, into a tragic figure of true love. His later verbal struggles with the famous abbot Bernard of Clairvaux over reason and religion also would also make him a hero of the soon-to-arrive intellectual dawn in Europe known as the Enlightenment.

Abelard's most lasting intellectual achievements, however, and the ones by which he is best remembered by scholars today, lie in the field of philosophy. They are summarized briefly later in this chapter and are important today because Abelard's students would go on to play key roles as kings, popes, philosophers, poets, politicians, theologians, and monks, influencing both current 12th-century philosophy and later 14th-century thought as well. First, it is essential, both in terms of appreciating his good writing and of understanding his famous love life, to quote him directly. Abelard wrote romantically that

> Now there dwelt in that same city of Paris a certain young girl named Heloise, the niece of a canon [an influential cathedral cleric] who was called Fulbert.... Of no mean beauty, she stood out above all by reason of her abundant knowledge of letters....
>
> We were first united in the dwelling that sheltered our love [Fulbert's house], and then the hearts that burned with it. Under the pretext of study we spent our hours in the happiness of love, and learning held out to us the secret opportunities that our passion craved. Our speech was more of love than of the books that lay before us; our kisses far outnumbered our reasoned words. Our hands sought less the book than each other's bosoms—love drew our eyes together far more than the lesson drew them to the pages of our text.... No degree of love's progress was left untried by our passion, and if love itself could not imagine any wonder as yet unknown, we discovered it. And our inexperience in such delights made us all the more ardent in our pursuit of them, so that our thirst for one another was still unquenched.[4]

Heloise herself underlined what Abelard said above: "Which queen, which princess," she wrote separately, "would not have envied my joys and my bed?"[5] This couple's great happiness, however, soon led to their great sorrow. Abelard explains to the reader that Fulbert and his kinsmen came to believe—quite incorrectly—that he was trying to get rid of Heloise by forcing her to become a nun. He explains how his enemies punished him by castrating him:

> Violently incensed, they laid a plot against me, and one night while I all unsuspecting was asleep in a secret room in my lodgings, they broke in with the help of one of my servants whom they had bribed. There they had vengeance on me with a most cruel and most shameful punishment, such as astounded the whole world; for they cut off those parts of my body with which I had done that which was the cause of their sorrow. This done, straightway they fled, but two of them were captured and suffered the loss of their eyes and their genital organs. One of these two was the aforesaid servant, who even when he was still in my service, had been led by his avarice to betray me.[6]

Abelard's strongest claim to fame rests not on his descriptions of love-making but on his philosophical work. Too complicated to be explained here in any detail but, by drawing very selectively from an article in the *Stanford Encyclopedia of Philosophy*,[7] some of the highlights of his thought can—*greatly oversimplified*—be mentioned here briefly.

1. Dialectics: This category includes works concerned with logic, philosophy of language, metaphysics, and philosophy of mind; ethics (analysis of moral worth and degrees of praise or blame for actions); philosophical theology (the nature of the Trinity); and practical issues (e.g., "For and Against"—a famous series of Abelard's 158 questions-and-answers on difficult religious issues).

2. Metaphysics: Abelard is the first great example of nominalism in the Western tradition. In metaphysics, a *universal* is what particular things have in common, namely their characteristics or qualities. Abelard holds that universals are mere words (*nomina*) and he devotes a great deal of effort to pouring cold water over the metaphysical excesses of his rivals.

3. Logic: Abelard was also the greatest logician since Antiquity and devised what is technically known as a "purely truth-functional propositional logic." This implies that every statement has exactly one "truth value," which is either true or false, and that every logical connective is "truth functional."

4. Philosophy of language: Much of Abelard's philosophy of language focuses on how a given class of expressions functions logically. Although a sentence says something, a sentence is not same thing as what it says. The semantic job of sentences is to *say* something, which is not to be confused with naming or denoting some thing. A sentence is true only if things are in fact in the way it says, and things make sentences true or false only by virtue of the way they are, and nothing further is needed. Thus the sentence "Socrates runs" is true when Socrates runs, and that is all that can be said or needs to be said.

5. Philosophy of mind: Abelard concludes that intentionality is a primitive and irreducible feature of the mind, our acts of *attending to things*. Different acts of attention are intrinsically different from one another: they are about what they are about in virtue of being the kind of attention they are. Much of Abelard's writings on logic and dialectic are devoted to working out the details of a way to explain mental content. This is now called an "adverbial theory."

6. Ethics: According to Abelard, traditional Christianity is radically "intentionalist," that is to say, *it is a person's intentions alone that ultimately determines the moral worth of given actions*. It is not just what we do or how act, but rather what our *intentions* were when we did these things. Suppose, for example, that a set of twins who are brother and sister are separated at birth, so that as adults neither knows that the other exists. Suppose, further, that they meet, fall in love, are legally married, and have sexual intercourse. Technically, this is incest, but

Abelard finds no fault with either party because *neither intended to do anything morally wrong.*

7. Theology: Abelard uses his "theory of identity" to comment on the Trinity, i.e., the three Persons of God. These Persons are essentially the same as one another, he says, since they are all the same concrete thing, namely God, but they differ from one another by definition: what it is to be the Father is not the same as what it is to be the Son, or what it is to be the Holy Spirit. Their unique properties, however, are all shared by God. Abelard concludes that while human reason alone cannot fully explain all of the above points, he claims that they do in fact validate his explanation.

22

Eustache

French Monk and Pirate

The text of *Eustache the Monk*, written in Old French with traces of the local Picard dialect, is the work of an anonymous poet who composed its 2,307 verses in octosyllabic rhymed couplets between 1223 and 1284.[1] Using the details of the life of Eustache Busket (c. 1170–1217) as a factual base, this poet creatively wove fact and fiction together into a tale that has many echoes of the legend of Robin Hood and of two similar medieval legends, one on Hereward the Wake, and the other on Fouke le Fitz. What follows here is a brief biography of Eustache himself.

Eustache was a younger son of Bauduin Busquet, a senior baron of the Boulonnais region of France. As a youth, he was probably trained as a knight, which would have been the usual profession for a young aristocrat. He also became an accomplished seaman, a skill he may have learned on his own in Italy. Legend has it that he also studied necromancy (black magic) in Toledo, Spain, but there is no proof of this.

When he was about 20 years old, he entered the Benedictine abbey at Saint Samer near Boulogne and became a monk, probably because as a younger son he would not have been able to inherit his father's title and his lands. Eustache left the monastery only after his father had been ambushed and killed by a local noble, Hainfrois de Heresinghen. In response to this murder, Eustache took his legal case to Renaud of Dammartin, the Count of Boulogne, and demanded justice.

To settle this dispute and in keeping with medieval law, a judicial duel was arranged. Under medieval law, the outcome of such a duel was held to show God's will decisively on such a matter. In this duel, Eustache's champion—his proxy in the fight—was killed. Although under the law this fact proved conclusively that Hainfrois was in the right, Eustache was nevertheless appointed seneschal (a senior position) by the Count of Boulogne while the count was away on an expedition with King Philip Augustus to recover territories in Normandy held by King John of England. Upon the count's return, however, Eustache was falsely accused of financial mis-management by his great enemy, Hainfrois. Perceiving that Hainfrois was trying to destroy him, Eustache then fled into the forests around Boulogne and became an outlaw. In retaliation, Hainfrois seized all of Eustache's properties. This, in turn, led Eustache to begin a dramatic campaign of outlawry against the Count.

The campaign becomes the mainspring of the long epic poem about Eustache but, in fact, only three of the many adventures cited in it have any historical basis. These three lasted for about one year (from early 1204 to early 1205), but in the hands of the poet they become a very long and riveting series of death-or-glory adventures. The poet composed the original text in octosyllabic rhymed couplets, which lends itself to a fast-paced narrative with a great deal of word play in archaic French that cannot be fully reproduced in modern English.

Some of Eustache's adventures are outlined at the end of this chapter because they offer us such unusual glimpses into workaday life in medieval France and England. First, however, it must be related what Eustache did between 1205 and his eventual execution in 1217 (he was beheaded by English sailors aboard an English ship in the English Channel at the end of the Battle of Sandwich).

In 1205, Eustache had left France for the English Channel where, as a French pirate, he seized English vessels as part of the long-running, on-again off-again, conflicts between France and England. As the modern historian Jill Eddison explains the state of play,

> Piracy was endemic in the Middle Ages. Men stole each other's ships; they looted each other's cargoes at sea or in port; they demanded ransoms from those captives likely to be able to pay and they threw useless crew members overboard into the sea. Life was cheap and often short. In an age when men easily and quickly resorted to violence, these were the universal, accepted facts of life....
>
> [Moreover,] on the one hand, the Channel was a highly important seaway, a rich commercial artery in the trade which formed the foundation for the rising economy of the western world. On the other, it was also a political frontier between two evolving, ambitious and belligerent monarchies, England and France.[2]

By November of 1205, Eustache had arrived in England, where he offered his services to King John as a pirate working directly for the king, and he was quickly accepted in the role. He then began to cruise the Channel, and soon captured the island of Sark, which he used as his base. During this piracy period, he received two safe-conduct passes from King John, which allowed him to return to England. The King must have been pleased with him, because as a reward for his maritime services he was also given lands in Swaffam, Norfolk. By 1209, he was still working for King John but now in the more exalted capacity of English ambassador to the Count of Boulogne. However, when King Philip learned that Eustache was living in France, he outlawed him. Always quick on his feet, however, Eustache was back in London in 1212 when the Count of Boulogne negotiated there a charter of allegiance with King John. But fearing that he would soon be betrayed, Eustache then left England for France, where he sided with King Philip.

It is possible that he was involved in the naval disaster at Damme, in what is now Belgium, in 1213. If so, he may have been responsible for the loss of the *Nef de Boulogne* during the English attack on King Philip's fleet. This was a huge ship, said to have been built with a very high bow and very high stern in the shape of a castle. The high bow and stern would have offered great tactical advantages during a fight at sea: sailors in either place could then fire their arrows and other weapons *down* at their enemy's decks below them.

The next year (1214) the English barons revolted against King John, and Eustache is on record as having supplied them with arms. As a result, his lands in Norfolk were confiscated. Nevertheless, he continued to be a power in the English Channel in 1215. The medieval chronicler and illustrator Matthew Paris reports that the king of France, Philip Augustus II (1180–1223), told a papal legate:

> Through our land I will willingly furnish you with a safe conduct, but if by chance you should fall into the hands of Eustache the Monk or of the other men of Louis [France's King Louis VIII] who guard the sea-routes, do not impute it to me [do not blame me] if any harm comes to you.[3]

In May 1216, a French fleet of 800 ships headed for England to support the Baron's War there, and in this process Eustache safely delivered King Louis to the Isle of Thanet, the most easterly point of Kent, England. Finally, on 24 August 1217, Eustache sailed to England himself to support Louis, but in the Battle of Sandwich his own ship was attacked by four English ships. He fought ferociously, but the English hurled small pots of finely-ground lime onto his ship, possibly by attaching them to heavy-duty arrows fired from powerful bows. These pots smashed against the upper parts of the ship and generated clouds of thick dust that was carried by the wind and quickly blinded Eustache's crew. The English sailors seized their advantage by swarming onto Eustache's ship and taking all the nobles there prisoner, to be held for ransom. Any members of Eustache's crew who seemed too poor to generate any ransom were probably simply pushed overboard to drown.

As for Eustache himself, he was found cowering in the bilges of the ship, where he offered his captors huge sums of money if they would spare his life. However, the English sailors hated him so much for his piratical life and his turncoat qualities that the most they would do for him was merely to let him choose on which side of his ship he wanted to be executed. His answer is not recorded, but what is clear is that he was immediately beheaded on one side or on the other.

Looking back at his eventful life as embellished in the manuscript in Old French mentioned at the beginning of this chapter, it is worth remembering that, throughout the Middle Ages, the concept of Satan (the Devil) had grown in people's minds to the point where they accepted Satan as a very active and very aggressive malignant supernatural force. It was certainly believed that Satan was bent on tormenting as many human beings as possible and then dragging their souls down into hell.

All this is relevant here because so much of the gratuitous violence in the story of Eustache was *considered at that time to be quite diabolical.* We learn this when Eustache allegedly studied black magic in Spain,

> While in Toledo, for one whole winter and a summer he lived down under ground in an abyss where he spoke to the Devil himself, who taught him black magic and unnatural tricks with which to fool and deceive everybody. He learned thousands of magic spells, evil tricks and charms....
>
> When Eustache had learned enough, he parted company with the Devil. The Devil told him his life would last long enough for him to accomplish a good deal of evil. He would fight wars against kings and counts and end his days struck dead at sea.[4]

As a final touch, toward the end of the poem, the ex-monk Eustache candidly and boldly tells the reader: *"J'ai un nom Mauferas"* ("My name is Do Evil"). This boasting about his underlying but hidden diabolical nature probably reflects the long-standing and never-resolved medieval concerns about how to understand and how to deal with the problem of evil. The *Stanford Encyclopedia of Philosophy*, for example, explains why this issue seemed to be so impossible for thinkers in the Middle Ages to resolve:

> Ancient [Greek] philosophy had speculated on evil, but the particularly pressing form the problem takes on in Christianity, where an omniscient, omnipotent, and benevolent God freely created absolutely everything besides himself [presumably including evil], first emerged in the Middle Ages.[5]

This is a philosophic problem that even today admits of no easy solution.

The Monk Matthew Paris

So Good at So Many Things

The English Benedictine monk Matthew Paris (c. 1200–1259) was based at St. Albans Abbey in Hertfordshire and was a man of a many talents.[1] He was at the same time an illustrator, a chronicler, a cartographer, and an artist, being especially skilled at producing beautiful, illuminated manuscripts. These manuscripts were hand-lettered books with painted decorations in bright colors and dyes, which included such precious metals as gold and silver. Their pages were also painstakingly made from the best-quality parchment (the processed animal skins, commonly calf, sheep, or goat). Monasteries produced such elegant, illuminated manuscripts between about 1100 and 1600.

Thanks to his energy and abilities, Matthew was an excellent mirror of his times. His artistic output included illustrations for his own chronicles; illustrations of saints' lives;, several hundred correctly-drawn and brilliantly-colored shields of arms, which were used to identify the armored nobility by sight; and some impressive maps of Britain, the Holy Land, and the world—all of which are milestones in the history of European cartography.

Matthew also wrote extensively and very well: his *Chronica majora* ("Greater Chronicle"), which he intended to be a "universal history of the world," gives us many modest but still very interesting (and sometimes downright damning) insights into life in his times. The *Chronica majora* is celebrated for the author's unprecedented use in it of over 200 archival and documentary resources. Indeed, it is one of the most important surviving documents in Latin Europe, i.e., the parts of Europe where the Romance languages, initially based on Latin, were spoken. Matthew wrote so much about history because he believed that his written history would reveal the sinful actions that had so often forged it. He hoped that his comments would encourage sinners to seek God's pardon for their many sins.

As a result of this literary process, the modern reader is much in the debt of the unknown scribe—probably a fellow monk at St. Albans—who made a "fair copy," i.e., a final corrected copy, now known as the manuscript "C," of Matthew's chronicle from 1189 to 1250. Although during his old age Matthew himself made numerous editorial changes in his own handwritten manuscript of the *Chronica majora*, generally dropping or softening many of his most critical remarks, these changes *were never made* in the fair copy C. For this reason, modern scholars are now able, by reading C, to understand what Matthew *really thought* before he saw the need for political correctness. For example, he deleted entirely his very disrespectful account of the archbishop's bad behavior toward the monks during the former's official tour of inspection of the monastery.

In some of Matthew's manuscripts, the entire upper half of a page contains a miniature drawing; in others, a drawing is reduced in size to take up only the bottom quarter of the page. Both sizes are tinted drawings, which were much cheaper and quicker to produce than painted illuminations. The figures he drew are said by specialists in the field to have a new and pleasing "roundness" to them, in contrast to the angular figures created by other more conventional contemporary artists.

As a chronicler/historian, Matthew received much of his information from what the English would now call "the great and the good," the important, well-connected people of his society. Indeed, one of his best informants was King of England Henry III himself: Matthew was on very friendly personal terms with him. During the course of the king's week-long visit to St. Albans in 1257, for example, King Henry kept Matthew close to his side, both by day and by night, because he wanted to be very sure what Matthew was writing was as accurate as possible. Matthew assures us that the king "guided my pen with much good will and diligence."[2] Matthew's real literary talent, however, lay in the fields of narrative and description, rather than in objective academic historical analysis as that concept is understood today.

Being a strong supporter of the older, well-established monastic orders against their newer rivals, namely, the secular clergy and the mendicant friars, Matthew was also vehemently opposed both to the hangers-on who frequented the court of Rome and to Henry III's many foreign relatives. As for the King himself, Matthew does seem to have liked him on a personal basis but did not support all of his policies. It is a matter of great regret for later scholars, however, that Matthew's work ends with his own death in 1259—which was just before the epic struggle in England began between Henry III and his barons.

Modern readers can still be grateful, however, for Matthew's willingness to lay out the seamier side of monastic life as well as its sunnier side. Retaining the tone and as much of the language of the original version as feasible, here is an edited and annotated version of what he writes about a prior and about a murderous monk:

> The prior, who was disgracefully squandering the substance of his little church and who had exceeded the bounds of moderation in his cups, got into an argument with one of his monks. This prior was trying, uncharitably and spitefully, to send the monk, whom he had summoned from the monastery of Cluny, back to Cluny against his will, despite the monk's perfectly reasonable reasons for not wanting to go back.
>
> But when the prior yelled at him fearfully, swearing that, willy-nilly, he must atone for his refusal to obey by going on a long pilgrimage alone and carrying his own food with him in a heavy leather sack, this devil of a monk, in a fit of violent anger or perhaps seized by madness, pulled out his knife [most medieval men carried a knife, both to cut their food and for self-defense] and disemboweled the prior, without any fear of perpetrating such a crime within the church precincts.
>
> When the fatally-wounded prior, with the death-rattle sounding in his throat, tried to summon the monks, or at least to arouse them, he could not do so because his windpipe had been closed. Again the monk rushed up to him and with frantic blows, three or four times repeated, buried the knife up to the hilt in his lifeless body. Thus this wretch, not without great dishonor and harm to the monastic order, and with the anger and vengeance of God on both sides, sent another wretch to Hell.
>
> I have narrated all this in full so that the reader, warned and prevented, will steer clear of such crimes, lest he be precipitated into a similar confusion by an angry God. The author of this crime was seized by those arriving at the place and was taken into custody tightly bound.[3]

Matthew was also a fine cartographer, drafting a unique itinerary for pilgrims that accurately showed the daily route from London to Rome in graphic detail. His sequence of pictures of the towns along that route indicated, very clearly, the best place to stay at the end of each day's travel. The result was that both intrepid travelers and timid stay-at-home viewers could follow the whole journey stop-by-stop, simply by looking at one picture after another—much like a modern-day comic strip.

24

Monastic Sheep Farming

More than 500 years ago, it was said—correctly—that "half of the wealth of medieval England rides on the back of the sheep" and that "sheep turn grass into wool," thus providing the essential raw material for the English woolen cloth-weaving industry.[1] The wool trade was one of the key factors in the flourishing of the medieval English economy. A symbolic but still current proof of this fact is that, ever since the 14th century, the presiding officer of the English House of Lords sits very solidly upon the Woolsack—a chair still stuffed with good-quality wool.

The best-written and most readable study of the history of the wool trade in England, and of the key role the monasteries played in it, is arguably Eileen Power's outstanding book, *The Wool Trade in English Medieval History*. It will be drawn upon often in this chapter. Published in 1941, her book contains the printed text of lectures she delivered at Oxford University in 1939. It certainly merits what the editor of the *Times Literary Supplement* said when it was first published: "This is *exposition*, not exhaustive discussion. As such it is brilliant."[2] Together with the other sources cited in this chapter, we will see how it was the wool trade that gave England such a key economic position in the Middle Ages. As Power puts it very well,

> [England's] commerce and politics alike were built upon wool. When her kings got themselves taken prisoner, like Richard I, the ransom was paid—with grumbling—out of wool. When they rushed into war with their neighbours, like the three Edwards, the wars were financed and allies bought—with more grumbling—out of wool....
>
> The very Lord Chancellor plumped himself down [in his office] on a wool-sack [a tangible sign of the great importance of the wool trade], and the kingdom might have set on its great seal the motto which a wealthy wool merchant engraved on the windows of his new house:
>
> > I praise God and ever shall
> > It is the sheep hath paid for all.[3]

Sheep farming was already an important industry in England at the time of the Norman Conquest in 1066. The incomplete statistics that survive from these early days indicate that, between them, the four shires (counties) of eastern England, the four shires of western England, and one great English monastery, namely, Ely Abbey, carried (i.e., had on their lands) about 292,000 demesne sheep.

As mentioned earlier, a demesne was a plot of medieval land that was part of a manor but it was kept by the owner of the manor for his own use, rather than being leased out to someone else as a tenant.

Nuns, for their part, had some 1,700 sheep grazing on the common land, i.e., land that was not enclosed by stone walls or by fences, in the Cotswolds. This is not surprising. In that era, sheep farming was increasing very rapidly: the growth of the population and the cloth trade in Flanders and northern Italy had greatly increased the *demand* for wool, while the founding of new monastic orders in England greatly increased the *supply* of wool.

The monastic orders in England also practiced sheep farming on a large scale. Ely Abbey, for example, had 13,400 sheep on its estates in six counties at the time of the Domesday Book in 1086. This work, whose title in Middle English meant "Doomsday Book," was a manuscript record of the "Great Survey" of much of England and parts of Wales. It was completed in 1086 at the order of King William the Conqueror, who wanted an accurate list of the lands, livestock, and all the other assets of his kingdom.

The Cistercians set up their own monasteries in the lightly populated dales and moorlands of Yorkshire and in the narrow valleys of Wales for two good reasons. The first was that their monastic doctrine directed them to find and then settle in and work in very isolated places where there were either none or at least very few other people—so that they would not be distracted from their single-mined pursuit of an ascetic, holy lifestyle.

The second reason was that the older orders had already settled in many of the other and more prosperous parts of the Midlands. In any case, the bottom line was that the Cistercians were so successful that, by 1300, in England alone there were almost 100 Cistercian houses, many of which had between 10 and 20 associated farms known as granges. These resembled modern farms and were free from the usual restraints and complications of communal feudal farming. They were up to 400 acres in size and were initially staffed by lay brothers (laymen who had chosen to live a religious life but without becoming monks) and later by full-time hired workers, farm servants, and laborers.[4]

Ultimately, the Cistercians and the Premonstratensians (another monastic order, founded in France in 1120) would become the best sheep farmers in the whole of England, and probably in the whole medieval world, although other monastic orders, e.g., the Benedictines, were major sheep farmers as well.

Collectively, numerical estimates vary but it is thought that the monasteries of England and France raised an annual total of at least 32,300 sheep. For example, the Benedictines had 13,000 flocks of sheep; the Norman nunnery of Holy Trinity in Caen grazed 1,700 sheep in Gloucestershire; the monks of Peterborough grazed more than 1,600 sheep and lambs; Meaux Abbey pastured 11,000 sheep on its estates; and the monks of Beaulieu had flocks totaling over 5,000 sheep.[5]

Nevertheless, the Cistercians were the real stars of sheep production. Indeed, they did so well financially that in 1193–1194, when the English were forced pay a very stiff ransom to free King Richard I from his captivity by the Emperor Henry VI, all of the wool produced that year by these two monasteries alone was sold, and the proceeds were used to pay the huge ransom.[6] This had been set at 150,000 silver marks, which was nearly three times the entire annual income of the English Crown.

It has been justly said that "a rising tide floats all boats." In England, the 12th and 13th centuries were a time of rising production, of more people, of growing settlements, and of technological advances. This rising tide stimulated many monasteries and lay estate owners alike to invest ever more heavily in producing sheep. A few figures from various years are revealing:

- The Bishop of Winchester had 29,000 sheep on his estates in 1259.
- The priory of St. Swithun's in Winchester kept 20,000 sheep there in the early 14th century.
- In 1303, Henry Lacy, Earl of Lincoln, had 13,400 sheep in Yorkshire, Lincolnshire, and other parts of southern England.
- The fenland abbeys of Peterborough and Croland had 16,300 sheep between them.[7]

The peak years of English demesne farming were the 13th and early 14th centuries. Thereafter, the drumbeats of pestilence (the Black Death, discussed later) and of war reduced agricultural prices. Agricultural profits fell as a result, the population declined, and farmlands and pasture lands ceased to expand. Local lords transformed themselves into a rentier class by leasing their lands rather than by overseeing them personally. The middleman dealer became ever more important. In brief, the earlier unregulated wool trade in England was now hemmed in by monopolies; by high taxes; and by the power of a financial body of English merchants known as the "Company of Merchants of the Staple," which held a near-monopoly on the wool trade.

From the monasteries' point of view, playing the wool market could be, financially, as risky a business as playing the stock market would be in a later day. In many cases, the monasteries sold their wool to Italian merchant bankers by means of advance contracts. Such contracts were usually valid for two or three years, but sometimes they were good for up to 20 years. Eileen Power says of these contracts,

> The reason [for the financial risk] is clear when we examine the contracts. In almost every case the [wool] merchants paid large lump sums in cash in advance ... and these were really loans made on the security of wool, which converted the transactions into credit deals ...
>
> Dealings were very lucrative to merchants who exacted heavy interest disguised in the price at which wool was valued or else took the form of an extra sack or two "gratis." But they constantly involved the monasteries in great difficulties....

Indeed, a former abbot of the Cistercian Pipewell Abbey was reduced to pleading with the monks always to remember that "It is so very easy to borrow, but so very hard to pay back!"[8] A sample wool contract of 12 May 1287, lightly edited below, makes it very clear that if a monastery could not deliver to the buyer the wool it had contracted for, then the buyer could legally force payment:

> [The abbot of the monastery in Meaux, France] came before the exchequer court and told the court that he, his monastery, and his successors were legally bound to deliver to Ricardo and Reynerio Guidicionis, Henrico de Podio and Thomasino Guidicionis and their fellow merchants of Lucca [Italy], eleven sacks of the better wool of his house, pressed and packed into round bales and weighed according to the ancient custom of the house, to be delivered to the merchants [of Hull, England, on 8 July 1289]....
>
> For which wool the abbot acknowledged he had received the full price in advance, which is to say 15 marks per sack. And if the abbot cannot deliver said wool to the merchants at the specified term, he agrees for himself, his monastery and for his successors as abbot that the exchequer might levy [seize] the wool or its value from the lands, tenements, goods and chattels of the house.[9]

It was the big monastic estates that played a key, spectacular role in turning England into one great "wool factory."[10] In 1322, for example, Canterbury priory alone had 14,000 sheep on its 40 different manors, with an average flock size of about 340 animals.

Overall, wool accounted for more than 20 percent of this priory's income. Its far-flung holdings allowed the monastery to move sheep at will from one manor to another, thus making the most efficient use of all its pasture-lands. It also made it easy to replace quickly any sheep lost to disease or injury, and to bring into the flock the most expensive and very best rams.

The Cistercians' unswerving pursuit of their simple and extremely ascetic way of life led them to unexpected and, quite probably, to very unwelcome financial successes in their new calling as master sheep-keepers. Choosing to settle in remote, lightly-populated regions, they selected what would become the Strata Florida Abbey in western Wales, a region which turned out to be ideal for extensive sheep farming. They were able to develop it very efficiently because all the Cistercian communities were under the direct control of their mother house in Cîteaux in France. This made it possible to profit from a common pattern of farms, working methods, and shared experiences, all of which, not surprisingly, led to great prosperity for the abbey.

The monks themselves worked very hard. Contemporary sources make it clear that the Cistercians could offer to buyers much better quality wool than their competitors, and that their wool was also cleaner and better prepared for shipment. This evidence of a superior Cistercian product, justifying a higher price, becomes more visible to modern scholars as they consider the monks' excellent sheep-breeding policies, their care and management of their sheep, their cleaning and sorting of the wool, and their grading and final delivery of the wool in bulk.[11]

At Strata Flora, they also cleared vast tracts of wasteland and, perhaps of equal importance, they also extended the widespread practice of transhumance, i.e., moving their flocks into upland sheep pastures during the dry summer months for the more nutritious grass growing in the hills, and then returning the sheep to the lowlands, where during the wet winter months the grass grew very well. To take but three of many possible examples of the transhumance practiced by the Church in the diocese of Maguelone in southern France, the bishop's sheep summered on the mountain plateau of Mende, nearly 100 miles away. Transhumance there involved the movement of many thousands of sheep. In the French region of Draguignan, in Provence, some 60,000 sheep and ewes traveled from the mountains back to the plains. In Italy, ecclesiastical institutions were important owners of arable lands; they relied on sheep to fertilize their estates and to provide meat and wool.[12]

An added benefit was that as the flocks were moved around the country, they also interbred and began to show distinctive regional variations which would later become standardized into different breeds. In this whole process, the monastic flock-masters led the way by moving rams or entire flocks of sheep from abbey to abbey as required. The net result was that the demanding breeding standards reached by the great medieval monastic estates in England during the 17th century would not be surpassed until the mid–18th century, or even later.

The Middle Ages were in fact an exceptionally good time to keep sheep. In the early 14th century, there were perhaps as many as 12 million sheep in England and Wales, with uncounted numbers of sheep also grazing in Scotland and Ireland. In England, many of them were kept in medieval monastic sheep granges (sheep farms) known as bercarias (*ber-cariae* in Latin)—a system of production pioneered by the Cistercian order but soon imitated by other orders.[13] The exact number of medieval bercarias is not known but based on the number of monastic sites, they are estimated to have totaled several thousand simple but very durable stone-and-earth structures designed to pen sheep.

One interesting historical aspect of the monastic wool trade worth discussing is focused on Rievaulx (pronounced "ree-VOH") Abbey, one of the largest and richest Cistercian houses, located in Yorkshire in the north of England.[14] Founded in 1132, this abbey had accumulated vast estates by the late 12th century and was very active in the wool trade. In the late 13th century, however, it fell onto hard times because of the inherent contradiction between its efforts to serve the community as a generous Christian monastery, on the one hand, and at the same to be a key player in the highly competitive wool trade, on the other.

In the late 13th century, the Cistercians' policy of advance sales of wool—selling wool forward by legally contracting to deliver a given amount and given quality of wool to Italian dealers at a specific date in the future—resulted in their permanent indebtedness to the dealers. This was an unescapable fact of life of life for the Cistercian monasteries of northern England, and one that often led to their own bankruptcies.

Such advance sales were the only way for a monastery to raise cash in a medieval economy in which the merchants were often quite rich but the agricultural producers were permanently short of money. Rievaulx Abbey, for example, always needed more money to expand its ambitious building programs; to provide open-handed hospitality to its many visitors; to contribute to the support of the poor; and to pay for food, lodging, and clothing for its 140 monks and for its even larger numbers of lay workers.

A reliable income was essential in social terms during the Middle Ages because a poor monastery would not be as able to discharge its obligations of religious practice and worship as well as a rich monastery. In addition, a poor monastery was much less likely to please its current donors and be able to attract rich new donors: such public relations efforts usually involved very costly hospitality and expensive gifts.

The income that Rievaulx earned from the sale of its wool was never reinvested simply in order to sell ever-increasing amounts of wool. It was instead used for religious activities that were believed to have a heavenly payoff in the future, both for the monks themselves and for the lay people of their community.

This abbey did in fact go through two bankruptcies, but these were not due to monastic incompetence. The reasons for them lay instead in the combination of two other causes, namely, the considerable mortality in the sheep flocks due to a disease known as sheep scab, and the continuing high levels of the abbey's spending on buildings and maintenance in the abbey complex itself. This spending was often financed by the need to borrow money at high interest rates.

Rievaulx, however, also had one important financial safety net that most other monasteries lacked. The English king himself wanted to preserve this abbey as a good source of ready money for the future. Moreover, he also needed to be seen—very publicly—as being a reliable supporter and protector of the Church itself. For both these reasons, Rievaulx Abbey was not likely to go out of business.

Before looking at the big picture of the overall international and national effects of the Black Death, the bubonic or pneumatic plague, on medieval farming communities, a few words may be useful on the small-scale sheep-raising "dale" of Nidderdale in Yorkshire, England, where one of the surviving classic sheepcotes is located.

The Black Death first reached Nidderdale in July 1349. It is now known—but of course it was *not* known then—that this was a lethal disease spread by the plague-infected fleas which lived on black rats. A bite from one of these fleas was all that it took to give a man, a woman, or a child an often-fatal case of bubonic plague, so called because of the bumps or "buboes" that soon appeared on their bodies. A few people did recover from this type of plague, but if a person's lungs were infected with the disease (which was known in this case as pneumonic plague), he or she was very likely to die—but not before this ill person had spread the disease to many other people by coughing. The disastrous bottom line was that nearly one-half of the population of Nidderdale would die of the plague.

The plague returned, and then left Nidderdale again, in the 1360s, killing more people in the process. By this time, it had made an enormous impact on the hamlet: whole families had been wiped out, and their loss forced important changes in how the land could be farmed. Some land was not farmed at all and was simply left fallow, waiting for better days. In the areas where people still lived, however, they had to decide how to farm the land with so few able-bodied people still available.

Most of Nidderdale was now being farmed by the lay-brothers of the abbeys. After the Black Death, however, there were no longer enough lay-brothers to work the local farms. The abbeys were therefore forced not only to hire new people to work the farms, but also to rent out some of their farms for money. This meant that fewer workers produced fewer crops, and this in turn reduced the income of the abbeys.

Looking at the Middle Ages in England as a whole, most of the countryside where farmers could grow their crops and raise their animals was still open (unenclosed) land. It was collectively known as the "commons."[15]

People traditionally shared it by using the "Open Field System," in which long thin strips of land were farmed by different families.

Over time, however, and with so much more land gradually becoming available because so many people had died, the common land was "enclosed" by dividing it up by means of stone walls and wooden gates. This process officially began as early as 1235 and slowly but surely created the lovely patchwork landscape of fields and stone walls in England that is still so much admired today.

If there was any *positive* effect of the Black Death in Nidderdale itself and in similar farming communities, it was that it caused a great shortage of agricultural labor. Seen in retrospect, it is clear that this fact heralded the "beginning of the end" of serfdom. Peasants could now demand better working terms: indeed, they could literally walk away from a given farm and go to work for someone else if their demands were not met. They were no longer, as a practical matter, tied to the same piece of land for their entire working lives.

25

Evaluating the Black Death

The Black Death, which was also known as the Plague, the Pestilence, or the Great Mortality, was a bubonic plague pandemic that occurred in Afro-Eurasia from 1346 to 1353. Its impacts on medieval life were pernicious and far-reaching. Caused by the bacterium *Yersinia pestis,* which may also cause septicemic or pneumatic plagues, it was by far the most fatal pandemic ever recorded in human history, killing an estimated 75 to 200 million people. Not surprisingly, the Black Death also generated severe religious, social, and economic upheavals in most regions, including in medieval Western Europe.

This pandemic originated either in Central Asia or in East Asia. Its first definitive appearance was in the Crimea in 1347. From there it was probably carried by fleas living on the black rats that travelled on Genoese slave ships. Once it came ashore, the Black Death was then carried by human fleas (which cause pneumonic plague) and by the accompanying person-to-person contact via aerosols. This process spread it much faster and much wider than would have been possible if the primary vector (a carrier of disease, especially an insect) had only been the rat fleas causing bubonic plague.

According to the medieval historians Philip Daileader, Ole Benedictow, and other sources, the probable death toll in Western Europe from the Black Death, and its side effects, ran along the following lines:

> For our own purposes in this book on monasteries, the most noteworthy losses were those suffered by the monks, friars, nuns, and priests living in the monasteries. They were hit hard because they were so vulnerable, due to their endless work caring for streams of patients suffering from the plague. For example, in the index of his 2004 book on the Black Death, the Norwegian scholar Ole J. Benedictow mentions at least 31 European monasteries and convents that were affected by this pandemic.[1]

Monasteries were especially numerous in England in the early 14th century, when there were perhaps as many as 500 different religious houses. The Black Death dealt them all a major blow, decimating the numbers of monks and nuns. Most of these institutions would never fully recover in the future.

In the meantime, however, there was a severe shortage of clergy. The many clerics who had died were often replaced by very lightly-trained inexperienced clergy who had no knowledge of what their predecessors had gone through. Although new colleges would be opened at the universities to train more male clergymen, the shortage of priests did provide new opportunities for laywomen to take on more extensive and more important public service roles in their local parishes.

On balance, it is likely that about half of the European population died of plague. In 1348, the disease spread so rapidly that before doctors or government officials could even try to detect its origins, about one-third of the population had already died. In very crowded cities, such as Paris, it was not uncommon for half of the people to die. In Italy, the population of Florence was reduced from between 110,000 and 120,000 inhabitants down to 50,000 in 1351. The death toll in London itself was approximately 62,000 people between 1346 and 1353. The plague did bypass some areas, with the most isolated places being less vulnerable to contagion. For example, plague did not appear in Flanders until the beginning of the 1400s, and some of the most remote rural parts of France, Finland, northern Germany, and Poland seem to have suffered least from it.

As a result of the plague and the acute labor shortages it caused, the peasants gradually became more empowered: they even revolted when their aristocratic former overlords tried to reestablish the pre-plague status quo. In 1358, for example, the peasantry of northern France rebelled, and in 1378 the guild members there revolted when some of their rights were taken away. The net result was that the social and economic structure of Western Europe was drastically and permanently changed.[2]

There must have been no end of true, heart-breaking but usually unrecorded stories about the onset of the plague. Here is one very moving account written by the Italian chronicler Agnolo di Tura, a shoemaker by profession, about his own ordeal in Sienna, Italy, where the plague arrived in May 1348. He tells us:

> Father abandoned child, wife husband, one brother another; And so they died. And none could be found to bury the dead for money or friendship. Members of a household brought their dead to a ditch as best they could, without priest, without divine offices ... great pits were dug and piled deep with the multitude of the dead. And they died by the hundreds both day and night.... And as soon as those ditches were filled more were dug....
>
> And I, Angolo di Tura ... buried my five children with my own hands. And there were also those who were so sparsely covered with earth that the dogs dragged them forth and devoured many bodies throughout the city. There was

no one who wept for death, for all awaited death. And so many died that all believed it was the end of the world.[3]

As if there was not already enough suffering caused by the Black Death itself, some zealots decided to inflict even more suffering on themselves through the process of self-flagellation, flogging themselves with small whips designed to draw blood. This movement became very popular after the Black Death, probably due to the widespread fear that the world was now quickly coming to its end, and to the belief that self-inflicted suffering, even just before death, might in some way atone for unforgiven sins. Alternatively, the flagellants may have believed that since clearly both the local physicians and the Church itself were powerless in the face of the Black Death, peoples' own actions—or inactions—would be totally useless as well. This led some people to opt instead for a short but merry life of last-ditch hedonism.

One of the few positive results of the Black Death, however, was a famous collection of novellas by the Italian author Giovanni Boccaccio (1313–1375). Known as *The Decameron*, this is a frame-story consisting of 100 tales told by a fictional group of seven young women and three young men who seek shelter in an isolated villa just outside Florence, Italy in order to escape the Black Death, which was then ravaging the city. Written in the vernacular of the Florentine language, *The Decameron* is now considered to be a masterpiece of early Italian prose. It can be thought of as a very forward-leaning book, namely, one which was oriented toward the coming Renaissance future, rather than simply evoking the many charms of the medieval past.

The skills that this book values most are the commercial and city-honed traits of quick humor, sharp repartee, sophistication, education, and high intelligence. In contrast, the old-fashioned traits of feudal piety and loyalty are shoved aside, as are ignorance, stupidity, and dullness. Moreover, the Church, its priests, and its dogmas all become satirical sources of comedy in *The Decameron*. This reflects the widespread discontent with medieval Christianity that arose from its massive failures to understand and deal successfully with the Black Death.

The effects of the Black Death on the monasteries and on other medieval landowners, the nobles and the gentry, were quite profound on two counts. The first was that the cost of labor increased very sharply because so many peasants and other workers were now dead and could not be replaced quickly, if at all. At the same time, the fall in the rental and other income of "middling" landowners, such as the medieval English yeomen who are so celebrated in song and story, made it difficult or impossible for them to hire enough farmhands to work on their land or domestic servants to work in their houses.

On balance, it can therefore safely be said that the Black Death constituted a major divide in the history of medieval Europe. It marked the end of a period of medieval growth and optimism. Construction work on cathedrals and monasteries ground to a halt, and some of these unfinished structures would remain unfinished well into modern times.[4]

Although this parallel is far from exact, one can also speculate that, just as it needed the massive public spending generated by World War II to lift the American economy out of the depression of the 1930s, so, too, it may have needed all the spending and the income generated by the Hundred Years War (1337–1453) to help offset some of the impacts of the Black Death.[5]

26

Fountains Abbey

This remarkably abbey, founded in 1132 and now a stately ruin, was so important its heyday that it merits a separate chapter. It was named for the many springs of water that gushed forth from its site while it was being built in Yorkshire, England.[1] Because Fountains Abbey embraced one of the biggest, most magnificent, and best-designed English landscapes, its ruins still constitute the stellar standard by which all the other medieval monasteries in Britain can best be judged today.

At the center of this World Heritage site are the remains of a famous 12th-century Cistercian monastery that became one of the biggest and richest monastic houses in England. The tower of its church is 168 feet high; the magnificent vaulted underground storeroom, known as the cellarium and 300 feet long, is an architectural gem; and Studley Royal Park, with its 650 acres of woodland and ornamental gardens, is just a short stroll away. For all these reasons, Fountains Abbey, now run by England's National Trust, always draws large numbers of visitors each year.

There had always been a tradition of monasticism in the north of England, especially in Yorkshire, where abbeys were being built as early as the 7th century. Remarkably, despite Viking raids and local civil wars (e.g., the victorious king William the Conqueror "harried the North"), these abbeys flourished. The most impressive of them all was Fountains Abbey, now Britain's largest monastic ruin. It was founded by 13 Benedictine monks from York, who after a dispute and riot had been expelled from the Benedictine house of St. Mary's Abbey there.

Inspired by the austerities being practiced at the nearby Cistercian monastery at Rievaulx, these dissident monks wanted to live under a much more demanding monastic rule than the increasingly lax Benedictine rule they had been living under until then. Thurstan, the Archbishop of York, kindly gave them land in the valley of the Skell River that had everything necessary for the construction of an abbey of their own, plenty of stone and timber and a reliable watercourse.

Having not yet been formally accepted by the Cistercian order, however, the monks sent emissaries to Abbot Bernard at the Cistercian monastery of Clairvaux in Burgundy, France. Their petition to join the order was accepted, and on their way back to Fountains they were accompanied by a monk skilled both in building timber monasteries of the approved type and in teaching monks the Cistercian way of life.

According to the official history of this abbey, its earliest days were dark indeed. The monks were forced to seek shelter from the endless rains by cowering under the branches of a big elm tree while they built a small wooden oratory and dug a vegetable garden. Legend has it that when their food supplies ran very low they were even reduced to nibbling on the most tender branches of the elm tree, which were a common winter fodder only for cattle.

The monks therefore urgently sent another emissary to France, this time to ask for permission to abandon Fountains entirely. Fortunately, before this monk was able to return to Fountains with permission to do so, three canons from York had joined the nascent abbey at this critical time, bringing with them enough money to keep it going. New recruits arrived as well, so when the community was formally admitted into the Cistercian order in 1135, it already had 35 monks and was about to embark on a period of rapid accumulation of wealth, power, and land that was to last well into the 13th century.[2]

The abbey grew to become very rich and to possess vast stretches of land across western Yorkshire. Much of its wealth came from trading wool and lead, two of the region's most abundant resources. Following the second half of the 13th century, however, the abbey fell upon hard times. To summarize some of them very briefly:

- Governed by 11 abbots over the years, it became financially unstable largely due to their forward selling of the wool crop.
- It was in poor physical condition by 1294; it had to deal with military unrest in the early 1300s, when the Scots invaded northern England; and it suffered heavy losses of manpower and income during the Black Death of 1348–1349.
- Moreover, as a result of the Papal Schism of 1378–1409, Fountains Abbey and other Cistercian houses were ordered to break off all their contacts with their mother house in Cîteaux.
- Some of the abbots of Fountains Abbey turned out to be incompetent or corrupt.

It might easily be imagined today that Fountains Abbey was always an unhurried place that favored serenity, contemplation, and calm.[3] Certainly this must have been true in its very earliest days, but for most of its working life it was a bustling, crowded, and indeed even an *industrialized* corner of medieval England.

In 2021, the National Trust announced the totally-unexpected discovery of the foundations of a medieval tannery at Fountains Abbey. Mark Newman, a Trust archeologist, said that this was a wonderful and very important discovery. Fountains Abbey is probably the most investigated Cistercian abbey in Britain, so as he put it, "when you discover a major building on this scale that was completely unknown, you don't get many of these in a career."[4] This discovery, made by ground-penetrating radar, revealed previously unknown monastic buildings, including one 52 feet wide and 104 feet long. They have lined pits and tanks around them, which proves that they are the remains of a tannery.

This produced the materials needed for clothing, e.g., weatherproof animal skin for the lay brothers' heavy outdoor work, and sheepskins for them to sleep under at night; belts; bedding; and monastic book bindings. Surprisingly close to where the monks lived and worked, a tannery of this size, spanning such a large area of the Fountains Abbey site, reveals an operation on a quasi-industrial scale.

In practice and taken as a whole, the abbey was therefore a very busy, noisy, dusty place where people were always coming and going, and where stone first had to be cut for new buildings and then installed in them. This was necessary because up to 200 lay brothers, 60 choir monks, 600 visitors, and the many servants of the abbey all needed places to live. Remarkably, this occurred at a time when only 700 people would have constituted a fair-sized population for a small town in early medieval England.

Because of its vast landholdings which stretched all the way across the north of England from coast to coast and which included land in more than 138 medieval villages, the abbey was largely self-sufficient. It had, on call, not only the raw materials it needed but also the trained administrators and laborers that were necessary to put everything to the right use at the right time. Much of the abbey's physical structure would grow rapidly through the 12th and 13th centuries, as did land donations to it and land acquisitions as well.

The Cistercians were experts both with water-driven machinery such as trip hammers, and with the fulling mills used to wash the abbey's wool before it was sent out for sale. Moreover, brewing at the abbey took place on a truly massive scale because of the need to provide several pints of beer and ale per person per day for hundreds of thirsty residents, guests, and servants. The daily baking needs were of course huge. Unfortunately the aroma of freshly-baked bread had to compete with the stench from the abbey's leather-working tanneries, which were not far away. Nevertheless, in 1535 the abbey still had such a high income that it was the richest Cistercian monastery in England. This prosperity was to be only short-lived, however.

After the Dissolution of the Monasteries by Henry VIII in 1539, the abbey's buildings and 500 acres of land were seized by the Crown and were sold to Sir Richard Gresham, a local merchant, for the considerable sum of more than £11,137. They were eventually resold to Sir Stephen Proctor, who used some of the abbey's stonework to build the Elizabethan mansion Fountains Hall in 1611, two rooms of which are now open to the public.

The closure and sale of a large religious house could easily have an enormous negative social and economic impact on any local community that had become dependent on it. Ironically, this does not seem to have been the case with Fountains Abbey. True, all the monks and their retainers had to leave, but the tenants themselves still remained in place and continued their agricultural work much as before but under new owners.

27

The Poisoned Chalice and Fatal Affray of Furness Abbey

Founded in 1123, this Cistercian abbey, which is located on the west coast of England near Barrow-in-Furness, Cumbria, was in its heyday the second-wealthiest and most powerful monastery in the whole country, being second only to Fountains Abbey itself. Today, Furness Abbey has some of the finest monastic ruins in England.

The monks of this abbey were large landowners and formed the most powerful institution in what was at the time a remote border territory. They were also very influential on the nearby Isle of Man, which lies in the Irish Sea about 60 miles west of the abbey. Their abbot therefore played an important role in the religious and secular administration of the region.

Being located only about 70 miles down the coast from Scotland, the abbey sometimes got caught up in clashes between the frequently-warring Scots and the English. When the Scottish leader Robert the Bruce invaded England in 1322, for example, the abbot decided that the only sensible course was to provide food and lodging for the Scottish troops and to support their leader, rather than risk having his abbey put to the sword.

The abbey became a preferred place of burial for the local elite men and women, who believed that the endless prayers of the monks would speed the passage of their souls through the pains of Purgatory to the eternal rest awaiting them in heaven. By the same token, kings and bishops funded the construction of many impressive buildings clustered around the cloister of the abbey. These reflect the size of the monastic community itself, which in the 13th century totaled about 100 monks and 200 lay brothers.

There was also some bad happenings. In about 1246, Abbot Lawrence Acclorne was reportedly murdered by three of his monks, who had poisoned the chalice he was using when celebrating High Mass. As if that were not enough, at about the same time there was also a fatal affray in the abbey's stable, most likely a stabbing, which involved a confrontation between the servants of a local noble and those of the abbot himself.[1]

Despite these negative events, Furness Abbey remained a prosperous and well-regarded community. Papal taxation records from 1291, for example, show that the tax bill for all its manors and estates came to more than £171—a sizeable sum at the time—and that in 1296 King Edward I held the abbey in such high regard that he directed the monks there to pray for the soul of his recently-deceased brother.

The abbey's very wealth, however, contributed to its final undoing. When Henry VIII dissolved the monasteries, the total wealth of the Church as a whole was assessed. Furness Abbey was found to have an annual income of £805, making it by far the wealthiest monastery in the region and the second-richest Cistercian abbey in all of England.

To protect both himself and the clerical and lay workers of the abbey, Abbot Pyle "voluntarily" surrendered the abbey to the Crown in the spring of 1537. Commissioners were then dispatched to the abbey to oversee the dispersal of the monks and lay workers and the destruction of the church and other buildings. "Ropes and other engines" were later used to topple the walls of the abbey and thus ruin it. By the late 18th century, the former abbot's lodging, the only building that had not been destroyed, was now being used as a simple farmhouse.[2]

The Furness Abbey complex is now an English "Scheduled Monument and Conservation Area," containing five significant buildings and related structures. Restoration work took place between 2008 and 2017, amid fears that part of the abbey could collapse if it were not restored.

28

Medieval Pilgrims

Pilgrimage, the importance of making a sacred journey, often under very difficult conditions, has been a familiar undertaking in many cultures of the world.[1] By the 4th century, pilgrimage had already become one of the most recognized and approved public expressions of Christian piety. Men and women of all ages, and from all walks of life, wanted to see with their own eyes some of the places where Jesus, his apostles, and other revered persons had lived, worked, and sometimes died.

Not only that, but the early Christians also saw human existence itself as "a pilgrimage through life," as the following four quotes from various historical sources will suggest[2]:

1. [Christians] live each in his native land but as though they were not really at home there [they are only sojourners on the earth]. They all share in the same duties as citizens and suffer all the same hardships as strangers. Every country is a fatherland to them, and every fatherland is a foreign land.... They dwell on earth but they are citizens of heaven [letter to Diognetus, 5, late 2nd century].

2. There are not one but *two* cities on earth: one earthly, and the other heavenly. Their members live alongside one another in this world but hold different values, expectations, and priorities. Christians should see themselves as pilgrims traveling through the world, using its resources but not being ensnared by them [after Augustine of Hippo, 354–430].

3. Let us think where we have our home [i.e., in heaven], and then consider how we might get there [*Seafarer* 117–118: Old English poem, date uncertain].

4. We are in the country of exile of this world; we are exiles, and always have been since the first parent of humankind broke God's commands; and so in sin we were sent on this miserable pilgrimage and now ever after we have to look for another homeland. [Bickling's Homilies II: a collection of 18 Old English homilies compiled in England by two anonymous scribes before the end of the 10th century.]

It should be noted that in the 320s and 330s, Constantine, the first Roman emperor to become a Christian, constructed sumptuous churches at several locations that were already popular tourist destinations. The distinctive features of these buildings were widely copied in other churches, tombs, and baptisteries throughout Europe. Octagonal glass bottles, echoing the forms of Constantine's churches in the Holy Land, were manufactured in bulk and found a ready market among these early pilgrims.

A major destination for many European pilgrims was the city of Rome, which was so much easier and safer to get to than the far-distant Holy Land itself. Rome was cherished as the home of many important martyrs, especially the apostles Peter and Paul. Constantine had caused great basilicas to be erected over their tombs, which pilgrims visited (as well as other locations in Rome), hoping for miraculous cures. Added attractions of Roman sites were the presence of holy relics, the bones or clothing said to be of the saints themselves: to see or handle these items was thought to confer some form of saintliness on the believer.

Although Rome was surpassingly rich in relics, many other places could offer some of their own. In the 11th and 12th centuries, for example, many pilgrims traveled to Santiago de Compostela in northern Spain, where relics of the apostle Saint James the Greater were believed to have been found in about 830. Moreover, in England, Canterbury appealed to English pilgrims, who flocked there to see the miracle-working relics of Thomas Becket, the archbishop of Canterbury who had been martyred by the knights of King Henry II in 1170 and who was canonized not long thereafter.

Before setting out on his or her journey, the prudent pilgrim usually asked for, and received, a blessing from the local bishop. In addition, if this pilgrimage was designed in whole or in part to serve as a penance for sins committed, a full confession was needed first. Then, spiritually well-prepared, the pilgrim donned a long, coarse cloak and carried a heavy leather bag, referred to as a purse, to carry a bit of food and water; a stout, wood walking staff; a broad-brimmed hat for protection against the sun; and a unique, shell-shaped, pilgrim-badge confirming that he or she was in fact en route to Compostela.

The most devout travelers prayed as they walked, and carried prayer books and even portable altars with them. Monasteries, conveniently located about one day's journey apart, provided the pilgrims with more substantial food, lodging, travel updates, masses, and prayers. Pilgrimage became so popular that many churches and monasteries even had to undertake major renovations in order to deal with the ever-larger crowds they were expected to host.

In Paris, for example, what is now the Basilica of Saint-Denis, a

Gothic-style cathedral located close to the city, was dramatically enlarged for this purpose by the remarkable Abbot Suger, whose French name is pronounced "Su-jaire," in the early 12th century. He rebuilt the rear of this abbey church with a majestic, dramatic, wall of stained glass windows which flooded the interior with colored light. Indeed, Suger single-handedly bequeathed a long-lasting popularity to this venerable church.

Today one can get a very good feel for it as a major pilgrimage center of Paris when it was first opened to the public in 1144. The French medievalist Régine Pernoud has described this event at some length along the following colorful lines, which are translated here:

> The road from Paris to Saint Denis was even more congested then than on the days of the annual fairs; pilgrims went there in droves; all the time, heavy carts laden with hay had to stop and make way for groups of priests or a party of nobles whose horses were stamping impatiently, while two dust-covered lay brothers were trying to push a flock of sheep in front of them as best they could.
>
> As they approached Saint Denis, the traffic was becoming even more dense: carts full of sacks of flour, barrels of wine, or mountains of vegetables were being forced into the entrances of little villages. Everything that the market-gardens of the Île de France [the historical center of Paris] could provide had been brought in; in this month of June, it had to come from far away. The King's sergeants, who had come to add their ranks to the sergeants of the abbey, had trouble channeling the hordes of people and animals.
>
> As far as the eye could see, grooms, clerks, and the lower orders were putting up tents on the edges of the fields surrounding Saint Denis in order to find shelter during the three days of ceremonies. They had not been able to find lodgings in the abbey itself or in the town houses, because all these were already taken by high-ranking people.[3]

The theory, practice, and literature of pilgrimage was so entrenched in medieval Europe that it set the tone both for real-life travel and for world-class literature. The nine Crusades, for example, which were mounted over a period of 200 years to conquer the Holy Land, were considered to be a unique and very meritorious form of pilgrimage, as were many of the individual heroic quests attributed to real or fictional knights.

On the literary front, the concept of pilgrimage strongly underlies Chaucer's celebrated *Canterbury Tales*, in which a diverse group of about 30 pilgrims who are en route to Canterbury in England, amuse themselves and pass their travel-time by recounting many interesting stories. The concept of the holy journey also underlies Dante's *Divine Comedy*, which leads the reader through Dante's metaphorical hell and purgatory before finally reaching heaven.

In the later Middle Ages, pilgrims also believed they should travel chiefly in order to win indulgences, the cancelling of spiritual punishment for sins confessed and forgiven. In 1300, Pope Boniface VIII even declared 1300 to be a jubilee year—one in which all pilgrims to Rome, once duly confessed, could receive a plenary indulgence, namely, a full dispensation from any punishment due to any sins committed over the course of an entire lifetime. To some purists and reformers like the mendicant orders, however, such a "blanket dispensation" of sin was thought to be less laudable than what today might jokingly be called the traditional "repent as you go" devotional exercises for the forgiveness of sins.

29

Goliards
Wandering Poets

Goliards were very free-spirited university students who were also low-level clerics.[1] Their unusual name might have come down to us from several possible sources, but the mythical Biblical giant Goliath, who fought King David, is often cited as the most likely of them. In the 12th and 13th centuries these Goliards were generally referred to by students and pranksters alike under the nickname of "Golias," a description which evoked a powerful reaction from some contemporary observers. One of these commentators tells us that

> There was in our own time a certain parasite, Golias by name, notorious alike for his intemperance and his wantonness. He was a tolerable scholar, but without any morals or discipline, who did vomit forth against the Pope and the Roman Curia [the Church] a series of famous [written] pieces, as adroit as they were preposterous, as imprudent as they were impudent, and of his own life and morals also, even writing his own epitaph at the last. What punishment might have been his, if the Curia had ever inflicted corporal punishment on him?[2]

The most important fact here, however, is that because they were officially clerics, the goliards could never be tried for their offenses by the civil courts but only by the far more lenient ecclesiastical courts. In practice, this amounted to a kind of diplomatic immunity which gave them free rein to do just as they pleased. It also gives modern readers today a unique insight into their remarkable subculture of medieval life.

Goliards wrote biting satirical poetry, sang scurrilous songs, and gave public performances, all designed to call attention to the many shortcomings they perceived in the Church, in the universities, and in the medieval status quo. The goliardic way of life itself basically arose from the need of bored younger sons to find a way to amuse and support themselves in an era when the policy of primogeniture always gave a family's title, land, and other assets only to the oldest son.

These younger sons, of whom there were a great many, were often sent off to the universities and monasteries to be taught theology, which was a requirement for any middle class, or clerical, career. However, many of these bright but lazy young men felt no attraction whatsoever toward the rigors of the religious life. Even if they had very much wanted to join it, there were in fact very few openings because of the great surplus of over-educated and under-motivated clerics who were always vaguely looking for a temporary job.

In the lack of anything better to do, many of the goliards passed their university days drinking wine, chasing women, living vagabond lives, and writing satirical anti-establishment poetry. One of the biggest and most famous collections of goliardic poetry is the German *Carmina Burana* ("*Songs from Beuren*" of c. 1225–1250), which includes about 315 poems and love songs, mostly written in Latin. Set to music in 1935 by Carl Orff, *Carmina Burana* is probably the most frequently performed choral work of the 21st century.

In some regions, goliards also staged a "Celebration of the Ass." In it, a donkey outfitted in a ridiculous costume was paraded to the rail around the altar of a local church, while a singer chanted a song of praise. Whenever he paused for breath, the audience would bellow: "He Haw, Sire Ass, He Haw!"

Most of the goliards were "students without masters"—that is, students who did not have any permanent teacher but who studied (if at all) only where, when, and with whom they pleased. However, it is precisely because of their footloose, promiscuous, irregular way of life—very similar to that of the hippies of the 1970s, it might well be said—that they can give us such a refreshingly candid glimpse into the seamier side of medieval university life. One of their lapidary songs is the well-known *Gaudeamus igitur* ("Let us rejoice"), which is still very widely used today both as a beer-drinking song in European universities and at formal university graduations. Originally based on a Latin manuscript of 1287, the English text of it is roughly as follows:

> Let us therefore rejoice
> While we are young.
> Let us therefore rejoice
> While we are young.
> After a pleasant youth
> After the troubles of old age
> The earth will have us.
>
> Life is short and all too soon
> We emit our final gasp;
> Death ere long is on our back
> Terrible is his attack;
> None escapes his dread grasp.

Long live our academy,
Teachers we cherish;
Long life to all the graduates;
And to the undergraduates;
Ever may they flourish.

Long live our society,
Scholars wise and learned;
May truth and sincerity
Nourish our fraternity
And our land's prosperity.

May our Alma Mater thrive,
A fount of education;
Friends and colleages, wherever they are
Whether from near or from afar,
Heed her invitation.[3]

It is thought that during the Middle Ages there were about 4,000 taverns in Paris alone, which sold a total of some 700 barrels of wine every day. Some 60 of these taverns were special favorites of the Paris students. This famous goliard poem, translated below from Latin, is probably a good example of them:

In a tavern to die
Is my resolution;
Let wine to my lips be nigh
At life's dissolution;
That will make the angels cry
With glad elocution,
"Grant this boozer, God on high,
Grace and absolution!"[4]

30

François Villon

Murder and Poetry in Medieval France

During the 15th century, the University of Paris issued many regulations trying to control its unruly students who were jokingly likened to the small flighty birds known as *martinets* ("swifts"). The best known of them today was the French poet François Villon, who was born in 1431 and died sometime after 1463.[1]

These young men were relatively well-educated but they had few if any means of support. They therefore wandered at will throughout Paris; engaged in petty crime; spent most of their endless free time in bars; and consorted with the *fillettes* ("girlies"), the young women of good looks and loose morals.

Villon was without doubt the most famous *criminal* graduate of the University of Paris in medieval times—following, entirely by his own choice, a sordid life of illegal excesses. As long as he was still a university student, he was also still a cleric and therefore could not be tried for his offences by anything but a church court.

After he received a master of arts degree, however, Villon killed a priest in a knife-fight in 1452 in self-defense; spent time in jail on numerous other charges; and was in such serious trouble so often that he was ultimately sentenced to death, i.e., to be "hanged and strangled."

Being very bright and articulate, Villon managed to talk his way out of this fatal penalty and was instead barred for 10 years from living in Paris. Always unrepentant, however, he wrote (in French) that, after his death,

> At least there will be a memory of me
> As one who was a merry madcap.[2]

It must be remembered that sudden or slow death was certainly no stranger in medieval Paris. It waited for victims in the filth of the roads, the alleys, and the tenements. It dangled in front of them from the gallows, where prosperous and healthy Parisians sometimes held midnight picnics near the rancid corpses swaying at rope's-end in the breeze. The certainty of death, and the urgent need to repent *right now*, was the main point of many vivid sermons preached by priests in the churches and by itinerant friars in the streets.

So many of Villon's low-life friends did in fact end up on the gallows that he paid an ironic but moving tribute to them in his famous *Ballade des Pendus* (*Ballad of the Hanged Men*). Two of its stanzas are given below in English:

> My brothers who live after us,
> Don't harden your hearts against us too,
> If you have mercy on us now,
> God may have mercy upon you.
> Five, six, you see us, hung out to view.
> When the flesh that nourished us so well
> Is eaten piecemeal, ah, see it swell,
> And we, the bones, are dust and gall,
> Let no one make fun of our ill,
> But pray that God absolves us all!

> The rain has soaked us, washed us: skies
> Of hot suns blacken us, scorch us: crows
> And magpies have gouged out our eyes,
> Plucked at our beards, and our eyebrows.
> There's never a moment's rest allowed:
> Now here, now there, the changing breeze
> Swings us, as it wishes, ceaselessly,
> Beaks pricking us more than a cobbler's awl.
> So don't you join our fraternity,
> But pray that God absolves us all.[3]

Villon himself was very lucky. In 1463 the *parlement* of Paris granted his appeal that his death sentence should be commuted to banishment from Paris for 10 years. At this point, then 32 years old, he disappears from the historical record for good. Perhaps to make up for his many crimes, however, he has left to posterity some very fine work.

One of the most famous lines of European secular poetry for example, is his rhetorical question *Mais où sont les neiges d'antan?* ("But where are the snows of yesteryear?")—a question that nostalgically evokes the fleeting beauty of all lovely women.

31

Limiting the Number of Monks

As indicated in the Preface, this book does not try to cover monastic life in any detail after about 1259, which can be considered to be near or at the very end of the High Middle Ages.

After that era, because of the economic problems and other constraints (discussed in this chapter), many of the Benedictine abbeys and priories that had flourished earlier now gradually slid into a downward spiral of decay.[1] Social and economic support for the monasteries tended to dwindle and, especially in England, monastic lands, buildings, and worldly goods would be seized by the king in the 1530s and sold or given to new owners. Well before then, the bottom line was that, for a variety of reasons, the number of monks who could easily be recruited to staff the monasteries fell sharply. The reasons for this sea-change included:

- Local decisions by the monasteries to accept only an ever-smaller number of child-oblates.
- Raising the age of admission to about 18 for young-adult candidates wishing to join monasteries.
- The growing appeal of the mendicant orders themselves, which attracted the most ascetically-motivated applicants who (1) wanted to travel and (2) did not have any interest in spending their entire working lives in only one monastery.
- Ever-increasing financial pressures, which forced the monasteries to tighten their belts and to reduce the size of their monastic staffs.

There were many clear signs of these changes. In 1200, for example, the abbey of Cluny imposed a limit on the number of its monks and accepted far fewer new recruits. The records of the Cluniac houses in England set a fixed quota of members that was not to be exceeded. In France, in 1234 the abbey of Corbie set an optimum number of only 40 monks. The abbey of Fleury limited itself to 45 monks. In 1340, the monks of Montéliou in southern France froze their number at 37 and slowed the whole application process. The Norman abbey of Mont-Saint-Michel set its number of monks at 40 to keep it within new financial limitations.

Sometimes monastic problems were more social than economic. Monasteries in Germany, for example, admitted as postulants only the sons and daughters of the local nobility. In one such case, Pope Benedict roundly criticized the management of the Reichenau monastery, which formerly had a community of 90 people. By 1339, due to its policy of social exclusiveness, only eight or ten monks were left—not enough to conduct religious services at an acceptable level.

In addition, many of the older monasteries in the European Middle Ages found that their dwindling annual incomes made it impossible for them to pay all the corrodies they had agreed to pay. A corrody was a pension, variously in the form of room-and-board, or food, or money, which was legally owed by a monastery to a lay person, who had often bought it as a long-term investment for himself and his wife. When the monastery could not pay the corrodian (the investor himself), to do so it was then forced to borrow funds from money-lenders at very high interest rates.

Another monastic problem of this era was what in canon law was known as *commendam* or *in commendam*. Essentially, this was the process of temporarily transferring, *in trust,* an ecclesiastical benefice, i.e., a source of income from a church source, to the custody of a given individual for whatever use he thought best. This process did not directly affect the potential *supply* of new monks but, when abused, it certainly could adversely affect the *quality* of abbots and other high-ranking church officials once they were in power. This fact may well have had a chilling trickle-down effect on monastic recruitment at the entry-level of the profession.

The *in commendam* issue dates from at least 379, when the Bishop of Milan mentioned, in a letter, a church that he had recently given *in commendam.* He wrote: "*Commendo tibi, fili, Ecclesiam quae est ad Forum Cornelii ... donc ei ordinetur episcopus.*" ("I entrust unto thee, my son, the church which is at the Cornelian Forum ... until a bishop is allotted to it.") In practice, a temporarily-unoccupied church property could be given to any responsible member of the church *in commendam*, to safeguard and manage it until a new permanent holder was found for it and was granted a legal title to it. A benefice held *in commendam* could also be used to provide an income for a temporary administrator of a church then in financial difficulty. Gregory the Great (590–604) gave vacant monasteries *in commendam* to bishops who had been driven out of their churches by the invading "barbarians" (the Germanic or other foreign invaders who did not speak Latin) or whose own churches were too poor to provide them with a respectable living.

This whole process, of course, easily lent itself to great abuses. In the 8th century, kings appointed their favorite layman-vassals as abbots *in commendum* over monasteries, simply as a way of rewarding them. These men did not have to provide any spiritual care for the monks under their charge, but they did have the right to manage—and to profit from—the financial affairs of a specific monastery, which was sometimes ruined financially as a result. Although the appointment of laymen *in commendam* was abolished in 1122, clergymen could still be named as commendatory abbots. This practice was used to give an income to a professor, a clerical student, a priest, or a cardinal, while another man actually carried out the daily responsibilities that this position involved.

Not surprisingly, abuses continued to flourish. Favored cardinals received multiple benefices. They acted like secular absentee landlords by increasing their personal possessions, rather than working for the well-being of the Church and its believers. Later, these arrangements were no longer only temporary but could instead be held for a lifetime. The end losers were, of course, the monasteries themselves, who were deprived of their income and some of their former prestige and were thus likely to drift downhill as a result.

A good example is the ancient abbey in Rome known in English as St. Paul's-Without-the-Walls. By 1409, it contained only six monks, two of which were absent. Its sad story is quickly and easily told:

> Its abbot was a secular cleric [a priest but not a monk], a cardinal in fact, who had received [the abbey] *in commendam* from the pope, and who enjoyed its revenues while residing in his palace in another quarter of the city. Any semblance of regular observance [of religious services] in the abbey had long since ceased.[2]

In the late Middle Ages—from about 1250 to 1500—English monasticism was not in very good shape, either. This is beyond most of the years covered in this book, but it is important to reveal a bit about the coming era.[3] For the monks and the canons regular, the late Middle Ages were a very difficult time indeed. Many of their institutions had landowners on a large scale and thus suffered from the economic and social consequences of the bubonic plague. In addition, ambitious abbots usually wanted to expand their monasteries or at least to keep them in a good state of repair. Both efforts were far more easily said than done at an era of dwindling incomes.[4]

To compensate for declining rents and rising labor costs, some abbots vigorously enforced their medieval rights as lordly landowners—a move that is thought to explain the noted hostility towards them displayed by rebellious peasants in 1381. Moreover, they also leased out more of their abbeys' lands and now took direct control of their monasteries' revenues by deleting the monastic income traditionally earmarked for their own lower-ranking monks.

The monasteries were especially hard-hit by Black Death mortalities; in some, half or more of the monks died. Moreover, new recruits for the English monasteries were not socially of high standing. They were drawn from the middling and smaller landowning classes and from the average persons of the towns. A sign of these more modest times was that the number of major abbots who sat as lords in Parliament declined in the late Middle Ages, and some abbots even persuaded the king to excuse them and their successors from any parliamentary service whatsoever.

In the smaller monasteries, matters could run downhill very rapidly in the absence of any effective monastic supervision. For example, when Bishop Alnwick of Lincoln paid an official visit to a monastery in Dorchester in 1441, he found that the canons were going fox hunting and hawking and were frequenting taverns. Women had visited the room of the monk Thomas Tewksbury in the evening. The abbot himself was accused of keeping no fewer than five mistresses at the monastery's expense.[5]

Conditions in English convents seem to have been comparable to those in the religious houses for men, though the convents tended to be poorer. Visitation records suggest that there were plenty of places where discipline had ebbed, but with some understandable male-female differences in tone. For example, the bishop had to caution the ladies of Nun Monkton "not to use henceforth silken clothes, and especially silken veils, nor precious furs, nor rings on their fingers nor tunics laced up or furnished with brooches ... after the manner of secular women."[6]

Still, sex was always a problem in the nunneries. At Catesby in 1442 Bishop Alnwick was told that the prioress had been discovered in the arms of the priest William Taylor; that the nun Isabel Barnet had borne a child fathered by the chaplain of the house; that at Godstow, Oxford scholars often visited the convent; and that Dame Alice Longsprey had been carrying on an affair with a chaplain whom she pretended was her relative. Nevertheless, despite such lapses, it is thought that the moral record of the convents was, on the whole, rather better than those of the male houses.[7] In broader terms, as a modern English medievalist has noted,

Traditionally, any study of English monasticism during the late Middle Ages entailed the chronicling of a slow decline and decay. Indeed, for nearly 500 years, historiographical discourse surrounding the Dissolution of Monasteries [by King Henry VIII] has emphasized its inevitability and presented late medieval monasticism as a lackluster institution characterized by worsening standards, corruption and even sexual promiscuity. As a result, since the Dissolution, English monks and nuns have been constructed into naughty characters.[8]

The bottom-line conclusion reached by this medievalist, however, was much more positive. He found that, in the medieval English monasteries of Lincoln and Norwich, reports of monastic sexual misconduct occurred only at very low and predictable rates. While nearly half of the monasteries he studied did have, over a 100-year-long period, some good examples of monastic sexual misconduct, the contemporary bishops were in fact much more concerned with the important economic and leadership issues facing them than with any failings of monastic chastity.

Moreover, these bishops were able to deal with such failings chiefly by selecting one or more remedies from what we may call their "ecclesiastical toolbox." These included high-level inspection visits by religious officials; compurgation—i.e., finding 12 men who were willing to swear they believed a defendant's oath that he was innocent; various degrees of penance; and written orders to erring monks telling them to repent and to behave correctly.[9] It is likely, however, that sexual scandals, even if infrequent, did tend to lower the public esteem in which monasteries and nunneries were held.

32

The Avignon Papacy

In the complicated historical eras variously known as the Babylonian Captivity of the Papacy (1309–1376) and as the Western Schism of the Roman Catholic Church (1378–1417), a series of popes reigned in Avignon and other locations, rather than in Rome, which had long been the traditional seat of the papacy.[1] To examine the adverse effects that developments in these two eras had on monasticism in the late Middle Ages, the first step must be to explain these eras in general terms and skipping most of their very complicated details.

The move of the papacy from Rome to the French city of Avignon basically arose from a struggle between the papacy and the French crown. This struggle culminated in the death of Pope Boniface XIII in 1303, shortly after his arrest and maltreatment by the forces of King Philip IV of France.

Following the death of Pope Benedict XI two years later, King Philip forced the deadlocked papal conclave to elect the Frenchman Clement V as pope in 1305. Clement, however, simply refused to move to Rome, arguing that it would be too dangerous a seat for him, and in 1309 he set up his own court in the safety of the papal enclave in Avignon, where it would remain for the next 67 years.

A total of seven popes would reign there—all of them French and all of them serving under the heavy hand of the French crown. Yves Renouard (1908–1965), arguably the most famous French scholar who studied the Avignon papacy, concluded that, because of their secure and stable location in Avignon, the popes were able—thanks chiefly to the continued support of the French crown—to transform the Church into a "pontifical monarchy."[2]

It should be noted that Catholic historiography grants legitimacy to the seven popes who resided in Avignon:

- Pope Clement V (1305–1314)
- Pope John XXII (1316–1334)
- Pope Benedict XII (1334–1342)

- Pope Clement VI (1342–1352)
- Pope Innocent VI (1352–1362)
- Pope Urban V (1362–1370)
- Pope Gregory XI (1370–1378)

Avignon became the favored location for the papacy when it was not in Rome because Avignon was so safe, being entirely surrounded by the lands of the papal fief known as Comtat Venaissin. This fief was firmly under the political and military control of the French king.

The many French cardinals who lived there quickly adopted very lavish life-styles that were far more suitable for high-ranking secular princes rather than living modestly as "men of God." More and more French cardinals, often the relatives of the pope-in-power at the moment, were also given very lucrative—but very undemanding—jobs in the sprawling church bureaucracy. In this refractory climate there were also two Avignon-based "anti-popes," i.e., men who, in opposition to the legitimately-elected pope, tried to usurp his position. They were Clement VII (1378–1394) and Benedict XIII (1394–1423).

At times between the 3rd and mid–15th centuries, the antipopes were supported both by powerful factions within the Church itself and by secular rulers. As a result, sometimes it was impossible for the clergy and the faithful alike to distinguish which of the two (or sometimes even *three*) rival claimants should be called "pope" and which "antipope." This was indeed the case between Pope Leo VIII and Pope Benedict V.

Benedict XIII was succeeded by three antipopes, who did not reside in Avignon and had little or no public following: Clement VIII (1423–1429), Benedict XV (1424–1429 or 1430), and Benedict XIV (1430?–1437).

The period from 1378 to 1417, when there were several rival claimants to the title of pope, is now known as the Western Schism. Sardonic local commentators reportedly joked that, during this troubled era, *no one got to heaven.* Conditions improved only in 1417, when Pope Martin V was elected and was accepted by all of the opposing factions. While all of the above was going on, the fact that the Church had become a great temporal power in its own right led to a number of major abuses of this power. Under Clement V and John XIII, for example, the Church directly controlled the distribution of lucrative benefices, rather than continuing the former practice of using Church-run elections for this purpose. Moreover, the Holy See and its cardinals could also profit from other streams of riches. Some of these included the following:

- A 10 percent tax, known as "tithes," on Church property.
- The income of the first year generated by a bishop newly-installed in his office, called "annates."

- Special taxes for crusades that would never in fact be launched.
- Waiving some key clerical requirements, such as the need for a man to be able to read in order to hold a benefice.

These income streams were generous enough to permit some popes, e.g., John XXII, Benedict XII, and Clement VI, to spend vast amounts of Church funds on lavish wardrobes for their personal wear and on silver and gold plates for their banquet entertaining. This endemic corruption at the top-most ranks of the Church must have had a trickle-down effect that corrupted some of the men in the lower ranks as well. For example, because a new bishop had to pay a year's income simply in order to keep his benefice, he was under enormous pressure to make enough money from his new office to pay off this debt. While the mendicants did not face this particular problem, Chaucer and other contemporary observers make it clear to us that the mendicants were often "on the take."

Such abuses chipped away at the public relations image of the Church and greatly strengthened the movements calling for a return to the simple poverty and selfless life-styles of Christ himself and his apostles. The current scale of this corruption was simply enormous. As the historian Barbara Tuchman tells us,

> Besides its regular revenues from the tithes and annates on ecclesiastical income and from dues from papal fiefs, every office, every nomination, every appointment or preferment, every dispensation of the rules, every judgment ... or adjudication of a claim, every pardon, every indulgence, and absolution, everything the Church had or was, from cardinal's hat to pilgrim's relic, was for sale....
>
> The collection and accounting of all these sums, largely handled through Italian bankers, made the physical counting of money a common sight in the papal palace. Whenever he entered there, reported Alvar Pelayo, a Spanish official of the Curia [the administrative institutions of the Holy See], "I found brokers and clergy engaged in reckoning the money which lay in heaps before them."[3]

The work force deployed to build and equip the lavish papal palace averaged about 600 men, despite occasional labor shortages caused by such tumultuous events as the Hundred Years War and the Black Death.

A high point (or a low point, depending upon one's own point of view) of the prodigious papal income and spending process was the construction, maintenance, and furnishings, wall hangings and mural paintings, of the massive fortress-and-palace of the popes in Avignon during the 14th century. Consisting of both the old palace of Benedict XII and the new palace of Clement VI, this was the biggest Gothic palace in the world, and since 1995 it has been on the World Heritage List of UNESCO.

The staff of the Curia, which had totaled only about 200 men at the end of the 13th century, had risen to 300 at the beginning of the 14th century, and reached 500 in 1316. These estimates do not include the more than 1,000 lower-ranking supporting officials who also worked in the palace. Such a swollen bureaucracy was but one of the many self-generated problems faced by the Avignon papacy.

Simony—that is, the buying and selling of ecclesiastical privileges (for example, pardons or benefices)—was very widespread during the Avignon Papacy and further tarnished the reputation of the Church. In addition, the papacy's public standing was also gravely damaged by its inability to reform itself; to end the 100 Years' War; and, during the Black Death, to provide for the living and the dying the holy sacraments which the Avignon Papacy itself had asserted were absolutely essential for salvation.

Assessment

The Inherent Features of Medieval Monastic Life in Western Europe

Only after the rules governing monastic life were first laid down in the 6th century did monasticism flourish in Western Europe. These rules, grounded in obedience and often in cloistered living, stressed the importance of the monks' intellectual work. Their painstaking studies, transmissions, and illuminations of biblical and literary Latin texts are among the most sturdy foundations of Western culture today.

Unlike the monks, however, who could not leave their own monasteries without permission from their abbot, the mendicant friars of later centuries were highly mobile, preaching widely and administering to all those who would listen to them. In time, they in fact became the most vital part of the Church itself.

Taken as a whole, the practices, liturgies, and medical knowledge of medieval monasticism were of great benefit during the recurrent years of war, invasion, famine, and plague. The monasteries also contributed to social stability by offering honorable careers to relatively well-educated men and women, as well as to the many manual workers on which the monasteries depended.

The eventual establishment of close to 900 religious houses in England alone, as well as the proliferation of them in continental Europe, speaks not only to the success of the monastic way of life. Monastic labor contributed significantly to the economy of the Middle Ages. In the 13th century alone, the Church could, in theory at least, call upon the services of up to 20,000 monks, canons, nuns, and members of the monastic military orders. Extensive public works programs recruited some of these men and women and set them to work on land reclamation, road building and maintenance, iron works, and various charitable ways to help the poor.

Although the monasteries always spent more than they earned and would ultimately be forced to economize by sharply reducing their intake of men and women who wanted to become monks or nuns, their single greatest economic success during the Middle Ages was producing wine. It was the Benedictine Order that did the most to develop the monks' special skills in this field. Not only did those in residence in the monasteries and nunneries drink wine themselves (usually, but not always, in moderation), but it was both a point of honor and a very good investment to pour out the best vintages to impress important guests. Indeed, wine production was so important that it influenced the growth of French towns and the politics of the national government itself.

What monastic wine production did for France, monastic sheep farming did for England. The wool trade pioneered by the monks was one of the key reasons for the prosperity of the medieval English economy. It was by ceaselessly "turning grass into wool" that huge numbers of sheep provided the essential raw material for the English woolen cloth-weaving industry.

The rise of the universities in the 12th century gradually evolved into one of the most important center of medieval life. After a long tussle over academic and religious issues, the masters—the professors—of the universities usually gained the upper hand and subsequently directed the students of the independently-minded mendicant orders to abide by university regulations, rather than adhering solely to dictates of their often-distant monastic superiors.

Over a period of time, the free-spirited students known as goliards proliferated in the universities. Having no interest in academic achievements, they took advantage of the legal protection afforded to them by their status as clerics and delighted in writing biting satirical poems criticizing many of the shortcomings of the Church and its monastic and mendicant orders.

Although not a goliard himself, the poet François Villon was the most famous *criminal graduate* of the University of Paris. Primarily known for his *ubi sunt* ("where are they now") poetry, he paid a moving tribute in verse to the many men who were hanged for their major or minor crimes and whose bodies dangled in the wind, every day on public display, from the gallows.

Today, despite the fact that he died before the University of Paris was founded, Peter Abelard is recognized as the intellectual cornerstone of that famous university. Totally committed to academic and religious studies, he was an exceptionally able man, being the founder of scholastic philosophy;, the greatest logician of the Middle Ages, the first great Nominalist philosopher, and, finally, a very fine writer. A creative free thinker, his tragic affair with his student, Heloise, resulted in his being castrated by his enemies, thus resulting in his also becoming a tragic figure of love.

Eustache, born 28 years after the death of Abelard, was no intellectual. Known as the French monk-turned-pirate, he is, however, another memorable figure of the Middle Ages. His swashbuckling tale serves as a prototype for later legendary and more admirable characters, such as Robin Hood. In the medieval era, however, distinctions between "good" and "evil" were rarely ambivalent, and the anonymous poet's account in Old French makes no bones about stressing Eustache's truly "diabolical nature."

For women, the Middle Ages was, generally speaking, a man's world. If she was of noble birth and had the necessary financial means, a woman could pursue an ascetical life in a nunnery among others of her social class. The explosion of nunneries that occurred from roughly 1070 to 1170, however, arose out of a complex of women's aspirations and opportunities facilitated primarily by the demographic and economic growth of the societies of which they were a part. This was a time for nuns like Hildegard von Bingen, women who could make their mark as abbesses and scholars largely because they could read and write in Latin. Beguines, who were very devout women but who lived outside the formal structure of the Church, managed to pursue their own vocation into the 21st century.

Not surprisingly, monks and friars are much better known today than their female counterparts, both because there were more assignment opportunities in the Church for men than for women, and because, knowing Latin, it was much easier for men to get their literary output disseminated widely, even when it was quite critical of the established order.

Jean de Venette (1307–after 1368), a Carmelite friar and French chronicler, is a good case in point. Writing in Latin, he gives us an eyewitness report on the events following the defeat of the French King Jean II le Bon (John II the Good) at the battle of Poitiers in 1356 during the Hundred Years War. Unique in his perspective, Jean de Venette, pointing to the sufferings and deprivations of the peasantry, implicitly condemns the plundering by the mercenaries and nobles in the wake of the English victory. In this instance, Jean de Venette serves as a valuable check on a historical event that his contemporaries might otherwise have conveniently decided to ignore.

The Black Death, i.e., the bubonic plague that swept through Western Europe and elsewhere, peaking in the years 1347–1351 and decimating life in the medieval world, also had unexpected, ironic benefits. The deaths of roughly 75 million to 100 million people resulted in acute labor shortages which ultimately befitted and empowered the surviving peasants and other manual workers. As a consequence, the highly conservative medieval economic and social pyramid was drastically and permanently altered.

Monasticism was greatly altered, too. The extremely corrupt Avignon

Papacy of 1309–1417 was very badly tarnished by its selling of pardons and benefices; by its failure to end the Hundred Years War; and by its failure to provide sacraments during the Black Death—the sacraments which the papacy itself had declared to be absolutely necessary for salvation.

Towards the end of the 14th century, the manuscripts and literature of the day mirrored the increasing disillusionment of the faithful. Latin gave way to vernacular languages, and Geoffrey Chaucer's *Canterbury Tales*, was written not only in Middle English but also reflected, very critically, the shifting public attitudes toward medieval religious professionals.

As an observer of contemporary life and people, Chaucer was both psychologically and sociologically insightful, satirizing human greed, lust, and earthly power, whether among the religious or the laity. A man of faith himself, his personal perspective on his times is expressed in part of the Clerk's Tale, where Chaucer ruefully notes: "This world of ours, it has to be confessed, / Is not so sturdy as it was of old."

As in Chaucer's pilgrimage, men and women of the time traveled chiefly in order the earn indulgences, i.e., the cancellation of punishment for sins confessed and forgiven, but also in order to see interesting new sights and to have new experiences. The following three observations might get at the heart of monastic life:

First: It was widely believed that the monastic way of life was *as close to the angels as we sinful human beings can ever hope to get.* The faithful felt that this way of life was therefore well-worth pursuing by any man or woman who had the ability and the financial resources to do so.

Second: Christian monasticism has had *remarkable staying-power.* By creating a new, alternate, and, to many believers, heavenly-sanctioned religious institution within the body of the established Church, abbots and monks created something new under the sun. Its continuing attraction is shown by the fact that there are about 3,600 Roman Catholic abbeys and monasteries in the world today.

Third: Medieval monastic life addressed, often successfully, many of the most important practical and religious issues of the day. As a result, the monastic orders usually had more than enough recruits.

APPENDIX 1

The Medieval Renaissance of the 12th Century

This remarkable intellectual and cultural renaissance witnessed the origins of the universities, towns, and the sovereign state; the recovery of Greek science and of much Greek philosophy; the revival of the Latin classics, poetry, and Roman law; the beginnings of Gothic art; the emergence of vernacular languages; and, last but never least, the exciting intellectual adventure of gingerly applying to medieval theology the bold new concept of humanism, namely, *secularism*.

The medieval renaissance was not self-evident to contemporary observers and was not widely reported by most later scholars, either. This state of affairs probably lasted until 1927, when the brilliant Harvard scholar Charles Homer Haskins chronicled it in his famous book of that year, entitled *The Renaissance of the Twelfth Century*. It is the chief source of much of what follows here.[1]

Haskins' basic point, as presented both in that book and his other writings, e.g., in *The Rise of Universities* published in 1923, is that between the years 1100 and 1200 a great river of knowledge flowed into Western Europe, chiefly through the Arab scholars of Spain.

The most industrious and most prolific of all these translators from the Arabic was the Italian scholar Gerard of Cremona. Before he died in Toledo in 1187, he had translated into Latin more than 71 Arabic works, many of them on scientific subjects. It is said that more of Arab science passed into Western Europe through the hands of Gerald of Cremona (1114–1187) than in any other way.[2] This influx included the works of Aristotle, Euclid, Ptolemy, and the Greek physicians; a study of arithmetic new to Western European eyes; and the long-forgotten texts of imperial Roman law. The importance of such a flood of learning cannot be overestimated today. As Haskins himself aptly put it,

This new knowledge burst the bonds of the cathedral and monastery schools and created the learned professions; it drew over mountains and narrow seas

175

eager youths who, like Chaucer's clerk of a later day, "would gladly learn and gladly teach," to form in Paris and Bologna those academic guilds which have given us our first and our best definition of a university, a society of masters and scholars.[3]

It is worth repeating here that the university is indigenous to Western Europe and is the greatest and most enduring achievement of the Middle Ages. Humanity will therefore always be in the debt of the usually-unnamed medieval monastics who helped to build and to sustain this most-valuable international institution.

APPENDIX 2

The Canticle of the Sun

This canticle was written by St. Francis in about 1224. The following translation from the Umbrian dialect was made by the Franciscan Friars Third Order Regular and has been shortened and lightly edited for use here:

> Most High, all powerful, good Lord,
> Yours are the praises, the glory, the honour, and all blessing....
>
> Be praised, my Lord, through all your creatures,
> especially through my lord Brother Sun,
> who brings the day; and you give light through him.
> And he is beautiful and radiant in all his splendour!
> Of you, Most High, he bears the likeness.
>
> Praised be You, my Lord, through Sister Moon
> and the stars,
> in heaven you formed them clear and precious
> and beautiful.
>
> Praised be You, my Lord, through Brother Wind,
> and through the air, cloudy and serene,
> and every kind of weather through which
> You give sustenance to Your creatures.
>
> Praised be you, my Lord, through Sister Water,
> which is very useful and humble and precious and chaste.
>
> Praised be You, my Lord, through Brother Fire,
> through whom You light the night, and he is beautiful
> and playful and robust and strong.
>
> Praised be You, my Lord, through Sister Mother Earth,
> who sustains us and governs us and who produces
> varied fruits with coloured flowers and herbs....
>
> Praised by You, my Lord,
> through our sister Bodily Death,
> from whom no living man can escape....
>
> Praise and bless my Lord,
> and give Him thanks
> and serve Him with great humility.

APPENDIX 3

"The Splendors of Avignon and the Evils of the Times"

This chapter draws on the judgments reached in 1969 by the French scholar Édouard Baratier (1923–1972), a specialist in the history of Marseille and of Provence, which were published that year in his book, *Histoire de Provence*. Selections from it, very lightly edited below, will offer modern readers both some interesting history and some vivid local color.

Baratier's views were very extensive and were presented in nearly 600 pages of text; paraphrased below are only the specific points he made when highlighting "the splendors of Avignon and the evils of the times."

Baratier explained that, in this era, papal power in Avignon was represented by a Church official who was appointed by the pope and who presided over both the politics and the laws of the city. In practice, however, there was a considerable difference between the long-settled permanent residents of Avignon, on the one hand, and the newly-arrived "courtesans," as they were called, on the other. The latter formed a great "crowd of new immigrants" who swarmed in and around the papal court. They included clerics who were assigned to assorted Church duties; lawyers; merchants; and numerous small-scale dealers in foods, artifacts, and services. Many of these men were Italians.

However, the arrival of the popes in Avignon (they knew the area well because some of them were originally from southwestern France) also tugged along in their wake a huge and motley clientele of parents, friends, compatriots, hangers-on, providers of food or other goods, and bureaucrats from all over southeastern France. Ironically, however, very few of these newcomers were from Provence itself. The bottom line, in any case, was that finding enough food and lodging in Avignon for all of them raised difficult administrative and logistical issues. Papal officers were even obliged to requisition private apartments and to impose taxes on homeowners there in order to deal with this unexpected flood of immigrants.

If living in Avignon was then increasingly expensive, it had many free or inexpensive compensations to offer. These included attending the public installations and the funerals of the popes; watching the regal comings-and-goings of visiting sovereigns and of resident ambassadors; eating and drinking very well; and simply enjoying the see-and-be-seen buzz of the city's streets at night. Large numbers of candles made of fine-quality fat lit up the pavements. The net result was that both the tone of urban life in Avignon and the physical appearance of the city itself were transformed by the very presence of the popes.

The countryside around Avignon shared in this prosperity. The enormous culinary needs of such a nearby big city were a great boon to the local farmers and to the men and women living in the small towns around Avignon. To some extent, most of them could participate in, and profit from, the growing number of chiefly Italian-backed businesses catering to the papal court.

Doing well economically was easier now because the general prosperity was also reflected in much lower interest rates. Moreover, later administrative reforms in the government structure of Provence would, at least in theory, help local residents to play, if necessary, a more active role in trying to defend their homes and crops against any roving bands of desperate, out-of-work, mercenary soldiers. This theory, however, was never put to the test.

The real "evils of the times," however, were not far off. The Black Death (bubonic plague) hit Provence and other parts of Western Europe hard in and after 1348. Entire families were wiped out; the plague became a pandemic, "surging here and there in certain towns and their environs until the middle of the 15th century."

Plague was not the only calamity that affected Provence and its neighbors: famines or at least food shortages were other curses. During the later Middle Ages, private and Church manors often tried to become self-sufficient in wheat or other grains. In these cases, there was not much trade after poor harvests: shortfalls then could spark a localized but still-deadly famine. Due to successive bad harvests in Provence, for example, there was an "especially cruel famine" between 1368 and 1375.[1]

APPENDIX 4

A Medieval Pilgrimage to Jerusalem

William Wey (1407?–1476) was an English traveler and author. He graduated from Oxford with both a master's degree and a divinity degree at some point before the autumn of 1430, when he became a Fellow of Exeter College in England. He later became a monk. His pilgrimage to Jerusalem took place in 1457.

The following account is drawn from *The Itineraries of William Wey*, published in London by the Roxburghe Club in 1857, and is used here from Harvard University's Geoffrey Chaucer Website (see bibliography). It is long but well worth reading because it gives such a good feel for medieval pilgrimage travel. Lightly edited here but with phrasing, spelling, and punctuation retained as in the original, it reads as follows:

A good provision when a man at Venice purposeth, by the grace of God, to pass by the sea unto Port Jaffa in the Holy Land and so to the sepulchre of our Lord Christ Jesu in Jerusalem. He must dispose him in this wise:

First, if ye go in a galley, make your covenant with the patron in the said galley in the overest stage [the top deck], for in the lowest under it is right smouldering hot and stinking. And ye shall pay for your galley and for your meat and drink to Port Jaffa and again to Venice forty ducats for to be in a good honest place and to have ease in the galley and also to be cherished [treated very well].

Also, when ye shall your covenant take [make an agreement with the captain of the ship], take good heed that the patron [the captain] be bound unto you, afore the manner of covenants with you. That is to say, that he shall conduct you to certain havens [ports] by the way to refresh you and to get you fresh water and fresh bread and flesh. Also, that he shall not tarry longer at none haven than three days at the most, without consent of you all. And that he shall not take into the vessel, neither going nor coming, no manner of merchandise without your will, to distress you in your places and also for tarrying of passage by the sea. And by the havens he shall lead you, if you will: in the water also. Also, that your patron give you every day hot meat twice, at two meals: in the morning at dinner and after noon at supper, and that the wine that ye shall drink be good and your water fresh (if you may come thereto) and also biscuit.

Also, ye must ordain for yourself and your fellow [servant], if you have any, three barrels, each of a quarter, which quarter holdeth ten gallons: two of these barrels shall serve for wine and the third for water. In the one barrel take [put] red wine and keep it ever in store, and tame it not [do not open it] if ye may till ye come homeward again without sickness cause it or any other need. For ye shall in this special note: an yet had the flux, if ye would give twenty ducats for a barrel ye shall none have after ye much pass Venice. And that other barrel shall serve when ye have drunk up your drinking wine, to fill again at the haven where ye next come to.

Also, ye must buy a chest to put in Your things; and if you may have a fellow with you, two or three. I would then buy a chest that were as a broad as the barrel were long. In the one end I would have lock and key and a little door, and lay that same barrel, that I would spend [use] first at the same door-end—for if the galleymen or Pilgrims may come there, too, many will take and drink thereof and steal your water, which you would not miss ofttimes for your wine. And in the other part of the chest ye may lay Your bread, cheese, spices, and all other things.

Also, you must ordain you biscuit to have with you [you must have your own food supplies at hand], for though ye shall be at the table with your patron, notwithstanding, ye shall ofttime have need to [have] your victuals, bread, cheese, eggs, fruit, and bacon, wine, and other, to make your collation [whatever you drink]. For sometime ye shall have feeble bread, wine, and stinking water: many times ye shall be full fain to eat of your own. ... Also take with you a little cauldron and fryingpan, dishes, platers, and saucers of tree [wood], cups of glass, a grater for bread, and such necessaries....

Also, buy you a cage for half a dozen of hens or chicken to have with you in the galley, for ye shall have need unto them many times: and buy you half a bushel of millet seed of Venice for them. Also take a barrel with you, closed [one that can be shut], for a siege [a toilet] for your chamber in the galley: it is full necessary that if ye be sick that ye not come not in the air [come up on deck]. Also, when ye come to haventowns, if ye will, buy eggs if ye come betimes to land, for then yet may have good cheap; for they be full necessary in the galley, sometimes fried with oil-olive and sometimes for a caudel [a mixed drink]....

Ye shall tarry in the Holy Land thirteen or fourteen days. Also, take good care of your knives and other small things that ye bear upon you, for the Saracens [the local Muslims] will go talking with you and make good cheer but they will steal from you what ye have, an they may [do so] ....

Also when ye shall ride to flume [River] Jordan, take with you out of Jerusalem bread, wine, water, hard cheese, and hard eggs, and such victuals as ye may have for two days, for there neither by the way is none to sell....

[When you come down again from the mountain where Christ fasted for forty days and forty nights], for nothing drink no water [do not drink any water; it is almost certain to be polluted], but rest you a little, and then eat bread and drink clean wine without water—after that great heat, water gendereth a great flux or fever, or both; then a man may haply lose his life thereby.

APPENDIX 5

Far-Ranging Friars

John of Montecorvino and Odoric of Pordenone

Between about the years 400 and 1600, many of the key Christian missionaries on the global scale were monks. Some excellent examples of these voyagers are Basil of Caesarea, Augustine of Hippo, Patrick of Ireland, and Augustine of Canterbury. They were all ideally suited for international cross-cultural missionary work because of their ascetic commitments to fasting, simplicity, austere lifestyles. They also had an admirable ability to flourish and to make friendships under the most rigorous conditions. To the names cited so far, two more can profitably be added who will probably not be known to non-specialist readers. These are the Italian friars John of Montecorvino, and Odoric of Pordenone. Each is of considerable historical and human interest.

Brother John of Montecorvino (1247–1328) was an Italian Franciscan missionary, traveler, statesman, founder of the earliest Catholic missions in India and China, and archbishop of Peking. He worked entirely alone, as a missionary in very distant foreign parts, for 11 years. The story of his many adventures is too long to recount here, but the modern reader is lucky to have online access to a letter he wrote from China, in about 1280, to the chief of his order in Rome, the Minister General of the Friars Minor (the Franciscans). Much of his letter reads as follows:

I, Brother John of Monte Corvino, of the order of Minor Friars, made my way to Cathay [China], the realm of the emperor of the Tartars, who is called the Grand Khan. To him I presented the letter from our lord the Pope, and invited him to adopt the Catholic faith ... but he had grown too old in idolatry.

However, he bestows many kindnesses upon the Christians, and in these two years past I am abiding with him. I have built a church in the city of Peking, which is his chief residence. This I completed six years ago; and I have built a bell-tower to it and put three bells in it. I have baptized there, as well as I can estimate, up to this time some six thousand persons....

I have myself grown old and gray, more with toil and trouble than with years, for I am not more than fifty-eight. I have got a competent knowledge of the language and character which is most generally used by the Tartars. [The Tartar language belongs to a branch of a Turkic language group. A reasonable guess is that Brother John could also get along in Chinese.]

And I have already translated into the language and character the New Testament and the Psalter, and have caused them to be written out in the fairest penmanship they have; and so by writing, reading, and preaching I bear open and public testimony to the Law of Christ.[1]

Turning now to Odoric of Pordenone (1286–1331), he was a late-medieval Italian Franciscan friar and missionary explorer. He traveled through India, the Greater Sunda Islands, and China, where he spent three years in Beijing. His narrative of these journeys is very well-documented because it has been preserved in no fewer than 73 Latin, French, and Italian manuscripts, the chief of which dates from about 1350 and is now kept in the Bibliothèque Nationale de France in Paris.

It is historically valuable because it includes accurate descriptions of Asian social and religious customs which had not been reported accurately before, if it all. His report was also an important source for the writings of John Mandeville, namely, a travel-adventure memoir which was a compilation of many different travelers' stories and was first circulated between 1357 and 1371 in French. Despite the extremely unreliable and often fantastical nature of the travels Mandeville describes, it was very widely used by reputable travelers—by Christopher Columbus, for example—as a reliable reference work. Many of the incredible reports in Mandeville, however, turn out to be badly-garbled versions of Odoric's own eyewitness descriptions.

Some passages on Odoric's book confirm him as having been a very perceptive traveler. He was the first European after Marco Polo to clearly mention Sumatra. The cannibalism and the community of wives that he reports there were accurate observations, either of Sumatra itself or of some nearby islands. Moreover, his description of sago, a starch food which is extracted from the pulp of the sago palm tree and which is still the staple food of the Papuans in Papua New Guinea, is generally accurate.

Finally, regarding his travels in China, his descriptions of the Chinese customs of fishing with tame cormorants, of letting one's fingernails grow to extraordinary lengths, and of binding women's feet all ring true, but they were not recorded by other travelers of the time. Odoric thus deserves credit not only for visiting such distant lands but also for writing about them so others could share his knowledge.

APPENDIX 6

"Lightning Chastises the Monks"

It was an article of faith during the Middle Ages that God and his angels were keeping such a close watch on all human activities that the sins of mankind would never go unnoticed. By the same token, God could easily invoke natural phenomena whenever necessary to bring sinners back into line.

The following account, drawn from the writings of the religious Inquisitor Étienne de Bourbon (1190–1261) in Burgundy, France, makes this latter point very dramatically. Translated and edited, it runs along the following lines:

> We must always remember that the Lord often punishes sacred places when they are profaned or when something dishonest is done there. Here is an account that I heard from the holy Abbot Jean de Belleville....
>
> At a certain abbey, which I will not identify here, just when all the monks were holding a service in their monastery's church, an earth-shaking clap of thunder was heard directly above the church.
>
> A huge bolt of lightning hit the church, setting fire to the floor and causing much other damage. It grievously wounded a number of the oldest monks, but entirely spared all the youngest monks—because they were innocent of any sins.
>
> The oldest monks, however, were all sinners, and the bolt damaged their bodies chiefly where they had sinned. It first hit all the oldest monks on the nose, but then burned all the hair off the lower parts of their backs, including their genitals, inflicting grave wounds. I do not remember how many of these old monks died.[1]

APPENDIX 7

The "Clerical Estate" in England in the Later Middle Ages

Because of the complexities of the many different types of clerical organizations in England from about 1348 to 1500, it is fitting to mention them briefly in this appendix rather than in the main body of the text itself. As the late medievalist Maurice Keen wrote in his remarkably clear and very well-organized discussion of this convoluted issue,

> Perhaps the most striking feature of the clerical estate at large was *the diversity of the kinds of people that it embraced*, and in order to make discussion of it manageable it has to be broken down into its component parts.[1]

Since the medieval Church in England, as in other Western European countries, was subject to both the authority of the Pope and the provisions of canon law, its clerical estate was probably similar, in general terms, to that existing in other major Christian countries. Using medieval England as an approximate template, then, one can discuss the state of religious affairs by highlighting some of the distinction between "regular clerks" and "secular clerks."

The regular clerks were the professed religious, i.e., those who had taken formal vows to follow the monastic rule of a given order and to embrace a life of personal poverty, chastity, and obedience. Most of these regular clerks were priests, though some were "lay brothers" who were not ordained. The regular clerks could be divided into two groups.

One group was the enclosed orders of monks, nuns, and canons regular who could not leave their own cloister without specific permission, and whose main assignment was to maintain the prescribed liturgical round of prayers and contemplation in their churches. These enclosed orders were endowed, i.e., they had external sources of income, but they had to administer the medieval estates on whose produce they lived.

The other group was the mendicants, the orders of friars whose vocation was apostolic and pastoral work outside the monastery, and who

186

worked directly with the local people, particularly those in the towns. Mendicants had to beg for their living.

The secular clergy had a far more diverse range of clerks than did the regular clergy. Many of the secular clergy were in minor orders. This meant that they had taken only the "first tonsure," which empowered them to perform some very limited duties in a church, such as being the parish clerk—or perhaps they had no clerical duties at all. They were permitted to marry, but were not eligible to hold any benefices. If they could prove that they had some degree of literacy, however, such as being able to read a Latin passage from the Bible, they might be able to progress slowly a little way up the ranks of the Church and become an acolyte—but never an ordained priest.

In contrast, the men in the major orders were all ordained, as sub-deacons, deacons, or priests. In order to hold a benefice, a man in these orders had to be at least a deacon, be 24 years old and planning to proceed to the priesthood. Although a deacon could preach and baptize, only an ordained priest could celebrate Mass. In order to be ordained, a deacon had to "show title," that is, he had to prove that he had the financial means to support himself as a priest. Since virtually all of these men already had the backing of religious houses, however, and since very little money was actually needed to show title, this was only a *pro forma* requirement.

There was, however, one important social and intellectual dividing line in the secular clergy between those who could safely be called the "clerical elite," on the one hand, and the "run of the mill" clerics, on the other: The long-term career prospects for, say, a brilliant graduate of Oxford University were enormously better than those of a man with a far more modest academic background from elsewhere in England.

Appendix 8

Monastic Rivalries in Medieval Paris

The Bishop of Paris was at the same time both a powerful lay lord who controlled many secular properties with many different temporal rights, and a powerful spiritual leader who was responsible for the religious and financial well-being of all the many churches and parishes in Paris.[1]

The great monasteries of the city, however, refused to agree that the Bishop of Paris did indeed have the authority to intervene in their own monastic affairs. Their objections were well-founded, being based on the fact that numerous papal letters had already given these monasteries important and long-standing exemptions from the authority of any bishop. These exemptions prevented the Bishop of Paris from ordaining the abbots; from bringing them to terms in his own court of law; and even, most remarkably, from supervising their own clergy in their own parishes.

The French theologian Peter the Chanter, who was an important member of the Cathedral of Notre-Dame in Paris, vigorously defended the rights of the Bishop of Paris against these exemptions. Peter argued that it was absurd for any church located in Paris to claim that it was not under the authority of the Bishop of Paris and was not subject to him.

Nevertheless, despite Peter's eloquence on this subject, in the end the Bishop of Paris still had to contend with some cases involving the monastic rights of the Paris abbeys of Saint-Denis and Sainte-Geneviève. Eventually, however, the Lateran council of 1215 did try to regulate monastic incursions into episcopal authority.

Chronology

313 The Emperor Constantine legalizes Christianity and makes it the official religion of the Roman Empire. Some Christian zealots, however, want to replace the physical martyrdom of the persecution era with the "private martyrdom" which was self-inflicted by some early monastic ascetics.

c. 342 The first Christian monk known to history by name is Paulus the Hermit.

356 Anthony of Egypt, one of earliest and most famous desert hermits, is an early leader of monasticism.

c. 397 The roots of French winemaking date from the wine-growing experiments of Martin of Tours, a former Roman soldier who had become a Christian and who founded the first monastery in France.

431 Pope Celestine sends Palladus to Ireland as the first bishop "to the Irish believing in Christ."

c. 500 The anonymous monk known only as Pseudo-Dionysius tries to resolve some of the important doctrinal issues, such as medieval mysticism, that were important to the early Church.

c. 500 The first monks settle on Skellig Michael, a small, cold, windswept, rocky island off the coast of Ireland.

502–1132 The eight major abbeys or monasteries discussed in this book, with their year of founding in brackets, are Sainte-Geneviève [502] and Saint-Germain-des-Prés [540s], both in Paris; Moissac [before 680] in France; St. Gall [719] in Switzerland; Fulda [744] in Germany; Cluny [910] in France; Mont-Saint-Michel [966] in France; and the imposing ruins of Fountains Abbey [1132] in England.

c. 517 The earliest monastic writing begins at about this time.

529 Benedict of Nursia is widely considered to be the father of Western monasticism, having founded the monastery of Monte Cassino in Italy in 529.

570–1338 Writing was such a popular medieval activity that during these years there were about 24 significant English, Norman, or Welsh authors, some of them monks, who wrote about the history of England in various languages.

c. 731 Bede writes his famous *Ecclesiastical History of the English People*.

c. 750 An anonymous commentator lists the many failings of the wandering lazy monks widely reviled as *gyrovagi*.

909 Duke William III of Aquitaine founds in France the great Benedictine monastery of Cluny. It would be led by a series of seven powerful and intelligent abbots who practiced a very efficient highly-centralized form of management that put Cluny's mother house in charge of all of its outlying monastic houses.

c. 1000 The German monastery of Reichenau becomes a famous writing school known for the fine quality of its hand-painted manuscripts.

1022 For both religious and political reasons, as a result of the "heresy of Orleans" in France, a dozen of the most learned canons of the cathedral of Orleans were burned alive in a wooden hut, on the orders of the Capetian king Robert the Pious.

1066 A contemporary account of the Battle of Hastings, won by William the Conqueror, quotes a local monk who may have had some firsthand knowledge of this fight.

c. 1070 The French monk William of Jumièges is the original compiler of a famous history known as the *Gesta Normannorum Ducum* ("Deeds of the Dukes of the Normans"), which was later expanded by two 12th-century monks, the chroniclers Orderic Vital and Robert Torigni.

1076 In Maule, a small but prosperous French city, local knights and other residents gladly donate land and other assets to the local monastery "for their souls' sake."

1081–1151 The life of Abbot Suger, head of the monastery of Saint-Denis and advisor to French kings.

1095 The first mention of armed monks occurs as part of the preparations for the First Crusade, launched in 1095, to liberate Jerusalem from Muslim control.

1098 The Benedictine monk Robert of Molesme leaves this order and founds a new and much stricter order known as the Cistercians. They would become famous for their land clearing, sheep farming, and austere but stunningly-beautiful monastic architecture.

c. 1107 Robert d'Abrissel, a controversial Breton hermit and monk, practices "spiritual marriage" with numerous women.

1113 Pope Paschal II establishes the Hospital of St. John of Jerusalem as an independent order to care for the Jerusalem pilgrims. Its members are known as the Hospitalers.

c. 1118 The founding of the Knights Templar, a monastic military order organized to protect Christian pilg.5rims in the Holy Land.

1130 At its heyday, the French monastery of Cluny was the apex of an enormous monastic empire of perhaps 10,000 monks.

1132 The founding of Fountains Abbey in Yorkshire, England. Today its ruins are still the standard by which all other medieval monasteries in Britain can best be judged.

c. 1140 *Gratian's Decretum* (*Gratian's Decree*), attributed to the monk Gratian, is a fundamental work on canon law. In his teaching of law, he presents to his students all the different sides of a given question, in the confident expectation that an acceptable solution will emerge from this process.

c. 1142 The brilliant monk Peter Abelard is famous for his colorful life, especially his torrid affair with his student Heloise, which results in his castration by his enemies, and for his outstanding philosophical and theological writings. In medieval scholasticism, the *sic et non* ("yes and no") method of debate championed by Abelard forces students to understand opposing points of view and to be intellectually willing and able to defend their own points of view.

1144 Medieval interest in alchemy begins with the English translation of an Arabic book on this subject.

1163–1345 Construction of the world-famous Gothic Cathedral of Notre Dame in Paris.

1179 Pope Alexander III orders that every cathedral must have a *magister* (a teacher) to teach Latin grammar, free of charge. Latin grammar was the cornerstone of academic knowledge in the Middle Ages.

c. 1179 Hildegard von Bingen is a German Benedictine abbess, writer, composer, philosopher, Christian mystic, monastery-founder, and polymath.

c. 1192 A new order of armed monks, the Teutonic Order, is created in the Holy Land.

1193–1194 Cistercian and other monks are superb sheep farmers who do so well financially that they can pay the very stiff ransom needed to free King Richard I from his captivity by the Duke of Austria. This ransom of 150,000 silver marks was nearly three times the entire annual income of the English Crown.

c. 1200 There are now about 17,000 to 18,000 monks, canons, friars, and nuns in England alone.

1200 Three excellent universities have now come into being in Western Europe, namely, Bologna, Paris, and Oxford.

1210 The Franciscan order is founded to preach the Gospel, more by personal example than by word alone. Many of its members worked among the urban poor.

1216 The Dominican order is founded to preach the Gospel, both by word and example. It is joked that the basic difference between these two orders is that the Franciscans trust first to *feelings*, while the Dominicans trust first to *reason*.

1221 Dominic sends 12 friars to England to establish a Dominican presence there.

c. 1247 The monks produce a great deal of wine each year but they also have to dispense most of it to their many thirsty guests; to their large household staffs; and, of course, to themselves.

c. 1250 Meetings of Beguines lead to the founding of hundreds of Beguine houses known as *beguinages*, many of which still survive today as historic cultural sites in the Netherlands and elsewhere.

c. 1250 The independence of the masters (professors) at the University of Paris faces a serious challenge on academic and political issues from the mendicants of the Dominican and Franciscan orders.

c. 1259 The English Benedictine monk Matthew Paris is at the same time an illustrator, chronicler, cartographer, and artist, being especially skilled at producing beautiful, illuminated manuscripts.

c. 1259 Many of the Benedictine abbeys and priories begin to slide into a downward spiral of decay, which makes it harder for them to find new recruits.

1260s A Spanish law code defines and explains monasticism in practice.

c. 1280 In the 13th and 14th centuries, Franciscan friars make their way to the Far East. Brother John of Monte Corvino reports, in a letter to the Minister General of his order in Rome, the results of his 11 years of solitary missionary efforts in China.

c. 1284 Creatively weaving together in Old French both fact and fiction, an anonymous poet tells us about the life and death of Eustache, a French monk turned pirate.

1287 *Gaudeamus igitur* ("Let us rejoice") is a famous drinking song of the student poets known as goliards, who patronize some of the 4,000 taverns in medieval Paris.

c. 1290 An account of this period gives the modern reader a good picture of how the monks of a 300-acre manor in England manage their property.

c. 1300 A satirical poem recounts how a friar impregnates a married woman in England.

c. 1300 In Paris at this time, clerics make up a significant part of the population. The Bishop of Paris himself is assisted by 51 canons; the 33 churches of the city also have their own curates, vicars, and chaplains. All told, there are about 20,000 members of religious orders living in Paris, some 10 percent of the total population. Thanks in large part to all the people directly or indirectly associated with the Church and with academic life, during the 13th century the University of Paris will become the most important university in the world.

1300 Pope Boniface VIII declares this year to be a jubilee year—one in which all pilgrims to Rome will receive a plenary indulgence, that is, a full dispensation of any punishment due to sins committed over an entire lifetime. Mendicant orders, however, think that such a "blanket dispensation of sin" is far too generous.

1303/1304 On behalf of King Philip of France, the Templars are falsely charged with heresies, blasphemies, and homosexuality. The Grand Master of the Templars is publicly burned alive at the stake. Philip keeps for himself much of the booty confiscated from the Templars.

1317 Church officials condemn the Beguine status, but this order will continue on quietly until the very last Beguine dies in 2018 at the age of 92.

1341–1366 Carmelite friar Jean de Venette writes his *Latin Chronicles*, which cover these years and describe the extreme disarray in France following the defeat of the French king Jean II le Bon (John II the Good) at the battle of Poitiers in 1356 during the Hundred Years War.

1346–1353 The Black Death, a bubonic plague pandemic, occurs in Afro-Eurasia during these years and becomes the most fatal pandemic ever recorded in human history, killing 75 million to 200 million people. It cuts a wide swath through the cities and monasteries of Western Europe, marking the end of a period of medieval growth and optimism.

1386 Geoffrey Chaucer's *Canterbury Tales* is a wonderful collection of 24 stories written in Middle English and mostly in verse. In it, the friars are strongly criticized for profiting personally from their supposedly selfless calling.

1400 At the Battle of Tannenberg in Poland, the monastic order known as the Teutonic Knights suffers such a crushing defeat that the Knights never recover from it.

c. 1417 A significant number of major abuses by the Avignon Papacy severely tarnishes the reputations of its popes.

c. 1463 The French poet François Villon is the most famous *criminal graduate* of the University of Paris. One of the best lines of European secular poetry is his rhetorical question, which nostalgically evokes the fleeting beauty of all lovely women: "But where are the snows of yesteryear?"

Chapter Notes

Preface

1. After Olson, *The Early Middle Ages*, p. 140.
2. After Olson, *The Early Middle Ages*, p. 166.

Introduction

1. After Southern, *Scholastic Humanism and the Unification of Europe*, pp. 138–129.
2. The best easily-accessible source on the French monastery of Cluny may be 'The Rise of Cluny" in Lawrence, *Medieval Monasticism*, pp. 76–99, which has been used here. In this connection, however, it must be remembered that the parts of France actually controlled by the central government in Paris varied enormously in size during the Middle Ages. At the end of the 12th century, for example, most of what is now western France was controlled directly or indirectly by other powers, e.g., England; local lords; lands of the Church; fiefs of French vassals; or lands disputed between England and France. (Source: After Lawrence, *Medieval Monasticism*, p. 16.)
3. After Thompson, *Le Monde Médéval*, p. 209.
4. After Smith, *The Early History of the Monastery of Cluny*, p. 1.
5. Quoted in Labarge, *Medieval Travellers*, p. 29.
6. This and some of the following comments are from Vaughan, *The Illustrated Chronicles of Matthew Paris*, pp. ix–x.
7. After M. Postan in the Preface to Power, p. vii, of *The Wool Trade in English Medieval History*. Emphasis added.

Chapter 1

1. After Scheibelreiter, *Church Structure and Organisation*, p. 677.
2. After Pounds, *An Economic History of Medieval Europe*, p. 392.
3. There are many tragic if poorly-documented stories in Paris folklore about the perils of the local wooden bridges . The Petit Pont [Little Bridge], for example, there is still remembered today because at least 13 of its predecessors have been destroyed since the first bridge was built there in Gallo-Roman times. During the Middle Ages, this bridge was especially famous for the very loud and very lively banter of all the market women who were selling food and goods there. Later, in 1718, two boats loaded with hay tried to pass beneath this bridge at the same time one night. That same night, a woman whose child had drowned in the Seine earlier in the day had set out in a boat in search of his body. She carried a burning wooden taper to light her way. Unfortunately, her boat collided with one of the barges laden with hay. It caught fire and soon burned down the Petit Pont. This bridge, however, was quickly replaced by a new bridge in the next year.
4. After Astic-Heisserer, *Paris medieval*, p. 3.
5. After Vespierre, *Guide du Paris Médiéval*, p. 15.
6. After Vespierre, *Guide du Paris Médiéval*, p. 65.
7. After Lawrence, *Medieval Monasticism*, p. 152.
8. After Janin, *The University in Medieval Life*, back cover.

9. After Barber, *The Two Cities*, p. 32.

10. After Baldwin, *The Scholastic Culture of the Middle Ages*, p. 35.

11. After Haskins, *The Renaissance of the Twelfth Century*, p. 33.

12. After Le Goff, *The Medieval Imagination*, p. 14.

13. Contemporary medival writers were well-aware that this three-component social theory did not in fact reflect current social reality. Some of them, for example, said there were in fact twelve social groups, divided by four categories of dignity—Church, nobility, bourgeoisie (rich townsmen), and the common people—most of which were then further subdivided into three levels of wealth. (After Potter, *France in the Later Middle Ages*, p. 56.)

14. After Cassard. *1180–1328*, p. 7.

15. After McKitterick, *The, Early Middle Ages*, p. 158.

16. Adapted from Southern, *Scholastic Humanism and the Unification of Europe*, p. 139.

17. After Barber, *The Two Cities*, p. 131.

Chapter 2

1. Quoted in Lawrence, *Medieval Monasticism*, p. 1.

2. After Evans, *Life in Medieval France*, p. 55.

3. After Lawrence, *Medieval Monasticism*, p. 263.

4. After Lawrence, *Medieval Monasticism*, p. 114.

5. After Cassard, *1180–1328*, p. 423.

6. After Lawrence, *Medieval Monasticism*, p. 230.

7. After Potter, *France in the Later Middle Ages*, p. 56.

8. After Lafaye, "Monastic Orders as Vehicles of Diffusion in Europe," p. 1, and Potter, *France in the Later Middle Ages*, p. 56.

9. After Lafaye, "Monastic Orders as Vehicles of Diffusion in Europe," p. 1.

10. Waddell, *The Wandering Scholars of the Middle Ages*, p. 178.

11. It was joked that the Austin Canons lived very well indeed. One medieval chronicler wrote, in contemporary French: "Blessed be holy Augustine! The canons

have a great plenty of fat morsels and good wine, and are very well provided for. Here I could very well endure, for I had rather live here than die." (Quoted in Evans, *Life in Medieval France*, p. 66.)

12. After Baldwin, *Paris, 1200*, pp. 247–248.

13. After Chaucer, *The Canterbury Tales*, pp. 10–11.

14. Drawn from Bruzelius, "The architecture of mendicant orders in the Middle Ages."

15. After Brundage, *Medieval Canon Law*, p. 22.

16. Brundage, *Medieval Canon Law*, pp. 3–4.

Chapter 3

1. After Jewish Virtual Library, "Nazirite," pp. 1–2. This is also the source for other points made in this chapter.

2. B.C.E. means "Before the Common Era"; C.E. means "Common Era."

3. After Library of Congress, "Scrolls from the Dead Sea: The Quran Community," pp. 1–2.

4. After "Overview of Medieval Monasticism," p. 2.

5. After Ward, *The Wisdom of the Desert Fathers*, p. xii.

6. After "Monasticism in Western Medieval Europe," p. 2.

7. After Baldwin, *The Scholastic Culture of the Middle Ages*, pp. 36–37.

8. The setting-up of great monasteries such as Monte Cassino and Nonantola Abbey, both in Italy, stimulated the patronage of art, especially the production of manuscripts. Monte Cassino would be sacked by the Lombards in about 577. Founded by Saint Anslem in 752, however, Nonantola Abbey became one of the chief training grounds for pre-Carolingian writing.

9. Cited in "Overview of Medieval Monasticism," p. 3.

10. From *The Rule of St. Benedict*, quoted in "Overview of Medieval Monasticism," p. 1. This same source has been used in some of the other points made in this chapter.

11. After "Early Medieval Philosophy," p. 13.

12. After Olson, *The Early Middle Ages*, p. 139.

13. Richard Fletcher, a modern scholar, noted that the gradual rise to dominance of the Benedictine rule was a slow process that spread over several centuries. In fact, the late antique and early medieval periods were marked by a ceaselessly proliferating diversity of rules: a monastic founder could devise his own rule for his own monks to follow. Monasticism was therefore very adaptable, transplantable, and flexible. (Source: Fletcher, *The Barbarian Conversion*, p. 91.)

14. Benedictine Rule, Prologue.

15. After Ozment, *The Age of Reform*, p. 83.

16. Bloch, *Feudal Society II*, p. 345.

17. Adapted from Lawrence, "Overview of Medieval Monasticism," p. 5.

18. After Lawrence, *Medieval Monasticism*, p. 265.

19. After Matarasso, *The Cistercian World*, p. xi.

20. After Guillier, *L'abbaye de Sémanque*, p. 22.

21. Hutchinson, *Medieval Ships and Shipping*, p. 89.

22. After Holmes, *Oxford Illustrated History of Medieval Europe*, p. 138.

23. After Matarasso, *The Cistercian World*, pp. 287–292.

24. Quoted by Barber, *The Two Cities*, p. 138.

25. After Evans, *Life in Medieval France*, p. 70.

26. Quoted by Lawrence, *Medieval Monasticism*, pp. 228–229.

27. The cathedrals of early medieval England were divided into two types: monastic and secular. In monastic cathedrals, the bishop took the place of an abbot and ruled both the cathedral monastery and diocese. A prior would be in charge of the monks. The secular cathedrals were ruled by the bishop and were staffed by secular canons, who lived separately and were not under a monastic Rule. (Source: Chisholm, "Monastic & Secular Cathedrals of Medieval England.")

28. Large monasteries were managed by an abbot, who traditionally had absolute authority over his institution. He was usually chosen by the senior monks, who he was supposed to but not *required* to consult on all matters of monastery policy. It was possible for a truly outstanding younger monk to be chosen as abbot. What he lacked in hands-on experience might be offset by the good chance that he would supervise the monastery for decades to come and thus provide, in troubled medieval times, the great blessing of stability. Monks were expected to bow deeply before their abbot and to kiss his hand in reverence. If an abbot broke the rules of his order, however, he could be removed by the Pope.

29. Quoted by Lawrence, *Medieval Monasticism*, p. 63.

30. Haskins, *The Renaissance of the Twelfth Century*, pp. 46–47.

31. After Burton, *Monastic and Religious Orders in Britain*, pp. 83–84.

Chapter 4

1. Cited by Lawrence, *Medieval Monasticism*, p. 23.

2. After Lawrence, *Medieval Monasticism*, p. 39.

3. After Pounds, *An Economic History of Western Europe*, p. 199.

4. After Cobban, *English University Life in the Middle Ages*, p. 3.

5. After Keen, *English Society in the Later Middle Ages*, pp. 248–249.

6. After Roux, *Paris au Moyen Âge*, p. 141.

7. After Barrow, *The Clergy in the Medieval World*, pp. 3–4.

8. After Barrow, *The Clergy in the Medieval World*, p. 5.

9. Tuchman, *A Distant Mirror*, p. 216.

10. After Miller, "Beguines," p. 3.

11. Quoted in Waddell, *The Wandering Scholars of the Middle Ages*," p. 179.

12. These points, lightly annotated and edited, are drawn from Waddell, *The Wandering Scholars of the Middle Ages*, pp. 179–181.

13. After Southern, *Scholastic Humanism and the Unification of Europe*, pp. 170–171.

14. After *World History Encyclopedia*, "The Daily Life of Medieval Monks: Recruitment."

15. After McKitterick, *The Early Middle Ages*, p. 154.

16. After Ursula Vones-Liebenstein in *The Cambridge History of Medieval Monasticism in the Latin West*, p. 766.

Chapter 5

1. The canons regular were, in effect, a hybrid order of "clerical monks." They represented an effort to give practical effect to the belief the Apostles were basically monks and that the secular clergy must therefore model their own lives after them. (Source: Lawrence, *Medieval Monasticism*, pp. 163–164.)

2. After Dyer, *Standards of Living in the later Middle Ages*, p. 98.

3. After Verdon, *La vie quotidienne au Moyen Age*, p. 222.

4. After Bove and Gauvard, *Le Paris du Moyen Âge*, pp. 12–14.

5. The first recorded Viking attacks were on three of the most famous monasteries in Ireland: Lindisfarne in 793, Jarrow in 794, and Iona in 795. Large numbers of Viking attacks are recorded on the Irish monasteries: the Irish monastic annals give us very detailed records on the monasteries that did survive these attacks. (Source: Holmes, *Oxford Illustrated History of Medieval Europe*, p. 107.)

6. After Michelin, *Paris*, p. 258.

7. The Viking attacks left no one untouched in the areas they raided. They focused on attacking wealthy establishments such as churches and monasteries, preferring to descend on a monastery when the faithful were gathered together to celebrate a saint's day and when a market was therefore being held. In addition to plundering the goods and money of the assembled laity, they also seized the chalices and ornaments of the monks. Captives were carried off into slavery, never to be seen again by their families. (Source: Dyer, *Making a living in the Middle Ages*, p. 44.) A medieval monk once wrote, on a stormy night on the coast: "Bitter is the wind tonight, it tosses the ocean's white hair, I need not fear—as on a night of calm sea—the fierce raiders from Lochlann [i.e., Norway]."

8. After McKitterick, *The Early Middle Ages*, p. 162.

9. After de Jong, *Carolingian Monasticism*, p. 623.

10. After de Jong, "Carolingian monasticism," pp. 646–647.

11. Ozment, *The Age of Reform*, p. 86.

12. After Evans, *Life in Medieval France*, p. 60.

13. After Abbaye du Mont-Saint-Michele, p. 1.

Chapter 6

1. After Fleming, *Britain after Rome*, p. 128.

2. After Burton, *Monastic and Religious Order in Britain*, p. 174.

3. After Evans, *Life in Medieval France*, p. 56.

4. After Dyer, *Standards of Living in the later Middle Ages*, p. 37.

5. After Dyer, *Standards of Living in the later Middle Ages*, p. 71.

6. After Dyer, *Standards of living in the later Middle Ages*, p. 185.

7. After Dyer, *Making a living in the Middle Ages*, pp. 28–29.

8. After Dyer, *Standards of living in the later Middle Ages*, p. 236.

9. These points are drawn from Chapter 7, "The Cloister and the World," pp. 101–134, of C.H. Lawrence's book on Medieval Monasticism.

Chapter 7

1. Key sources used in this chapter include Susan Rose, *The Wine Trade in Medieval Europe*; Ladonne, "Holy Vineyards"; and Vins de Bourgogne, "When time and man work hand-in-hand." Susan Rose's definitive book has been a key source in writing this chapter and in most but not all cases it has been endnoted accordingly.

2. After Rose, *The Wine Trade in Medieval Europe*, p. 39.

3. After Ladonne, "Holy vineyards," pp. 1–5.

4. After Dyer, *Making a living in the Middle Ages*, p. 208.

5. After Rose, *The Wine Trade in Medieval Europe*, p. 40. Some of the other points made in this short but excellent book are echoed in this chapter, but without endnoting every single one of them.

6. Quoted by Rose, *The Wine Trade in Medieval Europe*, p. 41.

7. After Rose, *The Wine Trade in Medieval Europe*, p. 42.

8. The comments and quotes used here are drawn from Rose, *The Wine Trade in Medieval Europe*, pp. 117–132.

9. Adapted from Rose, *The Wine Trade in Medieval Europe*, pp. 118–119.

10. After Sadourny, "Les transports sur la Seine," p. 239.

Chapter 8

1. Some of the points made in this chapter are drawn from both Lawrence, *Medieval Monasticism*, pp. 119–123, and Janin, *Four Paths to Jerusalem*, pp. 86–109.

2. After Lawrence, *Medieval Monasticism*, p. 121.

3. This account closely follows Janin, "A Pilgrimage in Arms" in *Four Paths to Jerusalem*, pp. 86–109.

4. After Fletcher, *The Barbarian Conversion*, p. 497.

5. Quoted by Janin, *Four Paths to Jerusalem*, p. 89.

6. Many of the comments in the following pages on the Knights Hospitaler and the Knights Templar are sourced to Janin, *Four Paths to Jerusalem,* pp. 99–101.

7. Quoted by Janin, *Four Paths to Jerusalem*, p. 99.

8. Quoted by Janin, *Four Paths to Jerusalem,* p. 100.

9. On very rare occasions, priests and monks apparently did engage in combat. For example, the Benedictine monk Abbon (c. 850–923), who was an eyewitness at the Viking ships' attack on Paris in 885, wrote a poem in about 897 which describes how a bishop and his abbot held their ground in the front ranks of the French fighters defending Paris. Abbon tells his readers how "one well-aimed millstone [dropped onto a Viking boat by the bishop and the abbot from a bridge into the River Seine at the height of the battle] sent the souls of six [Vikings] to hell."

10. After Turnbull, *Tannenberg 1410*, pp. 28–30 and back cover.

11. After Urban, *Medieval Mercenaries*, p. 275.

12. Quoted in Jenkins, "Monasteries and the Defence of the South Coast in the Hundred Years War," p. 4.

13. Quoted in Jenkins, "Monasteries and the Defence of the South Coast in the Hundred Years War," p. 14.

Chapter 9

1. Some of the points made in this chapter are drawn from Janin, *The University in Medieval Life.*

2. Some of the comments above come from Verger, "Patterns," pp. 60–62.

3. After Asztalos, "The faculty of theology," p. 415.fis

4. After Asztalos, "The Faculty of Theology," pp. 416–417.

5. The following points echo Janin, *The University in Medieval Life*, pp. 82–83.

6. Quoted in Janin, *The University in Medieval Life*, p. 82.

7. After de Ridder-Symoens, *A History of the University in Europe*, p. 160.

8. After Janin, *The University in Medieval Life*, p. 31.

9. Quoted by Tuchman in *A Distant Mirror*, pp. 30–31.

Chapter 10

1. Some of the following comments on scholasticism are drawn from Turner's 1912 entry in the Catholic Encyclopedia.

2. Thomas Aquinas's *Summa Theologica*, written c. 1270, famously included a discussion of several questions regarding angels, such as "Can several angels be in the same place"? The more modern joking version of this question is: "How many angels can dance on the point of a pin?" Such questions are *reductio ad absurdum* challenges to the excesses of medieval scholasticism.

3. After Turner, "Scholasticism," pp. 7–10.

Chapter 11

1. After Peters, *Inquisition*, pp. 40–41, and Zerner, *Hérésie*, p. 466.

2. Brundage, *Medieval Canon Law*, pp. 70–71. Emphasis added. This book is an excellent introduction to a very complex subject.

Chapter 12

1. After Lawrence, *Medieval Monasticism*, p. 104.
2. After Haskins, *The Renaissance of the Twelfth Century*, p. 73.
3. After Baldwin, *The Scholastic Culture of the Middle Ages*, p. 56.
4. After O'Donnell, "Cassidorus."
5. After Brundage. *Medieval Canon Law*, p. 179.
6. After Brundage,, *Medieval Canon Law*, p. ix and back cover.
7. After Nelson, "The Avignon Papacy," p. 1
8. After Musson, *Medieval Law in Context*, p. 10.
9. After Brundage, *Medieval Canon Law*, p. 48.
10. This and the following discussion are drawn from Musson, *Medieval Law in Context*, pp. 14–15.
11. After Brundage, *Medieval Canon Law*, pp. 11–12, 189.
12. The Anglo-Saxon Chronicles—a collection of seven manuscripts, in the form of a diary, written by monks living in England between the 9th and 12th centuries and covering a period of English history of over one thousand years—are not discussed here because of their length, complexity, and multiple authorship.
13. After Burton, *Monastic and Religious Orders in Britain*, p. 7.
14. Sciolino, *The Seine*, pp. 281–282.
15. Quoted by Morillo, *The Battle of Hastings*, pp. 18–19.
16. Some of the following points are drawn from Bouet, "Orderic Vital," pp. 1–2.
17. Bouet, "Oderic Vital," p. 1.
18. After Brundage, *Medieval Canon Law*, p. 48.
19. Quoted in Winroth, *The Making of Gratian's Decretum*, pp. 7–8.
20. After Haskins, *The Renaissance of the Twelfth Century*, pp. 97–98.

Chapter 13

1. Many of the points made in this chapter are drawn from Silverman's essay on monastic medicine which is listed in the bibliography, or from Goldiner's piece on medicine in the Middle Ages.

2. After Silverman, "Monastic Medicine," p. 11.
3. These points are drawn from Silverman, "Monastic Medicine," p. 16.

Chapter 14

1. After Campbell *et al*, "Alchemy and the Mendicant Orders of Late Medieval and Early Modern Europe."

Chapter 15

1. Adapted from Lawrence, *Medieval Monasticism*, p. 199, and Heer, *The Medieval World*, pp. 320–321.
2. Madigan, *Mystics, Visionaries and Prophets*," p. 96.
3. Quoted in Fordham University, *The Life and Works of Hildegard von Bingen*, p. 2.
4. After Power, *English Medieval Nunneries*, p. 238.
5. After Power, *English Medieval Nunneries*, p. 237.

Chapter 16

1. The source of many of the points made in this chapter is Miller, "Beguines," pp 1–14.
2. After Lawrence, *Medieval Monasticism*, p. 212.
3. Adapted from Lawrence, *Medieval Monasticism*, pp. 213–215.
4. This account follows Miller, "Beguines," pp. 5–14.
5. Miller, "Beguines," p. 12.

Chapter 17

1. After Ó Cróinín, *Medieval Ireland*, p. 35.
2. After Ó Cróinín, *Early Medieval Ireland*, p. 35.
3. Swan, "Ecclesiastical settlement in Ireland in the early medieval period," pp. 4, 8.
4. We do not have a text of Kirk's book.
5. Many of the points in this chapter come from Ó Cróinín, *Early Medieval Ireland*.

6. After Ó Cróinín, *Early Medieval Ireland*, p. 212. Emphasis added

7. After Jackson, *A Celtic Miscellany*, p. 279.

8. Bede complained strongly about the obstinacy of the [Irish] Celtic Church in regard to the celebration of Easter. He wrote: "Now the Britons [i.e., the Irish] did not keep Easter at the correct time, but between the fourteenth and twentieth days of the moon—a calculation depending on a cycle of eighty-four years. Furthermore, certain other of their customs were at variance with the universal practice of the Church. But despite protracted discussions, neither the prayers, advice, or censures of Augustine and his companions could obtain the compliance of the Britons, who stubbornly preferred their own customs to those in universal use among Christian Churches ... The Britons admitted that his teaching was true and right, but said again that they could not abandon their ancient customs without the consent and approval of their own people ..." (Source: "Paschal Calendar," p. 1.

9. After King, "The Book of Kells," pp. 1–4.

10. Quoted by Lawrence, *Medieval Monasticism*, p. 40.

11. The best reference source on this complicated subject is probably Ó Cróinín, *Early Medieval Ireland*, which has been heavily used in this chapter.

12. Quoted by Ó Cróinín, *Early Medieval Ireland*, p. 167.

13. Adapted from Ó Cróinín, *Early Medieval Ireland*, pp. 215–216.

14. After McKitterick, *The New Cambridge Medieval History*, p. 48.

15. Adapted from Ó Cróinín, *Early Medieval Ireland*, pp, 182–183.

16. Taken from a private communication of 21 June 2021 from Dr. Niav Gallagher of the Royal Irish Academy in Dublin

17. After Gallagher, "How the Franciscans arrived in Ireland," pp. 6–7.

Chapter 18

1. The bibliographic source of these two quotes is not known but they may come from the *Chronicle of Raoul Glaber* which was published in Paris in 1824 by J.L.-J. Brière.

2. Perrin, "Raoul Glaber," p. 1.

3. After Aubrey, "The White Mantle of Churches," p. 5. This quote has been very lightly edited.

Chapter 19

1. Sources used in this chapter are drawn in part from La letter volée cited in the bibliography.

2. After Dalarun, "Robert d'Arbrissel et les femmes," p. 2.

Chapter 20

1. The Middle English texts of these tales , and the modern English translations, come from Chaucer, *The Canterbury Tales*, pp. 8–14.

2. After Chaucer, *The Canterbury Tales*, pp. 8–9. It is possible that this statement has a double meaning, implying that carnal love is involved, too.

3. After Power, *Medieval People*, p. 110.

4. After Power, *Medieval People,* pp. 91–92.

5. After Scott-Robinson, "The Pardoner's Tale."

Chapter 21

1. The comments in this section are variously drawn from a Stanford Encyclopedia of Philosophy article on Abelard; from Jordan, *Europe in the High Middle Ages*, pp. 117–118; from Pernoud, *Héloïse et Abélard*, pp. 184–227; and from Janin, *The University in Medieval Life*, 179–181..

2. Quoted in Haskins, *The Renaissance of the Twelfth Century,* p. 168. The Biblical source is the Gospel according to Saint Matthew, Ch. 2, V. 18.

3. After Rashdall, *The Universities of Europe in the Middle Ages*, Vol. I, p. 57. Emphasis added.

4. Quoted in Janin, *The University in Medieval Life*, p. 180.

5. Quoted in Pernoud, *Héloïse et Abélard*, p. 67.

6. Quoted in Janin, *The University in Medieval Life*, p. 181.

7. See *Stanford Encyclopedia of Philosophy*, "Peter Abelard," pp. 1–20.

Chapter 22

1. After Kelly, *Eustache the Monk*, pp. 1–3. Most of the detailed points in this chapter come from Ohlgren, *A Book on Medieval Outlaws*, Chapter 3 on "Eustace the Monk," pp. 61–98.
2. Eddison, *Medieval Pirates*, p. 17.
3. Quoted in Eddison, *Medieval Pirates*, p. 65.
4. Quoted in Ohlgren, *A Book of Medieval Outlaws*, p. 66.
5. After *Stanford Encyclopedia of Philosophy*, "Medieval Philosophy," p. 13.

Chapter 23

1. One of the best sources on Matthew Paris is Vaughan, *The Illustrated Chronicles of Matthew Paris*. See Bibliography.
2. Quoted in "An Outline of English Fiction—Matthew Paris," p. 1.
3. Adapted from *The Illustrated Chronicles of Matthew Paris*, pp. 72–73.

Chapter 24

1. Quoted by Martin, "On the Sheep's back," p. 1.
2. This statement appears on the jacket cover of the book. The emphasis has been added.
3. Power, *The Wool Trade in English Medieval History*, p. 17.
4. After Dyer, *Making a Living in the Middle Ages*, p. 135.
5. After Burton, *Monastic and Religious Orders in Britain*, pp. 236–237.
6. After Power, *The Wool Trade in English Medieval History*, p. 33.
7. These estimates come from Power, *The Wool Trade in English Medieval History*, pp. 34–35.
8. After Power, *The Wool Trade in English Medieval History*, pp. 43–44.
9. Quoted in Bell *et al*, "Advance Contracts for the Sale of Wool in Medieval England," pp. 3–4.
10. This and some of the following

points in this chapter come from Martin, "On the Sheep's back," pp. 1–9.
11. After Donkin, "Cistercian Sheep-Farming and Wool-Sales in the Thirteenth Century," pp. 2, 8.
12. After Laumonier, "Sheep-Rearing in Medieval France," p. 5.
13. There were six different types of medieval granges: agrarian, sheep or cattle farms; horse studs; fisheries; and industrial iron-working complexes.
14. The following account is largely drawn from Jamroziak, "Rievaulx Abbey as a wool producer in the late thirteenth century," pp. 1, 217–218.
15. The phrase "the tragedy of the commons" was coined in 1833 by a mathematical amateur named William Forster Lloyd. He famously pointed out that, in this system, every famer who behaves entirely rationally is compelled to increase the size of his own herd , which is grazing (free of charge) on the commons. If every farmer does the same thing, *all will be ruined* because there will be too little grass for an ever-increasing number of cattle.

Chapter 25

1. After Benedictow, *The Black Death*, p. 417.
2. After Decameron Web, "Social and Economic Effects of the Plague," p. 1.
3. After Agnolo di Tura's 1348 report on the Black Death.
4. After Pounds, *An Economic History of Medieval Europe*, pp. 443–444.
5. Adapted from Benedictow, The Black Death, p. 391.

Chapter 26

1. Two of the best sources on Fountains Abbey are (1) the Historic UK article listed in the bibliography, and (2) the book by Mark Newman, The Wonder of the North: Fountains Abbey and Studley Royal.
2. After Newman, The Wonder of the North, pp. 13–14.
3. Some of the following comments are drawn from Newman, The Wonder of the North, pp. 20–23.
4. After Brown, "Archaeologists find

'missing link' in history of Fountains Abbey," p. 1.

Chapter 27

1. After English Heritage, "History of Furness Abbey," p. 4.
2. After English Heritage, "History of Furness Abbey," p. 9.

Chapter 28

1. The comments in this chapter have been drawn from different sources cited in the bibliography, i.e., Sorabella, "Pilgrimage in Medieval Europe," pp. 3–5; and the four "Pilgrims and Pilgrimage" pieces.
2. These quotes are taken from the "Pilgrim and Pilgrimage" entries in the bibliography.
3. After Pernoud, Aliénor d'Aquitaine, pp. 38–39.

Chapter 29

1. Sources used in this chapter include Janin, The University in Medieval Life; Waddell, The Wandering Scholars of the Middle Ages; and Lawrence, Medieval Monasticism.
2. After Waddell, The Wandering Scholars of the Middle Ages, p. 175.
3. After Janin, The University in Medieval Life, pp. 36–37.
4. After Janin, The University in Medieval Life, p. 37.

Chapter 30

1. Sources used here include Janin, The University in Medieval Life, pp. 92–94, and the full text of Burl, Danse Macabre.
2. Quoted and translated by Burl, Danse Macabre, p. 30.
3. Quoted in Janin, The University in Medieval Life, p. 94.

Chapter 31

1. Some of the points made in this chapter are drawn from Lawrence, Medieval Monasticism, pp. 257–261.

2. After Lawrence, Medieval Monasticism, p. 260.
3. Unless otherwise attributed, some of the immediately-following comments are sourced to Keen, English Society in the Later Middle Ages, pp. 260–270.
4. After Keen, English Society in the Later Middle Ages, pp. 260–261.
5. After Keen, English Society in the Later Middle Ages, p. 263.
6. After Keen, English Society in the Later Middle Ages, p. 266.
7. After Keen, English Society in the Later Middle Ages, p. 266.
8. Knudsen, "Naughty Nuns and Promiscuous Monks," Abstract, p. ii.
9. After Knudsen, "Naughty Nuns and Promiscuous Monks," Abstract p. iii.

Chapter 32

1. The phrase the "Babylonian captivity" of the popes in Avignon is thought to have come from the writer Petrarch, who described Avignon at that time as the "Babylon of the West."
2. After Renouard, La Papuaté à Avignon, p. 124.
3. Tuchman, A Distant Mirror, pp. 26, 27.

Appendix 1

1. In addition, a source used here is Janin, The University in Medieval Life.
2. After Haskins, The Renaissance of the Twelfth Century, p. 287.
3. Haskins, The Rise of Universities, pp. 4–5.

Appendix 4

1. After Baratier, "Rois Angevins et Papes d'Avignon," pp. 186–192.
   Appendix 5
1. After Tappan, "Brother John of Monte Casino: Letter to the Minister General of the Friars Minor in Rome, c. 1280," p. 1.

Appendix 6

1. After Cassard, 1180–1328, p. 202.

Appendix 7

1. This appendix is drawn in large part from Keen, English Society in the Later Middle Ages,, "The Clerical Estate," p. 246 and later pages. Emphasis added here.

Appendix 8

1. This appendix is drawn in large part from Baldwin, Paris, 1200, pp. 162–163.

Bibliography

Astic-Heisserer, Sophie. *Paris Médiéval*. Paris: Taride, 2015.

Asztalos, Monika. "The Faculty of Theology" in H. de Ridder-Symoens (ed.), *A History of the University in Europe Volume 1: Universities in the Middle Ages*. Cambridge University Press, 2003.

"At the Origin of the White Mantle of Churches." https://archeologie.orleans-metropole. fr/dossiers-thematiques-temoins-de-lhistorie/a-lorigne-du-blanc-manteau-deglises. Accessed 15 August 2021.

Aubrey, Dennis. "The White Mantle of Churches." https://vialucispress.wordpress. com/2011/04/09/the-white-marble-of-churches-dennis-aubrey. Accessed August 19, 2021.

Baldwin, John W. *Paris, 1200*. Stanford University Press, 2010.

———. *The Scholastic Culture of the Middle Ages, 1000–1300*. Lexington: Heath and Company, 1971. Cambridge University Press, 2003, pp. 409–441.

Baratier, E. "Rois Angevins Et Papes D'Avignon (XII-XV Siècles)" in Édouard Privat (ed.). *Historie De La Provence*. Toulouse: Univers de la France, 1969, pp. 169–217.

Barber, Malcolm. *Two Cities: Medieval Europe 1050–1320*. (Second Edition). New York: Routledge, 2004.

Barrow, Julia. *The Clergy in the Medieval World: Secular Clerics, Their Families and Careers in North-Western Europe, C. 800-c. 1200*. Cambridge University Press, 2015.

Bartlett, Robert (ed.). *Medieval Panorama*. London: Thames & Hudson, 2001.

Bell, Adrian R., Chris Brooks, and Paul Dryburgh. "Advance Contracts for the Sale of Wool in Medieval England: An Undeveloped and Inefficient Market?" University of Reading, ISMA Centre, February 2005. Accessed May 3, 2021.

Benedictow, Ole J. *The Black Death 1346–1353: The Complete History*. Woodbridge: Boydell, 2006.

Bennett, Matthew. "The Experience of Civilian Populations During the Hundred Years War in France 1330–1440." British Commission for Military History Newsletter (undated). https://www.medievalists.net/2009/12/the-experience-of-civilian-populations-during-the-hundred-years-war-in-france-1330-1440. Accessed August 21, 2021.

Berkhofer, Robert F. "Oxford Biographies: Saint-Denis." https//:www.oxfordbiographies. com/view/document/obo-9780195396584-obo978011955396584-0100.xml. Accessed August 23, 2021.

Bienvenu, Jean-Marc. *Aux Origins D'un Ordre Religieux: Robert D'Arbrissel Et La Foundation De Fontevraud*. Actes des congrès de la Société des historiens médiévistes de l'enseigenment supérieur public. May 1974, accessed March 19, 2021. pp. 119–135.

Bloch, Marc. *Feudal Society*. Vol. II: *Social Classes and Political Organization*. London: Routledge, 1995.

Bolli, Christine. "Cluny Abbey." https://www.khanacademy.org/humanities/medieval-world/romanesque-art/romanesque-art-in-france/a/cluny-abbey. Accessed April 6, 2021.

Bork, Robert, and Andrea Kann. *The Art, Science, and Technology of Medieval Travel*. Aldershot: Ashgate, 2008.

Bouet, Pierre. "Oderic Vital (c. 1114/41)." https://mondes-normands.caen.fr/france/ensavoirplus/sources/odericvital.htm. Accessed March 20, 2021.

Boureau, Alain. "The Circulation of Heresies in Medieval Europe" in *The Notebooks of the Historical Research Center,* February 4, 2008, pp. 19–30. https://journals.openedition.org/ccrh/3421. Accessed August 11, 2021.

Bove, Boris, and Claude Gauvard. *Le Paris Du Moyen Âge*. Paris: Belin, 2014.

Brown, Mark. "Archaeologists Find 'Missing Link' in History of Fountains Abbey." https://www.theguardian.com/science/2021/oct/25/archaeologists-find-missing-link-history-fountains-abbey. Accessed October 25, 2021.

Brown University. "Decameron Web: Boccaccio's Life and Works." https://www.brown.edu/Departments/Italisn_Studies/dweb/boccaccio/life1_en.php. Accessed May 13, 2021.

———. "Decameron Web: Social and Economic Effects of the Plague." https://www.brown.edu/Departments/Italian_Studies/dwb/plague/effects/social.php#:~:text. Accessed May 9, 2021.

Brundage, James A. *Medieval Canon Law*. New York: Longman, 1996.

Bruzelius, Caroline. "The Architecture of the Mendicant Orders in the Middle Ages: An Overview of Recent Literature." *Antiquité/Moyen-Âge,* February 2012, pp. 365–386. Accessed March 27, 2021.

Bugyis, Katie-Ann Marie. Book review of *The Cambridge History of Medieval Monasticism in the Latin West,* Vols. 1 and 2, in the *Journal of the American Academy of Religion* 89 no. 2, June 14, 2012, pp. 787–791. https://academic.oup.com/jaar/article/89/2/787/6298382. Accessed November 27, 2021.

Burl, Aubrey. *Danse Macabre: François Villon—Poetry & Murder in Medieval France*. Thrupp: Sutton, 2000.

Burton, Janet. *Monastic and Religious Orders in Britain, 1000–1300*. Cambridge University Press, 1997.

Campbell, Andrew, Lorenza Gianfrancesco, and Neil Tarrant. "Alchemy and the Mendicant Orders of Late Medieval and Early Modern Europe." *Ambix* 65, no. 3, 2018. Accessed July 25, 2021.

Canneva-Tétu, Odile, and Jean-Benoit Héron. *Comprendre Les Abbayes Et Les Ordres Monastiques*. Rennes: Éditions Ouest-France, 2019.

Cartwright, Mark. "The Daily Life of Medieval Monks." https://www.worldhistory.org/article/1293/the-daily-life-of-medieval-monks/. Accessed August 5, 2019.

Cassard, Jean-Christophe. *1180–1328: L'Âge D'Or Capétien*. Paris: Belin, 2014.

Cavill, Paul. "Life as Pilgrimage in Anglo-Saxon Christianity: From Exile to Heavenly Home." https://www.york.ac.uk/projects/pilgrimage/contents/as_life.html. Accessed May 15, 2021.

Centre des Monuments Nationaux. "Cluny: History of the Monument." www.cluny-abbaye.fr/Explorer/Histoire-du-monument. Accessed November 29, 2020.

———. "Mont-Saint-Michel Abbey." www.abbaye-mont-saint-michel.fr/en/Explore/L-histoire-de-abbaye-du-Mont-Saint-Michel. Accessed April 10, 2021.

La Chancellerie des Universités de Paris. https://www.sorbonne.fr/en/the-sorbonne/history-of-the-sorbonne/la-fondation-de-la-sorbonne-au-moyen-age-par-le-theologien-robert-de-sorbon/. Accessed July 29, 2021.

Chaucer, Geoffrey. *The Canterbury Tales*. London: Penguin, 1996.

Chisholm, Mary. "Monastic & Secular Cathedrals of Medieval England (*circa* 1200)." www.exploringbuildinghistory.co.uk. Accessed April 11, 2021.

"Cluny" in *Le Guide Du Patrimoine, Paris*. Paris: Hachette, 1994, pp. 167–172.

Cobban, Alan B. *English University Life in the Middle Ages*. London: UCL Press, 1999.

———. *The Medieval Universities: Their Development and Organization*. London: Methuen & Co., 1975.

"Curnosky." *Traditional French Cookery*. London: Ebury Press, 1989.

Dalarun, Jacques. "Robert D'Arrissel Et Les Femmes." https://www.persee.fr/doc/ahass_0395-2649_1984_num_39_6_283125. Accessed March 17, 2021.

de Jong, Mayke. "Carolingian Monasticism: The Power of Prayer" in *The New Cambridge Medieval History,* Rosamond McKitterick (ed.), Vol. II, c. 700-c. 900. Cambridge University Press, 1995, pp. 622–653.

de Ridder-Symoens, H. (ed.) *A History of the University in Europe: Vol. 1: Universities in the Middle Ages.* Cambridge University Press, 2003.

Donkin, R.A. "Cistercian Sheep-Farming and Wool-Sales in the Thirteenth Century." No date. Accessed May 4, 2021.

Douglas, David C. *William the Conqueror.* Yale University Press, 1999.

Dyas, Dee. "Pilgrims and Pilgrimage: Life as Pilgrimage in Early Christian Writers," and "Patterns of Pilgrimage in England c.1100-c.1500." https:www.york.ac.uk/pilgrimage/content/tradition_bc.html. Accessed May 15, 2021.

Dyer, Christopher. *Making a Living in the Middle Ages: The People of Britain 850–1520.* Yale University Press, 2009.

_____. *Standards of Living in the Later Middle Ages: Social Change in England c. 1200–1520.* (Revised Edition). Cambridge University Press, 2020.

"Early Medieval Philosophy: Ancient and Christian Roots" in *Encyclopedia.com.* https:www.encyclopedia.com/history/news-wires-white-papers-and-books/early-medieval-philosophy-ancient-and-christian-roots. Accessed December 1, 2021.

Eddison, Jill. *Medieval Pirates: Pirates, Raiders and Privateers, 1204–1453.* Strond: History Press, 2013.

English Heritage. "History of Furness Abbey." english-heritage.org.uk/visit/places/furness-abbey. Accessed August 20, 2021.

Esteves, Ana. "The Forgotten Renaissance: The Renaissance of the Twelfth Century and How It Changed the World." https:historyofyesterday-com/the-forgotten-renaissance-340f353f43ed. Accessed July 29, 2021.

Evans, G.R. *Fifty Key Medieval Thinkers.* New York: Routledge, 2002.

Evans, Joan. *Life in Medieval France.* London: Phaidon, 1957.

Fleming, Robin. *Britain After Rome: The Fall and Rise, 400 to 1070.* London: Penguin, 2010.

Fletcher, Richard. *The Barbarian Conversion: From Paganism to Christianity.* Berkeley: University of California Press, 1999.

Fontaine, Jacques. "Education and Learning" in Paul Fouracre (ed.), *The New Cambridge Medieval History.* Cambridge University Press, 2015, pp. 735–759.

Fordham University. "The Life and Work of Hildegard Von Bingham (1098–1179)." https://sourcebooks.fordham.edu/med/Hildegard.asp. Accessed March 10, 2021.

Gallagher, Niav. "How the Franciscans Arrived in Ireland c. 1231" in History Ireland, https://www.historyireland.com/medieval-history-pre-1500/two-nations-one-order-the-franciscans-in-medieval-ireland/, pp. 6–7. Accessed June 20, 2021.

Gaskill, Malcolm. "Philosophical Vinegar, Marvellous Salt—The Experimental Fire: Inventing English Alchemy" in *London Review of Books,* July 15, 2021, pp. 15–16.

Gautier-Ernoul, Joëlle. "Robert D'Arbrissel." https://prieuresfontevristes.wordpress.com/robert-darbrissel. Accessed March 17, 2021.

Goetz, Hans-Werner. "Monasteries and Monastic Life" in *Life in the Middle Ages* (trans. Albert Wimmer, ed. Steven Rowan). University of Notre Dame Press, 1993, pp. 93–106.

Goldiner, Sigrid. "Medicine in the Middle Ages." *Heilbrunn Timeline of Art History: Essays.* https://www.metmuseum.org/toah/hd/medm/hd_medm.htm. Accessed August 16, 2021.

Guillier, Gérard. *L'abbaye De Sénanque: Une Architecture De Sérénité.* Sainte-Remy-de-Provence: Editions Équinoxe, 2006.

Harvard University. "Harvard's Geoffrey Chaucer Website: William Wey's Itinerary for a Pilgrimage to Jerusalem." https://chaucer.fas.harvard.edu/william-weys-itinerary-pilgrimage-jerusalem. Accessed May 15, 2021.

Haskins, Charles Homer. *The Renaissance of the Twelfth Century.* Harvard University Press, 1927.

_____. *The Rise of the Universities.* Cornell University Press, 1965.

Haverkamp, Claus-Peter. After review entitled *Images of Saône-et-Loire.* Paris, June 2011, pp. 20–23.

Heer, Friedrich (trans. Janet Sondheimer). *The Medieval World, 1275 to 1535*. New York: New American Library, 1961.

Historic England. "Medieval Monastic Sheep Farm (bercaria), 500m North-east of Whittodean Farm." https://historicengland.org.uk/listing/the-list/list-entry/1011292. Accessed May 4, 2021.

Historic UK. "Fountains Abbey." https://www.historic-uk.com/HistoryMagazine/DestinationsUK/Fountains-Abbey. Accessed May 1, 2021.

History Ireland. "Medieval History (pre–1500)." https://www.historyireland.com/medieval-history-pre-1500/two-nations-one-order-the-franciscans-in-medieval-ireland/ Accessed June 11, 2021.

Holmes, George. *The Oxford Illustrated History of Medieval Europe*. Oxford University Press, 2001.

Hugo, Victor. *Notre-Dame de Paris*. Oxford University Press, 2009.

Hutchinson, Gillian. *Medieval Ships and Shipping*. London: Leicester University Press, 1997.

Infobretagne. "Blessed Robert D'Arbrissel." www.infobretagne.com/arbrissel-robert.htm. Accessed June 1, 2021.

"Irish Missionary Monks and the Celtic Church" in Michelin, *The Green Guide: Ireland*. Greenville: Michelin Maps and Guides, 1996, pp. 95–96.

Jackson, Kenneth Hurlstone. *A Celtic Miscellany: Translations from Celtic Literatures*. London: Penguin, 1971.

James, Edward. *Britain in the First Millennium*. Oxford University Press, 2001.

Jamroziak, Emilia. "Rievaulx Abbey as a Wool Producer in the Late Thirteenth Century: Cistercians, Sheep, and Debts" in *Northern History* 40, no. 2, 2003, pp. 197–218. July 19, 2013. https://www.tandonline.com/doi/abs/10.1179/nhi.2003.40.2.197?journalCode=ynhi20. Accessed May 3, 2021.

Janin, Hunt. *Four Paths to Jerusalem: Jewish, Christian, Muslim, and Secular Pilgrimages, 1000 BCE to 2001 CE*. Jefferson: McFarland, 2002.

_____. *Medieval Justice: Cases and Laws in France, England and Germany, 500–1500*. Jefferson: McFarland, 2004.

_____. *The University in Medieval Life, 1179–1499*. Jefferson: McFarland, 2008.

Jenkins, John C. "Monasteries and the Defence of the South Coast in the Hundred Years War." July 10, 2012. https://www.academia.edu/2172260/Monasteries_and_the_Defence_of_the_South_Coast_in_the_Hundred_Years_War. Accessed August 31, 2021.

Jewish Virtual Library. "Nazarite." https://www.jewishvirtuallibrary.org/nazarite. Accessed January 8, 2021.

Jolliffe, John (ed.), *Froissart's Chronicles*. London: Penguin, 1967.

Jordan, William Chester. *Europe in the High Middle Ages*. London: Penguin, 2002.

Keen, Maurice (ed.). *English Society in the Later Middle Ages, 1348–1500*. London: Penguin, 1990.

_____. *Medieval Warfare: A History*. Oxford University Press, 1999.

Kelly, Thomas E. (trans.), Stephen Knight (ed.), and Thomas H. Ohlgren (ed.). "Eustache the Monk: Introduction." https://d.lib.rochester.edu/teams/text/eustache-the-monk-introduction. Accessed April 1, 2010.

Kelty, Fr. Matthew. "Aspects of the Monastic Calling." Trappist, Kentucky: Abbey of Gethsemane c. 1970.

King, Laura. "The Book of Kells." www.people.vcu.edu/-djbromle/color-theory/color04/laura/bookofkells.htm. Accessed October 13, 2021.

Knudsen, Christian D. "Naughty Nuns and Promiscuous Monks." PhD dissertation, Graduate Department of Medieval Studies, University of Toronto, 2012. Accessed April 16, 2021.

Koeningsberger, H.G. *Medieval Europe, 400–1500*. Harrow: Longman, 1987.

Kreutz, Barbara M. *Before the Normans: Southern Italy in the Ninth and Tenth Centuries*. Philadelphia: University of Pennsylvania Press, 1991.

Labarge, Margaret Wade. *Medieval Travellers: The Rich and the Restless*. London: Phoenix, 1982.

Lafaye, Anne-Julie. "Monastic Orders as Vehicles of Diffusion in Europe" in *Encylopédie d'historie numérique de l'Europe* [online]. https://ehne.fr/en/node/12413. Accessed September 10, 2021.

Laumonier, Lucie. "Sheep-Rearing in Medieval France." https://www.medievalists. net/2021/01/sheep-rearing-medieval-france. Accessed June 7, 2021.

Lawrence, C.H. *Medieval Monasticism: Forms of Religious Life in Western Europe in the Middle Ages*, fourth edition. New York: Routledge, 2015.

Ldonne, Jennifer. "Holy Vineyards." https://tasteoffrancemag.com/trending/holy-vineyards. Accessed February 16, 2021.

Le Goff, Jacques (trans. Arthur Goldhammer). *The Medieval Imagination*. University of Chicago Press, 1988.

La letter volée. "413. Robert D'Arbrissel, Founder of Fontevraud Monastery." Lettrevolee. irht.cnrs.fr/Robert.htm. Accessed June 1, 2021.

Library of Congress. "Scrolls from the Dead Sea: The Qumran Community." https://www. loc/gov/exhibits/scrolls/late.html. Accessed January 8, 2021.

Little, Lester K. "Moines Et Religieux" in Jacques Le Goff and Jean-Claude Schmitt, *Dictionnaire Raisonné De L'Occident Médiéval*. Paris: Fayard, 1999, pp. 741–757.

Madigan, Shawn. *Mystics, Visionaries and Prophets: A Historical Anthology of Women's Spiritual Writings*. Minnesota: Augsburg Fortress, 1998.

Martin, Richard. "On the Sheep's Back: The Rise and Fall of English Wool." December 2012. Accessed May 3, 2021.

Matarasso, Pauline. *The Cistercian World*. London: Penguin, 1993.

McKitterick, Rosamond. (ed.). *The Early Middle Ages: Europe 400–1000*. Oxford University Press, 2001.

———. *The New Cambridge Medieval History*. Cambridge University Press, 1995.

Mendelssohn, Stéphanie. "Angolo Di Tura Del Grasso." https://provincedesienne. com/2020/04/07/agnolo-di-tura-del-grasso. Accessed June 25, 2021.

Metropolitan Museum of Art. "Heilbrunn Timeline of Art History: Monasticism in Western Medieval Europe." Revised March 2013. https://www.metmuseum.org/toah/hd_mona_htm. Accessed November 26, 2020.

Miller, Tanya Stabler. "Beguines." https://wrldrells.org/2020/09//04/beguines. Accessed March 14, 2021.

Molinier, Auguste. "Jean De Venette." https://www.persee.fr/doc/sshf_0000-0000_1904_num_4_1_949_ff_0020_0000_2. Accessed August 22, 2021.

"Monks and the Middle Ages in Nidderdale: Information Sheets." Upper Nidderdale Landscape Partnership Educational Resources. No date. Accessed May 3, 2021.

Morillo, Stephen. *The Battle of Hastings: Sources and Interpretations*. Woodbridge: Boydell, 1996.

Musson, Anthony. *Medieval Law in Context: The Growth of Legal Consciousness from Magna Carta to the Peasants' Revolt*. Manchester University Press, 2001.

Nelson, Lynn Harry. "The Avignon Papacy, 1305–1378." www.vlib.us/medieval/lectures/avignon.html. Accessed June 21, 2021.

Neville, Grace. "Franco-Irish Relations in the Later Middle Ages." https://www.persee.fr/doc/irlan_0183-973x_1980_num_5_1_2200. Accessed November 2, 2021.

Newman, Mark. *The Wonder of the North: Fountains Abbey and Studley Royal*. Woodbridge: Boydell, 2015.

Nicholson, Helen. *Medieval Warfare: Theory and Practice of War in Europe, 300–1500*. New York: Palgrave Macmillan, 2004.

Ó Cróinín, Dáibhí. *Early Medieval Ireland* second edition. New York: Routledge, 2017.

O'Donnell, James O. "Cassidorus." http://faculty.georgetown.edu/jod/texts/cassbook/chap5.html. University of California Press, 1979. Accessed June 2, 2021.

Ohlgren, Thomas H. (ed.). *A Book of Medieval Outlaws: Ten Tales in Modern English*. Thrupp: Sutton, 2000.

Olson, Lynette. *The Early Middle Ages: The Birth of Europe*. New York: Palgrave Macmillan, 2007.

"An Outline of English Fiction—Matthew Paris." https://www.ped.muni.cz/weng/outline_of_english_fiction/terms/matthew_paris.html. Accessed April 10, 2021.

"Overview of Medieval Monasticism." https://www3.dbu.edu/mitchell/monasticoverview. htm. Accessed December 8, 2020.

Ozment, Stephen. *The Age of Reform, 1250–1550: An Intellectual History of Late Medieval and Reformation Europe.* Yale University Press, 1980.

Paris, Matthew. *The Illustrated Chronicles of Matthew Paris: Observations of Thirteenth-Century Life* (trans. and ed. Richard Vaughan). Cambridge: Corpus Christi, 1993.

"Paschal Calendar." https://penelope.uchicago.edu~grout/encyclopaedia_romana/ britannia/anglo-saxon/earlychurch/paschal.html. Accessed April 20, 2021.

Pedersen, Olaf. *The First Universities: Studium Generale and the Origins of University Education in Europe.* Cambridge University Press, 2000.

Pernoud, Régine. *Aliénor D'Aquitaine.* Paris: Albin Michel, 1965.

———. *Héloise Et Abélard.* Paris: Albin Michel, 1970.

Perrin, J. "Raoul Glaber, the Historian of the Year 1000." https://www.histoire-pour-tous. fr/biographies/3196-raoul-glaber-lhistorien-de-lan-mil.html. Accessed August 11, 2021.

Peters, Edward. *Inquisition.* University of California Press, 1989.

Peters, Justin. "Christian Monastic Initiation." An unpublished Religious Studies paper submitted on June 12, 2019 to the University of Missouri at Columbia, Missouri.

Phillips, Helen, Dee Dyas, and Judith Weiss. "The Becket Story: Chaucer's Canterbury Tales." https://www.thebeckestory.org.uk/pilgrimage/canterbury-tales. Accessed May 15, 2021.

———. Patterns of Pilgrimage in Medieval English Literature." https://www.york.ac.uk/ projects/content/med_liter.html. Accessed May 15, 2015.

Potter, David. *France in the Later Middle Ages.* Oxford University Press, 2002.

Pounds, N.J.G. *An Economic History of Medieval Europe* second edition. New York: Routledge, 1994.

Power, Eileen. (trans. and ed. 1928). *The Goodman of Paris [Le Ménagier De Paris]: A Treatise on Moral and Domestic Economy by a Citizen of Paris, C. 1393.* Woodbridge: Boydell, 2006.

———. *Medieval English Nunneries C. 1275 to 1535.* Cambridge University Press, 1922.

———. *Medieval People.* London: The Folio Society, 1999.

———. *The Wool Trade in English Medieval History.* Oxford University Press, 1949.

Rashdall, Hastings. (FM Powicke and AB Emden, eds.). "The Monastic Colleges" in *The Universities of Europe in the Middle Ages.* Volume III: *English Universities, Student Life.* Oxford University Press, 1969, pp. 184–190.

———. *The Universities of Europe in the Middle Ages.* Vol. 1: *Salerno, Bologna, Paris.* Oxford University Press, 1969.

Rendu, Jean-Baptiste and Jacques Guillard. *Abbayes & Monastères De France.* Nanterre: Massin, 2013.

Renouard, Yves. *La Paupauté á Avignon.* Luçon: Editions Jean-Paul Gisserot, 2004.

Robinson, Revd. Canon Joseph. "Temple Church." Norwich: Jarrod 1997.

Rockwell, Anne F. "Suger, French Abbot." https://www.briteannica.com/biography/Suger. Accessed August 23, 2021.

Rolland, O. "Suger." https//archeologie.culture.fr/saint-denis/en/abbot-suger-circa-1081-1151. Accessed August 23, 2021.

Rose, Susan. *The Wine Trade in Medieval Europe 1000–1500.* London: Bloomsbury, 2011.

Rousset, Paul. "Raoul Glaber Interprèle De La Pensée Commune Au Xle Siècle." https:// www.persee.fr/doc/rhef_0300-9505_num_36_127_3084. Accessed August 16, 2021.

Roux, Simone. *Paris Au Moyen Âge.* Paris: Hachette, 2003.

———. *Paris in the Middle Ages.* (Jo Ann McNamara trans., preface by Andrew Hussey.) London: The Folio Society, 2014.

Sadourny, Alain. "Les Transports sur La Seine aux Vllle et XIVe Siècles." Actes des congrès de la Société des historiens médiévalistes de l'enseignement supérieur public, 7e congrès, Rennes, 1976, pp. 213–244. https://www.persee.fr/doc/shemes_1261_9078_act_7_ 1235.

St. Catherine of Sienna Roman Catholic Church. "Differences Between a 'monk' and a 'friar'?" https:www.stcatherinercc.org/single-post/2018/01/19/whats-the-difference-between-monk-and-friar. Accessed February 5, 2021.

"Saint-Denis Cathedral Basilica." https://uk.tourisme93.com/basilica/abbot-suger.html. Accessed August 24, 2021.

Schreibelreiter, Greg. "Church Structure and Organization" in Paul Fouracre (ed.), *The New Cambridge Medieval History* 1, c.500-c.700. Cambridge University Press, 2005, pp. 675–709.

Sciolino, Elaine. *The Seine: The River That Made Paris.* New York: Norton, 2020.

Scott-Robinson, Richard. "The Pardoner's Tale." https://reflection.eleusinianmo.co.uk/medieval-literature/red-book-of-shalfleet/canterbury-tales/pardoners-tale. Accessed June 4, 2021.

Silverman, Benjamin C. "Monastic Medicine: A Unique Dualism Between Natural Science and Spiritual Healing." https://www.medievalists.net/2011/03/monastic-medicine-a-dualism-between-natural-science-and-spiritual-healing/. Accessed August 12, 2021.

Smith, Julia M.H. *Europe After Rome: A New Cultural History 500–1000.* Oxford University Press, 2005.

Smith, L.M. *The Early History of the Monastery of Cluny.* Oxford University Press, 1920.

Smither, Edward. "Meet the Missionary Monks." Richmond: IMB, 2019. Accessed August 8, 2021.

Sorabella, Jean. "Heilbrunn Timeline of Art History: Pilgrimage in Medieval Europe." https://www.metmuseum.org.toah/hd/pilg/hd_pilg.htm. Accessed May 15, 2021.

Sot, Michel. "Pélerinage" in Le Goff, Jacques and Jean-Claude Schmitt. *Dictionnaire Raisonné De L'Occident Médiéval.* Paris: Fayard, 1999, pp. 892–905.

Southern, R.W. "Peter Abelard." https://plato.stanford.edu/entries/abelard/. Stanford University. Revised August 8, 2018. Accessed March 29, 2021.

———. *Scholastic Humanism and the Unification of Europe.* Vol. 1: Foundations. Oxford: Blackwell, 2002.

Stenton, Frank. *Anglo-Saxon England* third edition. Oxford University Press, 2001.

Swan, Leo. "Ecclesiastical Settlement in Ireland in the Early Medieval Period" in Acts du 11Ie congrès international d'archéologie médiévale (Aix-en-Provence, 28–30 Septembre 1989). Année 1994, 3, pp. 50–56. https://www.persee.fr/doc/ascam_000-3000_act_3_1 1042. Accessed September 9, 2021.

Sweet, Alfred H. "The English Benedictines and Their Bishops in the Thirteenth Century." *American Historical Review* 24, no. 4 (July 1919), pp. 565–577. https://www.jstor.org/stable/1835808. Accessed November 23, 2021.

Tappan, Eva March. "Brother John of Monte Corvino—Letter to the Minister General of the Friars Minor in Rome, C. 1280." https://sourcebooks.fordham.edu/source/1280corvino2.asp. Accessed August 7, 2021.

Thompson, John M. *Le Monde Médiéval.* Washington, D.C.: National Geographic, 2010.

Thornton, Gillian. "Meet the Greatest and Most Outlandish Chronicler of the Middle Ages." *Hertforshire Life.* https://www.greatbritishlife.co.uk/people-everything-you-need-to-know-about-st-albans-cathedral-s-7291850. Accessed June 7, 2021.

Tuchman, Barbara. *A Distant Mirror: The Calamitous 14th Century.* New York: Ballantine Books, 1979.

Turnbull, Stephen. "Tannenberg 1410: Disaster for the Teutonic Knights." Oxford: Osprey, 2008.

Turner, William. "Scholasticism" in the *Catholic Encyclopedia,* vol. 13. New York: Robert Appleton, 1912. https://www.newadvent.org/cathen/13548a.htm. Accessed August 12, 2021.

Urban, William. *Medieval Mercenaries: The Business of War.* Barnsley: Frontline Books, 2015.

Verdon, Jean. "Les Femmes" in *La Vie Quotidienne au Moyen Âge.* Paris: Perrin, 2015, pp. 230–235.

———. "Se Consacrer à Dieu" in *La Vie Quotiedienne au Moyen Âge.* Paris: Perrin, 2015, pp. 221–238.

Verger, Jacques. "Patterns" in H. de Ridder-Symoens. *A History of the University in Europe.* Cambridge University Press, 2003, pp. 35–68.

Vespierre, Bernard. *Guide Du Paris Médieval*. Paris: L'Harmattan, 2006.

Vins de Bourgogne. "Bourgogne Wines: When Time and Man Work Hand-in-Hand." https://www.bourgogne-wines.com/winegrowers-and-expertise/passionate-winegrowers-with-ancient-savoir-faire,2323,9380.html?. Accessed 16 February 2021.

Vones-Liebenstein, Ursula. "Similarities and Differences Between Monks and Regular Canons in the Twelfth Century" in *The Cambridge History of Medieval Monasticism in the Latin West*. Toronto: Cambridge University Press, 2020, pp. 766–782.

Waddell, Helen. *The Wandering Scholars of the Middle Ages*. Mineola: Dover Publications, 2002.

Ward, Benedicta. *The Wisdom of the Desert Fathers*. Oxford: SLG Press, 1986.

Wilken, Robert Louis. *The First Thousand Years: A Global History of Christianity*. Yale University Press, 2013.

Wilson, David M. *The Bayeux Tapestry*. London: Thames & Hudson, 2004.

Winroth, Anders. *The Making of Gratian's* Decretum. Cambridge University Press, 2000.

World History Encyclopedia. "The Daily Life of Medieval Monks: Recruitment." https://www.ancient.eu/article/1293/the-daily-life-of-medieval-monks/. Accessed April 3, 2021.

Zerner, Monique. "Hérésie" in Jacques Le Goff and Jean-Claude Schmitt. *Dictionnaire Raisonné De L'Occident Médiéval*. Paris: Fayard, 1999, pp. 464–481.

Index

213